D1258172

The History of Accounting

This is a volume in the Arno Press collection

The History of Accounting

Advisory Editor
Richard P. Brief

See last pages of this volume for a complete list of titles

THE LATE NINETEENTH CENTURY DEBATE OVER DEPRECIATION, CAPITAL AND INCOME

Richard P. Brief, editor

ARNO PRESS

A New York Times Company

New York — 1976

Editorial Supervision: SHEILA MEHLMAN

Reprint Edition 1976 by Arno Press Inc.

DEPRECIATION THEORY IN HISTORICAL PERSPECTIVE
is reprinted by permission of The Accountant

THE HISTORY OF ACCOUNTING
ISBN for complete set: 0-405-07540-5
See last pages of this volume for titles.

Manufactured in the United States of America

Publisher's Note: All the items in this anthology have been reproduced from the best available copies.

Library of Congress Cataloging in Publication Data
Main entry under title:

The Late nineteenth century debate over depreciation,
capital, and income.

(The History of accounting)
Reprint of articles which originally appeared in The Accountant and in Law journal reports between 1876 and 1894.
1. Depreciation--Addresses, essays, lectures.
2. Capital--Accounting--Addresses, essays, lectures.
3. Income accounting--Addresses, essays, lectures.
I. Brief, Richard P., 1933- II. Title.
III. Series.
HF5681.D5L27 658.1'5242 75-18458

ISBN 0-405-07542-1

PREFACE

At the First International Symposium of Accounting Historians which was held in Brussels in October, 1970, Professor B. S. Yamey and I discussed the idea of reprinting some of the classic works in accounting. This anthology begins to implement that proposal.

The subject of this collection is the late nineteenth century debate over depreciation, capital, and income. It begins with comments in *The Accountant* on the first "modern" paper dealing with the depreciation problem. It also includes other articles on depreciation theory by Guthrie, Murray, Bogle, Ladelle and Turner.

As a theory of depreciation began to evolve, accountants also became embroiled on questions concerning the nature of capital and income and they were vigorously debated. These debates are exemplified in the writings of Best, Wade, Cooper, Welton, Payne and Laurence.

The controversy was fueled by a number of legal decisions in the last two decades of the century, most notably *Dent v. The London Tramways Company (Limited)* (1880), *Lee v. Neuchatel* (1889) and *Verner v. The General and Commercial Investment Trust (Limited)* (1894). Any reference to the nineteenth century accounting environment would be incomplete without emphasizing the important influence of the courts on the development of accounting thought.

The arrangement of the material in chronological order is intended to provide insight into the process by which accounting theory was first formulated. This process had three ingredients. First, scholarly papers of an expository nature were presented at the regular meetings of the various accounting societies in Great Britain. Second, accountants reacted to the judicial decisions which had implications for this theory. Third, *The Accountant* provided the medium for the discussion which, as the reader will no doubt observe, was lively, penetrating and timely.

The first paper, "Depreciation Theory in Historical Perspective," is intended to serve as an introduction to this volume. It appeared in *The Accountant* nearly a century after Mather's paper on depreciation.

Richard P. Brief
New York
June, 1975

CONTENTS

Bogle, J. D. S.
THE WRITING OFF OF DEPRECIATION ON THE WASTING ASSETS OF A JOINT STOCK COMPANY (Reprinted from *The Accountant,* December 21, 1889). London, 1889

Glasgow Institute of Accountants Debating Society
OBLIGATION OF COMPANY TO PROVIDE FOR DEPRECIATION OF WASTING ASSETS BEFORE DECLARING DIVIDENDS (Reprinted from *The Accountant,* December 14, 1889). London, 1889

Ladelle, O. G.
THE CALCULATION OF DEPRECIATION (Reprinted from *The Accountant,* November 29, 1890). London, 1890

Welton, T. A.
ON THE PROFIT OF COMPANIES AVAILABLE FOR DISTRIBUTION (Reprinted from *The Accountant,* December 13, 1890). London, 1890

Cooper, Ernest
NOTES ON MR. T. A. WELTON'S PAPER "ON THE PROFIT OF COMPANIES AVAILABLE FOR DISTRIBUTION" (Reprinted from *The Accountant,* January 3, 1891). London, 1891

Payne, Alex W.
THE PRINCIPLES UPON WHICH THE ASSETS OF A JOINT STOCK COMPANY SHOULD BE VALUED FOR BALANCE SHEETS (Reprinted from *The Accountant,* February 13, 1892). London, 1892

Laurence, P. O.
THE CAPITAL OF A COMPANY WITH SPECIAL REFERENCE TO ITS REDUCTION (Reprinted from *The Accountant,* January 21, 1893). London, 1893

VERNER V. THE GENERAL AND COMMERCIAL INVESTMENT TRUST (LIMITED) (Reprinted from *Law Journal Reports,* Vol. 63, Chancery Division, 1894). London, 1894

Turner, E. Hartley
THE DEPRECIATION OF MACHINERY AND PLANT (Reprinted from *The Accountant,* June 16, 1894). London, 1894

Cooper, Ernest
CHARTERED ACCOUNTANTS AND THE PROFIT QUESTION (Reprinted from *The Accountant,* November 24, 1894). London, 1894

DEPRECIATION THEORY IN HISTORICAL PERSPECTIVE

Richard P. Brief

ALTHOUGH the history of thought has been essential to the progress in almost every discipline, accountants have traditionally neglected the subject. Unfortunately, primary sources for the study of accounting history are not generally available to those who might otherwise make use of such materials. Of course, copies of ancient book-keeping texts have been discussed in the literature, but these references too frequently leave the reader with the impression that, prior to the twentieth century, accounting was an underdeveloped discipline. This view is simply incorrect. Accounting thought reached a much higher level of sophistication by the end of the nineteenth century than most students of the subject realize; and these early discussions of accounting problems are relevant to, and do shed light on, contemporary issues.

Without a doubt, the best single source of historical information on accounting is *The Accountant*,[1] a weekly periodical that was first published in England at the end of 1874 and which continues into the present. It is apparent, however, that few of those who have an interest in accounting history have had the opportunity to examine the early issues of this publication which contain a wealth of information in the form of articles, reprinted lectures, debates, editorials, and other materials on diverse topics in accounting, business and economics.

John Mather's paper, 'Depreciation in relation to the audit of accounts' (January 8th, 1876), is the first work on depreciation that is mentioned in *The Accountant*, and also probably the first paper by an accountant on the subject. Mather's talk was divided into three sections: (1) auditor's responsibility; (2) principles; and (3) cases. The auditor, according to Mather, 'did not feel his responsibility any the less because it was not legal or pecuniary, but moral, affecting his conscience and reputation, rather than his pocket.'

With respect to principles, nothing charged to capital should be valued above cost, and ordinary repairs must not be capitalized. When depreciation was omitted or deemed insufficient, the auditor should call attention to this finding in his certificate [*sic*]:

> 'The omission or apparent undercharge should be specifically reported, if it was proposed to pay a dividend on the basis of the accounts in question.'

Dividends out of capital

In the last quarter of the century the interpretation of 'paying dividends out of capital' and the problem of determining 'profit available for dividends' were inextricably connected with depreciation. Accountants sought first of all to clarify theory, and second, to understand their responsibility in these matters. However, they were offered little assistance from judicial and statutory authority which failed to specify rules of accounting behaviour. This dissatisfaction with legal institutions is one of the dominant themes in the period.

In this paper it is not possible to elaborate on the numerous and interesting discussions concerning the accountant's responsibility and the debates concerning the legislation of accounting behaviour during the period: for example, articles on why accounting practices cannot be legislated are certainly relevant to contemporary problems. Stimulating work on the auditor's certificate (*sic*) may be found in 1883 and 1884, and Ernest Cooper's paper, 'Chartered Accountants as Auditors of Companies' (November 13th, 1886), contains a well-documented history of the subject. Another noteworthy treatment of this same subject was 'The Duties and Responsibilities of the Public Accountant', by Arthur Lowes Dickinson (July 26th, 1902).

It is also important to realize that not all of the information that would be of interest to a student of accounting thought may be found in formal articles. Consider, for example, the following remarks in a letter by L. R. Dicksee (March 1st, 1902):

> '. . . Even with regard to such important questions as the value of assets, provision for depreciation, the assessments of profits earned, and the distribution of unrealized profits, the Courts have shown a marvellous disinclination [to provide] principles for the safe guidance of the auditor. . . . No doubt it has acted wisely in adopting this course,

[1] Dates in parentheses throughout refer to *The Accountant* unless otherwise stated.

however, because any attempt to state explicitly what the duties of auditors are in all cases would afford the best possible excuse in such cases for the insufficiency of the audit that has been performed.'

The controversy is fascinating. In general, *The Accountant* was sharply critical of existing statutes:

> 'Is there a single word in the whole of the Acts restraining the payment of dividends out of capital? There is not; what is said seems to amount to this, that the payment of dividends out of capital *can* be made. . . .
>
> 'What are accountants doing towards drawing up formal suggestions on this and other equally important points on which the Companies Acts are notoriously at fault? Not going to sleep, let us hope.' (December 12th, 1885.)

Legislation or not

Here, then, is the beginning of the great debate that lasted during the remainder of the century. Can dividends be paid out of capital? What is the difference between capital and income? Must a provision for depreciation be made before declaring a dividend?

On the one hand, some accountants wanted stricter laws to define 'proper' accounting behaviour:

> 'Existing law is deplorably defective, and . . . the chartered accountants acting through their Institute should be the first to move in the matter, and not allow the work to be done, and the honour to be appropriated by other and less capable hands.' (December 19th, 1885.)

This view was expressed by accountants as early as 1881:

> 'A shareholder is entitled to know, not what is the true value of his shares, for that in most instances is a matter of opinion, but *how* the value of fixed assets has been estimated – whether at cost, at a valuation . . ., or otherwise, and what sums have been placed in reserve or written off for depreciation, running out of leases or other decreases in value. . . .
>
> 'Much of the information . . . might be given if the legislature made its publication compulsory upon all.' (June 4th, 1881.)

On the other hand, some believed, along with Dicksee, that legal requirements to charge depreciation before declaring dividends would be 'injurious to companies and the public. . . . It would stop all enterprise because it would be absolutely impossible for companies to pay dividends in the early years of their existence.'

In the same spirit:

> 'There is nothing improper in this [returning interest on capital during construction], and as I don't approve of too much grandmotherly legislation in a free country where people should learn from their own experience how to take care of themselves, I don't approve of the State preventing undertakings being floated with an inducement of this sort.' (December 4th, 1886.)

One of the most interesting characteristics of accounting literature in this period relates to the insights one obtains into the nineteenth century business environment. Conversely, the nineteenth century business environment permitted a free and uninhibited exchange of views and this is one of the major reasons why historical discussions of accounting problems are so interesting, useful and relevant to contemporary problems.

This early stage of the development of accounting ideas reflects the profound influence which legal institutions had on accounting thought. It is perfectly apparent that most of these early thoughts on capital and income were profoundly influenced by such institutions. These controversies frequently reflected the major judicial rulings and statutes (e.g., January 16th, 1886 and December 14th, 1889). Unlike the subject of economics, 'a subject for the most part relegated to the whitewashed rooms wherein the gas flickers, and to public houses on a Sunday evening' (December 15th, 1888), accountants were forced to deal practically with problems having abstruse theoretical dimensions.

Theory of depreciation

Another major paper on depreciation appeared in 1883: Edwin Guthrie, 'Depreciation and sinking funds' (April 21st, 1883). Here we find the clearest exposition to date of a theory of depreciation.

Guthrie defined depreciation as a cost equal to the value of the asset that is 'consumed' during the year. While not exactly measurable, it is based on the assumption of a certain term of useful existence of machinery or building. Declaring that the depreciation problem concerns the recoupment of capital outlay and not profit and loss, Guthrie also lists different methods and rates that might be used to calculate depreciation.

In this lecture we also find the first reference to the present-day concept of 'going-concern' and its corollary the 'cost' principle, i.e., that 'matter and things in permanent working position must not be treated as following the fluctuations of the market' (though the use of 'valuation' to check depreciation was admissible).

As was the practice in those days, most papers were reviewed by members of the various accounting societies. William Harris commented on Guthrie's views (September 1st, 1883). He argued that 'it is what property would fetch, not what it cost, that settles value' and that the accounts therefore should reflect current values and 'let tomorrow look after itself.' The 'cost versus value' controversy continues to plague accountants today.

Harris also urged further investigation of the appreciation problem and called for an empirical study of depreciation:

> 'If we could only get a few examples of the actual figures showing the cost of the plant of a concern, the amount spent for repairs, the amount written off for depreciation and the amount realized by the sale of the materials . . . we should perhaps have the most interesting and most reliable paper on depreciation that has ever been written.'

Early textbook on depreciation

Shortly after Guthrie's lecture, Ewing Matheson's articles appeared in a periodical called *The Engineer*. This series of papers on depreciation were not reprinted in *The Accountant*, but were published in book form.[2] *The Accountant*, in editorial comments, expressed pleasure upon hearing of the publication of Matheson's work (December 29th, 1883). At the same time, it noted that:

> 'Since they [Matheson's articles] were published, numerous letters have appeared from manufacturers and others, many of whom take exception to the sound principles laid down and endeavour to show that the depreciation of plant is often rendered difficult by lack of profit and that in such cases it may be postponed.'

When the work appeared in book form, however, *The*

[2] *Depreciation of Factories*, by Ewing Matheson (E. & F. Spon, 1884).

Accountant was very disappointed that Matheson did not actually show how to compute the rate of depreciation (November 15th, 1884). Matheson brilliantly responded to this criticism (January 3rd, 1885):

> 'Simple and rudimentary as some of my suggestions may appear to you, and to your readers, my own experience tells me how often the simplest rules are neglected, and even apparently unknown to those whose capital is at stake.
>
> ...'[Regarding] the absence from my book of exact rates of depreciation for different classes of plant, I am more on my ground, and I venture to assert that any positive statements of rates would be more likely to mislead than inform.... Fixed rules are impossible, and examples, if offered for imitation, dangerous.'

Matheson then provides an example to clarify his argument and shows that about ten variables are relevant to the determination of the proper rate of depreciation.

Most accountants would probably agree with Matheson's argument. One also might wonder, for example, how these issues would have been dealt with now in the United States if tax laws and other legislation had not prescribed depreciation rates. Indeed, the implication of the argument that the use of deterministic accounting procedures results in illusory and misleading accounting measurements is not given sufficient attention today.

At about the same time that this dialogue took place, there was a note (November 29th, 1884) about the views of an 'eminent accountant in the north of England'. These ideas about the depreciation problem were unusual because they suggest certain fundamental economic consequences that might be associated with the advent of modern depreciation accounting. The economic historian might usefully consider them.

Speaking of 'money retained out of profits' for depreciation, this eminent accountant said that:

> 'It enables managers and directors to undertake continual new work without consulting their shareholders. It is only another way of providing fresh capital or avoiding a call, which might be resisted by those interested if it came in that form; and further in cases where you have several classes of shares upon which the capital is not equally paid up, or where you have debenture holders as well as ordinary shareholders, the rights of the respective parties are prejudicially affected by what can only be styled the misappropriation of funds intended for a specific object.'

Nineteenth-century accountants demonstrated an awareness of the economic implications of accounting practices. This subject is not given much attention in the present age.

Adam Murray's work on depreciation was the next major piece to appear (November 5th, 1887). However, his treatment of the problem differed very little from Guthrie's earlier work. Murray advocated basing depreciation on replacement cost, and this is probably the first reference to that concept.

The editorial comments on Murray's paper that appeared in *The Accountant* (November 12th, 1887) are in many ways more interesting than the paper itself. They were extremely critical, saying that the paper 'does not exceed expectations'. This language is rather strong, considering the fact that Murray was one of the leading accountants of the day.

Specifically, the paper was criticized on the following points: (1) the argument that charging less depreciation for an old machine if new machines are cheaper, i.e., if replacement cost is less than original cost, was considered erroneous; (2) the failure to comment on the proposal to compel limited companies to state in their articles the rate of depreciation to be charged; and (3) the failure to criticize replacement accounting which is 'notoriously practised in his district'. It is this kind of lively discussion that makes *The Accountant* such an interesting and valuable source of information on the history of accounting.

The most outstanding contribution to depreciation theory in the nineteenth century was O. G. Ladelle's brilliant essay, 'The calculation of depreciation' (November 29th and December 6th, 1890).[3] Ladelle died of typhoid fever at the age of 28 before he was able to deliver the paper. One can only speculate about what his impact on accounting theory would have been, had he lived.

A novel concept

Ladelle saw the depreciation problem as one in which a group of speculators buy an asset, with each person being assigned the expected benefits for a particular year. For these uncertain benefits they must jointly agree on the proportion of the original cost each must pay. In his words:

> '... Assume, for convenience of illustration, that a large number of persons, numbered from one upwards, purchase as a joint venture, an asset, which they do not propose to use simultaneously, but agree to use for a year apiece, in turn, and that we are asked to determine the method of apportioning the cost between them. For, if we can do this, it is quite clear that the union of all these persons, into one firm can make no difference to our calculations, and that the same figures, will give the amounts which the firm ought to charge to each year in its accounts.'

The general depreciation method derived by Ladelle is almost identical to the so-called present value method of calculating depreciation. This method has been given other names such as the annuity method, compound interest method, economic depreciation, etc., and it has been discussed by numerous writers,[4] especially in the last two decades. However, Ladelle's use of the problem of dividing cost among joint speculators as an analogy to structure the problem of allocating cost among joint time periods distinguishes his theory from all other work on the problem.

Value of accounting history

What conclusions may be drawn from this brief survey of nineteenth century depreciation theory? First, most of the issues related to the problem of accounting for assets were extensively discussed and debated in the last century. The contemporary theorist could derive greater benefits from this material than is commonly realized.

Second, the *laissez-faire* environment in which the accounting thought developed provides the modern accountant with a new perspective to view his problems. Valuable new insights into current issues can be obtained from studying the literature from the earlier period.

Third, these historical documents shed additional light on the problems of economic development in the nineteenth century, on the business environment, and on the development of the accounting profession. Much more work needs to be done in studying and synthesizing this early work.

---

[3] Reprinted and commented upon by Professor Brief in the *Journal of Accounting Research*, Spring 1965.

[4] For example, *The Theory of Imperfect Competition*, by Donald Dewey, Columbia University Press (New York, 1969) at pp. 146–7.

[SUMMARY OF]
DEPRECIATION IN RELATION TO THE AUDIT OF ACCOUNTS

J. Mather

MANCHESTER INSTITUTE OF ACCOUNTANTS.

QUARTERLY MEETING.

The members of the Manchester Institute of Accountants held their quarterly meeting on Monday evening. The President, Mr. ADAM MURRAY, took the chair.

The first business was the reading of the minutes by the secretary concerning an inquiry that had been made by the Council of the Institute into a case that had been reported to them with reference to the charges made by a Manchester accountant in an estate under liquidation. The Principal had charged fifteen shillings an hour for his own time; seven shillings and sixpence per hour for that of his principal clerk, and from three shillings and sixpence down to one shilling and ninepence for his other clerks. A charge of forty per cent. on the salaries paid to the clerks of debtors was also made. The following resolutions were adopted by the Council:—"The Council having had submitted to them, for their opinion thereon, a bill of charges made by an accountant as trustee to an estate under liquidation, have carefully considered the same, and resolve as follows:—

"1. That the rates charged by the trustee for himself and his principal clerk are unusually high for work of this description.

"2. That the percentage charged upon the salaries paid to the clerks, not being clerks of the trustee, is a charge unknown to, and unrecognised by the Council.

"3. That in the opinion of the Council the remuneration to the trustee should in all cases be determined by the creditors, or by a committee of their number who have the means of judging of the value of their services and nature of the duties discharged, and that in the resolution appointing a trustee the principle of remuneration should be set forth."

The Report went on to say that every gentleman present at the special Council meeting appeared to be of opinion that the making of such charges would bring the profession of accountants into discredit.

Mr. F. POPPLEWELL said that the total charges made by the accountant in the case in question were about twenty-five per cent. of the debtor's assets.

Several gentlemen remarked that the only fault which they could find with the resolution, was that its terms were too mild. Ultimately, a motion approving of the action of the Council was proposed by Mr. R. E. JOHNSON, seconded by Mr. G. NESBIT, and unanimously carried.

Mr. J. MATHER then read a paper on "Depreciation in relation to the Audit of Accounts." The subject was treated under three heads:

1. As to what extent an auditor was responsible in respect of the item of depreciation in a balance sheet which he certified.
2. What principles should guide him in discharging his responsibility.
3. A few cases drawn from actual experience by way of illustration.

In reference to the first point, the paper set forth that as a rule an auditor did not feel his responsibility the less because it was not a legal or a pecuniary, but only a moral responsibility, affecting his conscience and reputation rather than his pocket. An auditor without a conscience was not only a monstrous anomaly, but, considering his opportunities for mischief, he might be called a member of the "dangerous classes." He believed, however, that the number of such was small. In the case of public companies the shareholders were the clients, generally the confiding clients of the auditor, and the auditor's certificates ought to imply—1, that from an adequate investigation of the accounts he was satisfied there was no intention to mislead, *i.e.* that the figures submitted were *per se* strictly honest and *bonâ fide*; 2, that nothing charged to capital account was valued above its cost; 3, that no ordinary repairs had been charged to plant; 4, that when the item of depreciation was omitted or seemed insufficient, he had received explanations which would satisfy him of acting solely on his own behalf and for his own interest. Failing any of these points, the auditor's certificate, or his report to the shareholders, should implicitly call attention to the facts; and in the fourth case, whatever be the explanation, the omission or apparent undercharge should be specially reported, if it was proposed to pay a dividend on the basis of the accounts in question. With regard to the second point, the simplest and broadest principle for regulating the value and depreciation of plant might be said to be its known capacity under normal circumstances to produce profit, subject, however, to its cost being fixed as the maximum value. He threw it out as a point of some interest for discussion, whether it was preferable as a matter of account to credit the depreciation yearly in the account to which it related, or, on the other hand, to open a special account as a sinking fund. He strongly inclined to the second plan whenever fixed rates were adhered to. It would be interesting to know how many members of the Manchester Institute of Accountants had met with a tendency on the part of directors or managers of businesses to undervalue their plant. He had himself only found one instance of such a tendency, and it was so rare that accountants might well be excused for being a little off their guard when they met with it. Mr. Mather, in conclusion, cited several cases to show the importance of an auditor's attention being called to depreciations and valuations.

DENT *Versus* THE LONDON TRAMWAYS COMPANY (LIMITED), NOVEMBER 16, 1880

[WITH A FOOTNOTE ON DAVISON V. GILLIES, MARCH 14, 1879]

JESSEL, M.R. 1880. Nov. 16. } DENT *v.* THE LONDON TRAMWAYS COMPANY (LIMITED).

Tramway Company—Repairs—Depreciation—Loss of Capital—Reserve Fund—Ordinary Shareholders—Dividends out of Capital—Preference Shareholders—Dividends depending on Profits of Particular Year.

The articles of association of a tramway company provided that "no dividend should be declared except out of profits;" that the directors should, with the sanction of the company, declare annual dividends "out of profits," and that the directors should, before recommending a dividend, set aside "out of profits," subject to the sanction of the company, "a reserve fund for maintenance, repairs, depreciation and renewals." For several years previous to the year 1878, *no proper reserve fund had been set aside by the company, and no sufficient sum had been expended by the company in the maintenance, repairs and renewals of their tramways, so that in the year* 1878 *they had become much out of repair. The company had for several years previous to, and also for the first half-year of,* 1878 *paid dividends on their ordinary shares, and had declared a dividend for the half-year ending the* 31*st of December,* 1878. *In an action by a shareholder to restrain the directors from paying the dividend, and it appearing that the amount available for the dividend was less than the sum required for the renewal and repairs of the tramways,*—Held, *that the company could only declare a dividend out of net profits, and that there could be no net profits until the tramways had been restored to a proper state, and provision for that purpose had been made out of the company's assets; and an injunction was accordingly granted to restrain the directors from paying to the ordinary shareholders the dividend declared.*

Certain preference shares had been issued by the company to bear a preferential dividend "dependent upon the profits of the particular year only." A dividend had also been declared on the preference shares for the half-year ending the 31*st of December,* 1878, *but the directors declined to pay the same until the capital of the company*

Dent v. London Tramways Co.

***had been restored by the amount previously improperly** paid away in dividends. For **the year** 1878 the accounts of the company **shewed a** net profit, after making due pro**vision** for repairs, depreciation and re**newals,** and to place the tramways of the **company** in the same condition on the 31st **of** December, 1878, as they were in on the **1st of** January, 1878, sufficient to pay the **stipulated** dividend to the preference share**holders**:*—Held, *that the preference share**holders** were co-adventurers for each par**ticular** year only, and inasmuch as the **accounts** for the year 1878 shewed a net **profit** on the working of that year, after **making** all due provision for repairs, depre**ciation** and renewals, sufficient for the pay**ment of** a dividend to the preference share**holders,** that they were entitled to be paid **such** dividend without deduction, and that **they were** under no liability to recoup the **amounts** which had previously been im**properly** paid away in dividends.*

Motion for judgment.

From the statement of claim it appeared that the defendant company was incorporated under the Companies Acts on the 14th of December, 1870, with a capital of 250,000*l.*, divided into 25,000 shares of 10*l.* each, the whole of which capital had been issued and fully paid up.

That a special resolution of the company was duly passed and confirmed in March, 1874, whereby it was resolved that the capital of the company should be "increased by the issue of 8,000 shares of 10*l.* each, bearing a preferential dividend of 6*l.* per cent. per annum, over the present shares of the company dependent upon the profits of the particular year only."

That in accordance with the resolution 8,000 preference shares of 10*l.* each had been issued and were fully paid up, and that during the year 1878 and at the time of action brought, the plaintiff was the holder of 100 fully paid-up preference shares.

That in the half-year ending the 30th of June, 1878, the company had earned profits sufficient for the payment of a dividend of six per cent. per annum both on their preference and ordinary shares, which dividend was paid, leaving a balance of profits amounting to 2,522*l.* 12*s.* 3*d.*, part of which, to the amount of 2,400*l.*, was specially set aside to meet the six months' interest on the preference shares to fall due on the 31st of December, 1878.

That in the half-year ending the 31st of December, 1878, the company earned profits sufficient for payment of a dividend at the rate of six per cent. per annum upon the preference shares, and at the rate of six per cent. per annum on the ordinary shares; and at a general meeting of the company held on the 20th of February, 1879, such dividend was duly declared and became payable to the plaintiff and other preference shareholders in the company.

That the company refused to pay such dividend, and that the sum of 30*l.* was due to the plaintiff in respect of his preference shares.

That the tramways and works of the company were in a state of efficiency and good working order, and that no expenditure beyond the expense occasioned by ordinary wear and tear was required.

The plaintiff, who sued on behalf of himself and all other preference shareholders, claimed a declaration that he and the other holders of preference shares were entitled to a dividend on their shares at the rate of six per cent. per annum for the half-year ending the 31st of December, 1878, payment of such dividend and ancillary relief.

The amended statement of defence admitted the issue of the preference shares, but alleged that from the year 1871 down to the end of 1878, the accounts of the company were made up so as to shew a considerable net balance of profits in each year available for the payment of dividends to the shareholders in the company, and that on the faith of these accounts and that proper provision had been made for all legitimate and proper expenses and deductions chargeable against revenue, and that the balances were in fact properly available for the payment of the dividends, that the company had paid dividends to their ordinary and preference shareholders.

That the company had only recently ascertained that from the year 1871 to the end of the year 1878 the accounts of the company had been kept and made up in an improper and misleading manner; that the company had been thereby deceived, and that no proper sums had been expended and no proper allowance had been made for and in respect of the maintenance, repairs, depreciation and renewals of the tramways property and buildings, rolling stock and horses belonging to the company; and that the amounts from time to time actually charged against the revenue in respect of such maintenance, repairs, depreciations and renewals were grossly inadequate, and were far below what ought properly to have been so charged.

That during the years 1871 to 1878 inclusive the actual net profits of the company, after making allowance for the matters aforesaid, amounted in the aggregate to the sum of 26,950*l.* 9*s.* 6*d.*, but that, owing to the improper manner in which the accounts had been kept, they shewed during the same period a net balance of profits of 141,411*l.* 8*s.* 2*d.*, and that (with the exception of a sum of 10,090*l.* 17*s.* 4*d.*, being the net balance of profits appearing on the face of the accounts for the half-year ending the 31st of December, 1878) the whole of such sum had been paid away by the company during the above years in dividends to their ordinary and preference shareholders and scripholders.

That the only fund which, according to the accounts of the company in their improper form, was available to meet the diminution in value of the capital of the company was the reserve fund of the company, amounting to a sum of 2,723*l.* 15*s.* 8*d.*

That the accounts for the year 1878 purported to shew a net balance of profits for the year of 21,178*l.* 10*s.* 10*d.*

Paragraph 20 of the statement of defence was as follows:—

"If a proper proportionate amount had been charged against the revenue of the year 1878 for the matters referred to in paragraph 6" (being in respect of maintenance, repairs, depreciation and renewals), "the accounts would have shewn, as the fact is, that there was a balance of revenue, and in that sense a net profit of only 14,932*l.* 5*s.* 4*d.*, whereof the sum of 5,953*l.* 14*s.* 2*d.* is attributable to the half-year ending the 30th of June, 1878, and the sum of 8,978*l.* 11*s.* 2*d.* to the half-year ending the 31st of December, 1878."

That on the faith of the accounts for the half-year ending the 30th of June, in accordance with a resolution of the company, dividends at the rate of six per cent. per annum for the half-year were paid to the preference shareholders, and of three per cent. per annum to the ordinary shareholders. That on the 20th of February, 1879, the company resolved to pay dividends at the rate of six per cent. per annum to the preference and ordinary shareholders for the half-year ending the 31st of December, 1878.

In March, 1879, in an action of *Davison* v. *Gillies* (1), on a motion for an injunc-

(1) JESSEL, M.R. 1879. March 14. — DAVISON *v.* GILLIES.

This was a motion by the plaintiff on behalf of himself and all other shareholders of the London Tramways Company, for an injunction to restrain the defendants, the directors of the company, from applying any part of the assets of the company which represented capital, or ought to be retained to represent capital, in the payment of dividends on the shares in the company, and from submitting to the shareholders any resolution to confirm or permit the payment of dividends out of capital, or summoning any meeting for the purpose of authorising payment of dividends, without first fully and properly disclosing to all the members of the company the true state of the capital, and other accounts of the company, and without disclosing the fact that no dividends could be paid except out of assets, which ought to be retained to represent capital.

The motion was based on the facts stated in the defence in *Dent* v. *The London Tramways Company*, that the tramways had become worn out, requiring the expenditure of a large sum for repairs, which had not been properly provided for by the company in their accounts, and that in consequence the company had no right to pay the dividend declared on the 20th of February, 1879, until the tramways were restored to a proper state, and until the amount expended out of capital had been replaced. The other facts are sufficiently stated in the judgment.

Mr. Chitty and *Mr. Stirling*, for the plaintiff.

Mr. Davey and *Mr. Romer*, for the defendants.

THE MASTER OF THE ROLLS.—The articles of association, which are binding on the directors and on the company, are very plain. The 107th article is this: "No dividend shall be declared except out of the profits of the company." A general meeting can-

Dent v. London Tramways Co.

tion, which by consent was turned into the trial, the Master of the Rolls granted an injunction restraining the directors from paying the dividend to the ordinary

not get over that. The dividend can never be declared but out of the profits, and the allegation on the part of the plaintiffs is that this dividend is not declared out of profits at all—that there are no profits available. The right to declare a dividend depends on the facts. The word "profits" by itself is a word which is certainly susceptible of more than one meaning, and one must ascertain what it means in these articles. The 103rd article says this: "The directors shall, with the sanction of the company, in general meeting, declare annual dividends, to be payable to the members out of the profits of the company, not exceeding the rate of six per cent. per annum for each year on the paid-up capital for the time being of the company; and of one-half of the profits of the company above that amount, and they shall declare the other half of such surplus profits to be payable to the scripholders." Scripholders are another class who are not shareholders, who have subscribed moneys, and are to be entitled to half the surplus profits. It is quite clear that whatever their profits are, they are profits of the same kind: half the surplus is to go to the shareholders, and the other half to the scripholders.

Then the next article is this: "The directors shall, before recommending any dividend, set aside out of the profits of the company, but subject to the sanction of the company in general meeting, such sum as they think proper, as a reserve fund for maintenance, repairs, depreciation and renewals." It is quite plain that the profits mean something after payment of the expenses, because you do not get a reserve fund at all until you have paid your current expenses. It is obvious that the word "profits" means net profits. The next article is this: "The directors shall also, before recommending any dividend, set aside out of the profits of the company a sum equivalent to one per cent. per annum on the amount of the paid-up capital for the time being, as a contingencies fund." There again "profits" obviously mean net profits. The result therefore of the articles, as I read them, is that a dividend shall only be declared out of net profits.

Then I have to consider the question, What are net profits? A tramway company lays down a new tramway: of course, the ordinary wear and tear of the rails and sleepers, and so on, causes a sum of money to be required from year to year in repairs. It may or may not be desirable to do the repairs all at once; but if, at the end of the first year, the line of tramway is still in so good a state of repair that it requires nothing to be laid out on it for repairs in that year, still, before you can ascertain the net profits, a sum of money ought to be set aside as representing the amount by which the wear and tear of the line has, I may say, so far depreciated it in value so that that sum will be required at some future period. Take the case of a warehouse: supposing a warehouse keeper, having a new warehouse, should find at the end of the year that he had no occasion to expend money in repairs, but thought that, by reason of the usual wear and tear of the warehouse, it was 1,000*l.* worse than it was at the beginning of the year, he would set aside 1,000*l.* for a repair or renewal or depreciation fund, before he estimated any profits; because, although that sum is not required to be paid in that year, it is still the sum of money which is lost, so to say, out of capital, and which must be replaced. I should think no commercial man would doubt that that was the right course—that he must not calculate net profits until he had provided for all the ordinary repairs and wear and tear occasioned by his business. In many businesses there is a regular sum or proportion of some kind set aside for this purpose. Shipowners, I believe, generally reckon so much a year for depreciation of a ship as it gets older. Experience tells them how much they ought to set aside, and whether the ship is repaired in one year or another makes no difference in estimating the profits, because they know a certain sum must be set aside each year to meet the extra repairs of the ship as it becomes older. There are very many other businesses in which the same thing is done.

That being so, it appears to me that you can have no net profits unless this sum has been set aside. When you come to the next year, or the third or fourth year, what happens is this: As the line gets older the amount required for repairs increases. If you had done what you ought to have done—that is, set aside every year the sum necessary to make good the wear and tear in that year—then in the following years you would have a fund sufficient to meet the extra costs. Now, when I come to look at these articles, I think that is what is intended, and that that is the meaning of the reserve fund. What the company intended to do was this: Inasmuch as they knew that a sum for maintenance, repairs, depreciation and renewals would be wanted, and inasmuch as they knew that, according to the ordinary commercial rules, they ought not to calculate the net profits until they had provided for what was sure to happen, they said, "We will set aside a sum of money which we will call a reserve fund for those purposes;" although not expended during the year, it is a reserve fund set aside for expenditure in the following years, taken out of profits before a dividend is earned. It appears to me, therefore, that these articles do recognise what seem to me sound commercial principles. That being so, from year to year, as the line got older, it would get worse, and would no doubt require a larger expenditure every year for repairs and renewals as a general rule. I say "as a general rule," because sometimes the repairs might be so extensive as to make the renewal of a large portion of the line requisite in one year, and then the next year there might be a falling off in the amount required; but, as a general rule, as the line got older it would require more money.

Now, the line having been established seven

shareholders, on the ground that the same would be a payment out of capital, and that for some years no proper allowance had been made in the accounts in respect of maintenance, repairs, depreciation and renewals.

The defendant company then submitted that the preference shareholders were not entitled to be paid any dividends out of the moneys of the company until the company, by means of sums earned since the 30th of June, 1878, increased their reserve fund by the sum of 114,460*l*. 18*s*. 8*d*., by which the capital had been diminished, or until the preference shareholders had accounted to the company for the sums of 1,969*l*. 18*s*. 6*d*., 4,800*l*. and 3,572*l*. 16*s*. 9*d*., which had been improperly paid by the company to them as dividends in the years 1874, 1875 and 1876.

The defendant company denied that the tramways were in a state of efficiency or good working order, and they alleged that a considerable sum would have to be expended before the tramways would be in a state of efficiency or good working order, and to renew the company's rolling stock, and to provide funds for the renewals of their leases, and to provide the company with horses and other necessary and proper amount of stock.

Messrs. Waddell, the accountants, furnished to the directors a report in March, 1880, on the accounts of the company, with a view to giving an opinion as to the amount of profit available for the preference dividend for the year 1878; and they stated that, in their opinion, following the judgment in *Davison* v. *Gillies*, the proper course was to reserve out of revenue each year a contribution towards the ultimate repairs equivalent to the wear and tear for that year, and that, treating the accounts for the year 1878 on that basis, there still remained the above-mentioned profit of 14,932*l*. 5*s*. 4*d*.,

years, I find an eminent engineer telling me, in his affidavit in support of the motion, that to put it in a good state of repair will require 80,000*l*.—in other words, if you take the deterioration of the line from want of repair from its commencement, it is worth 80,000*l*. less than it was at starting; that is the summary of that gentleman's evidence. He also thinks that the repairs, or the greater part of them, should be done at once. That is a matter of opinion on which engineers may fairly differ and do differ. The defendants' engineer, who, I am told, is also an eminent engineer, says he thinks they should not be done at once, but should be done gradually. But still, as I said before, they have to be done. That sum of money is required, or something like it. I cannot ascertain from the affidavit of the defendants' engineer what sum he considers sufficient. I have no doubt he would fix a much smaller sum. However, for the purpose of my judgment, I am willing to take a very large discount off the 80,000*l*., because it is a very much larger sum indeed than is required to wipe away the whole of the dividend the company have declared. Therefore one need not consider whether it is 80,000*l*. or 40,000*l*.—either sum would do; but a very large sum it is, and the defendants' engineer does not tell me how much.

I do not wish to prejudice any future application the company may make under the leave I am going to reserve to them, but I will say that unless they give me something a great deal more definite as to the amount actually required for putting the line into repair than I have at present, I should certainly not be of opinion that the amount they propose to divide among the shareholders is fairly divisible. [His Lordship then commented on the account for the half-year ending the 31st of December, 1878, observing that the existing "reserve fund" was altogether inadequate for the purposes of ordinary maintenance, and that the "contingency fund" was not applicable to such purposes. His Lordship then continued:] That being so, on the present evidence I am satisfied that there are no profits at present available for division. It may happen that there would have been profits, if the company had properly applied the surplus of former years. I must say, looking at the accounts of the company, it appears to be a flourishing company, and I hope nothing I say will damage its future success; but still I am bound by the articles to say that no dividend is to be paid except out of profits, that there are no profits available, and therefore I grant the injunction asked. At the same time, I wish to give the defendants every possible opportunity of shewing that there are profits available, and I also feel that my intervention is likely to be injurious to the company. If the defendants can shew at any time that there are profits available for the purposes of this dividend, I will give them an opportunity of doing so; and therefore I give them leave to move to dissolve the injunction I now grant.

The injunction granted was to restrain the defendants from authorising or making any payment out of the assets of the company in respect of the dividend declared in February, 1879, on the ordinary shares.

By consent the motion was afterwards treated as the trial of the action, and thereupon the injunction was made perpetual.

Solicitors—W. Heggerty; H. C. Godfray.

---

more than sufficient for the payment of the preference dividend of the year.

The plaintiff now moved for judgment on the admissions in the defence, and by consent the above report was referred to.

Mr. Davey and *Mr. Stirling*, for the plaintiff.—According to the terms of the resolution under which the preference shares were issued, the preference shareholders are entitled to a preferential dividend dependent upon the profits of each year; and, as it appears from the defence, and also from Messrs. Waddell's report, that there was a net profit for the year 1878, after making all allowance for expenses and wear and tear of that year, we submit the preference shareholders are entitled to their dividend, whatever payments may have been made out of capital in previous years, and that their position is entirely different from that of the ordinary shareholders whose rights were determined in *Davison* v. *Gillies*. The plaintiff for the present purpose has only to consider the year 1878, and if improper payments have been made to the shareholders in preceding years, that is a matter for which the directors may be personally liable, or the shareholders may be under a liability to refund, but it cannot affect the plaintiff's right to a dividend for the year 1878.

They were stopped.

Mr. Chitty and *Mr. Romer*, for the defendant company.—We submit that no dividend can be paid to the preference shareholders until the amount has been made good which has been previously improperly paid away in dividends, and not expended or set aside, as it should have been, in or towards the repairs, depreciation and renewals of the tramways. There is really no net profit to divide until the tramways of the company have been restored to that state of efficiency which they would have been in if those moneys had been so expended. But, in any event, the preference shareholders, before they receive any dividend, should at least make good the sums which have been improperly paid to them as dividends. According to the articles of association which were considered in *Davison* v. *Gillies*, no dividend can be declared except out of net profits; and so far as regards the payment of a dividend, the preference shareholders stand in no better position than the ordinary shareholders, and should only be paid out of sums which are really profits.

THE MASTER OF THE ROLLS.—I have no doubt what ought to be my decision on this question. What would have become of the action of *Davison* v. *Gillies*, if it had gone to trial and been fully argued out, I do not know, but the order made on the motion for injunction seems to have been the right order on the then state of facts, although I think it has been assumed that I then decided a great deal more than I did really decide. The present question is, to my mind, a very simple one. There is a bargain made with the company that certain persons will advance them money as preference shareholders—that is, that they shall be entitled to a preferential dividend of six per cent. over the ordinary shares of the company, "dependent on the profits of the particular year only." That means this, that the preference shareholders only take a dividend, if there are profits for that year sufficient to pay their dividend. If there are no profits for that year sufficient to pay their dividend they do not get it—they lose it for ever; and if there are no profits in one year, and twelve per cent. profit the next year, they would only get six per cent., and the other six per cent. would go to the ordinary shareholders. So that they are, so to say, co-adventurers for each particular year, and can only look to the profits of that year. Now, what happened was this: the company improperly allowed their tramways to get out of repair, and paid away their receipts to the ordinary shareholders in the shape of dividends. The result was, that on the 1st of January, 1878, the tramways were very much out of repair, and wanted a large sum to put them in a proper state of efficiency.

Notwithstanding that, the company did work, and they earned a good deal of money, and the profits for the year 1878 were upwards of 14,000*l.*; and the dividend required being only six per cent. on 80,000*l.*, it is quite clear they earned

Dent v. London Tramways Co.

more than sufficient to pay the preference shareholders, supposing these were fairly earned profits. Now, to see whether they were fairly earned profits, I must look at the report which I have before me of the eminent accountants, Messrs. Waddell, who say they were. They say in effect that, considering the state of the tramways on the 1st of January, 1878, and their state on the 31st of December in that year, after setting aside sufficient to make good the wear and tear for that particular year and paying all expenses, there was a net balance of 14,932*l.* 5*s.* 4*d.* profit. Now that is admitted by the statement of defence, paragraph 20. [His Lordship read the paragraph, and continued:] Therefore, if "profits for the year" have any meaning at all, these were the profits for the year. "Profits for the year" mean, of course, the surplus in receipts after paying expenses and restoring the capital to the position it was in on the 1st of January in that year. I have had the advantage of having Mr. Waddell present in Court, and ascertaining from him that his report in the sense I have stated is expressed according to his meaning, and that there is no mistake in the admission in the defence—that is, that there was an actual net profit for the year 1878 of over 14,000*l.*

Then what is there to argue? The argument for the company amounts to this, that inasmuch as they have improperly paid to their ordinary shareholders very large sums of money which did not belong to them, they are entitled to make good that deficiency by taking away the fund available for the preference shareholders to an amount required to put the tramways into proper order. When the argument is stated in that way it is clear it cannot be sustained. The company have either a right to recover back from their shareholders the sums overpaid or not. If they have a right they must recover them. If they have no right to recover them, *a fortiori* they have no right to recover them from the preference shareholders, and of course still less right to take away the dividends from the preference shareholders. It appears to me the defence is founded on a misconception, and I am afraid a misconception of what I was supposed to have decided on a former occasion; but I have no hesitation in making the declaration which I am asked to make in deciding in favour of the plaintiff on the present occasion. There will, therefore, be a declaration that the preference shareholders are entitled to be paid the dividend for the half-year ending the 31st of December, 1878.

Solicitors—King & Peto, for plaintiff; Harrison, Beal & Harrison, for defendant.

DEPRECIATION AND SINKING FUNDS

Edwin Guthrie

MANCHESTER ACCOUNTANTS' STUDENTS' SOCIETY.

At a Meeting of the Manchester Accountants' Students' Society, held on the 2nd inst., Mr. Edwin Guthrie read the following paper on

DEPRECIATION AND SINKING FUNDS.

Of all the interesting questions which arise for consideration in connection with accounts—especially commercial accounts—those in relation to depreciation and sinking funds are the most open to controversy. It is not in respect of the fact of chargeability itself that differences of view arise, but as to vo ume and mode of charge. They are not as a rule precisely measurable quantities, but such as must be assessed at discretion and judgment, based upon observations and experience.

They are elements of charge more or less important, as the case may be, in every profit and loss account, of manufacturers or traders, whose business involves the employment of machinery, or the ownership of business premises. The incidence of charge under these heads bears also in many directions beyond the circle of trade pure and simple. Every balance-sheet or statement of affairs is consequently affected.

Having regard to the character and motives of this society, I propose to make this paper in a great measure illustrative, and if I am successful in presenting a distinct view of the *principles* involved in the assessing of these charges, I shall be content, without attempting to elaborate the more complex phases which are presented in certain financial circumstances.

First let us take the comprehensive case of a manufacturer; and though the question may appear a very simple one, let us first put and find the answer to the question, what is a manufacturer? And what is involved in the performance of the acts necessary to his business? A manufacturer is one who produces goods for sale; production implies consumption, the value and volume of consumption represents the cost of the produce, the difference between the volume or value of that which is consumed and the volume or value of that which is produced is the profit or loss of the manufacturer.

How important then that the volume or value of that which is consumed should be accurately ascertained. To ascertain that volume or value of cost, every constituent element must be ascertained, weighed, and measured. What are they in this case? What does the manufacturer consume? Raw material, stores, labour-direct, outside services, machinery and buildings. These heads of cost may be subdivided indefinitely, but under them are grouped the elements of cost of most manufacturers. In a manufacturing concern all these things are consumed, and at the liquidation of his business there is no difficulty in finding the precise ultimate result of the operations; but our object at the moment is to ascertain the state of affairs *ad interim*, our friend the manufacturer desires to know yearly or half-yearly how he is faring. He is, we say, consuming material, stores, labour, outside services, machinery and buildings; there is, however, an essential difference between the four first named and the two last named of these elements of cost. The difference is (and in this relation it is the only difference), that the first enumerated are consumed absolutely within the period concerned except a measurable residue for immediate consumption in the succeeding period, while the last enumerated are consumed over a number of years. From year to year, neither the precise value consumed, nor the residue of value carried on from year to year, is exactly measurable. We have, therefore, to base these interim half-yearly or yearly accounts upon the assumption of a certain term of useful existence of the machinery or building. This term is called the "life" of the machine or building.

Herein is indicated the *principle* upon which we have to make our assessment, and base our interim charges.

The following may be taken as a representative case:—

A. B. undertakes a lease of 21 years of certain land and buildings, subject to a stated annual rental. Certain necessary alterations involve an outlay upon the buildings of £2,100, and machinery at a first cost of £21,000 is laid down. In this case, the rent having, of course, gone along with other specific charges in the profit and loss account, we have to provide for the recoupment of the £2,100 outlay upon the buildings. To accomplish this in the period, the rule is, to divide the outlay over the number of years of the lease, so that, at the period of liquidation, the realisation of the general assets will yield a return equal to the total original sum expended.

If it occurs to you at this point to remind me that, a 21 years' annuity of £100 does not represent the present value of £2,100, we should not disagree; I should simply remind you in response that my subject is not that of profit and loss, but of recoupment of capital outlay, the annual capital deficiency of specific outlay. In a trading concern the question of interest on such specific outlay is upon current account in the general undertaking, and the proper division of profit and loss account into part one and part two; the former being the trading division, the latter the proprietary division, is the proper place of adjustment to equalise the charge between year and year of the trading account.

That is not the subject of the evening, I mention it only to anticipate any apparent obstacle which may have presented itself to the minds of any students who may have given attention to actual problems.

By the mode of treatment practised, the account really bears a larger charge in the earlier years of the term—by reason of the larger burden of interest incurred—than the later years, but this is in fact generally counterbalanced by the additional cost of repairs in the later years.

If the expenditure be not outlay upon structural alterations, as supposed in the case given, but simply purchase-money, the same rule is generally practised, that is to say, the equal division of the purchase-money over the number of years.

If this is done advisably and with the deliberate intention of lightening the burden of the future, the defence of this practice is a good one: but as a matter of actuarial precision it is not the true practice, nor is there in this item the consideration of any counterbalancing expenditure. The annual value of the expenditure based upon the rate of interest required as by a landlord, say 5 per cent., should be ascertained, and that amount written against the outlay after charging interest. In this way the incidence of the charge against the working account, which we have already called part 1 of profit and loss account, will be equal throughout the period.

The same rule will apply to all sinking funds where it is provided that interest and redemption of principal money should be covered by equal annual instalments.

If there should be additional expenditure during the term of the lease, the same rule will apply.

Having provided for the restoration of the capital expended in an original outlay absolutely irrecoverable in its whole amount, we have now to consider how fairly to provide for the restoration of the capital expenditure upon moveable machinery.

For simplicity's sake, let us assume in the first instance that the machinery is of one kind and of equal average length of life. First observing that the difference between this item of depreciation of machinery and the sinking fund covering the cost of the buildings abandoned at the end of the lease, viz. that while in the latter case there is no valuable residue, in the former there *is* a valuable residue, we have to assess in the case of machinery the amount of the value of the residue at the end of its "life." That assessment is necessarily arbitrary, resting entirely upon the exercise of judgment based upon observation and experience. Assume that in the case in point, the life of the machinery is the term of the twenty-one years' lease, and that the assumed residuary value is about one-fourth of the original outlay, the cost of the consumption of the machinery is about £15,750 over the period. Are we then to follow the principle settled in the case of leases, and divide this quantity into 21 equal parts to ascertain the annual cost of the depreciation of machinery? and if not, why not? and how otherwise is the residue to be reached within the term?

If the expenditure upon machinery was the same definite sum as the expenditure upon buildings under a lease, we should have to say, treat it in the same defined way; but experience shows that there are comparatively few cases where an original expenditure suffices the purposes of a manufacturer. Improvements upon machinery already acquired, and the introduction of entirely new machines, bring about in the course of a term of years, such irregularities of value, and the proportions of value consumed and left, that at the end of the term the differences of values would be so irregular, and the number of machines and of the different articles of plant so great, that in a large works it would require the employment of an actuary to keep a precise account of what was, after all, a matter of general judgment, subject to the incidence of the whole range of commercial contingencies. In some works there is a perpetual renewal of "life," by the continual partial introduction of new machinery, so that, a certain point of reduction—the point of realisable value—being once reached, the value remains permanent. Moreover the ratio of the diminution of realisable value is greater in the earlier than in the later years of the life of machinery.

These arguments point to, and the last mentioned consideration, I think, clenches the principle upon which depreciation of machinery should be rated, and that is, after prudentially assessing the residual value, ascertain what rate of discount upon the diminishing annual value will serve to reach that residual value. Thus, the rate of 6 per cent. will write down the sum of £21,000 to £5,726, which approximates the estimated residual value at the end of the twenty-one years, the depreciation over the whole period being £15,274. This is designed to provide for the variations incident to additions and displacements.

The basis of average is thus part of the principle upon which rates of depreciation may be settled.

At this point the question may very properly be put, If the *realisable value* at the end of the assumed period of life is to be assumed, why is not this, the principle of valuation, to apply at every rest or period throughout the life? I think we shall find no difficulty in arriving at the conclusion that such would not be a true system of interim assessment. Manufacturers and traders do not construct business premises or lay down special plant in the intent of a short period. It would seldom pay to do so. A large, irrecoverable outlay is generally expended in the preparation of a factory, and unless speedy destruction overtakes any certain business, the method of treatment for annual accounting is as of a "going concern." Otherwise, since all machinery may be said to be second-hand when once it has turned round, and perhaps unsaleable then at half its cost of first purchase and erection, a depreciation of 50 per cent. would probably not be sufficient to represent the *realisable* value at the end of the first year. Manifestly the career of the business contemplated must have an assumed term, and the cost of the consumption of machinery and other erections must be attributed to the whole term assumed.

For fuller occasional satisfaction, prudent manufacturers will periodically call in professional valuers, having the necessary special experience, to value their plant and machinery, not necessarily annually, but perhaps every three, seven, or ten years, according to the nature of the case. But every valuation so taken for purpose of the proprietor's account, should be made with regard to normal cost rather than to the value on the day of valuation. Matter and things fixed in a permanent working position must not be treated in account as following the fluctuations of the market, for it is not a trading item that is in question, such as stock-in-trade, which can be sold any day without interruption to the works. Such a valuation is for purpose of check, and for ascertaining that a fair proportion of capital outlay is being brought into account to return the value expended within the period of its remunerative exhaustion.

In assessing such amount care should be taken that in any case of uncertainty as to amount of annual charge for depreciation of machinery and other outlay, the higher rather than the lower rate should be taken as the safer, not only from ordinary prudential considerations, but in order that, in the event of some extraordinary contingency, such as the supersession of existing machinery and appliances by new inventions, the blow should not be heavier than need be under such extraordinary circumstances.

On the other hand, to introduce into profit and loss account too great a charge for depreciation may be as disastrous as the making of too small a charge, for by so doing, selling prices of the product manufactured may be fixed so high as to prevent the necessary volume of business.

Let us consider now the relation of the cost of repairs to depreciation and annual value of property in account. Ought repairs under all conditions to be a charge direct to profit and loss account, or may they be capitalised and go in augmentation of the capital values?

On this question we cannot fix an unvarying rule. In cases where the expenditure is a regular quantity, it is clearly best to charge all expenditure to profit and loss account direct, and leave the regular rate of depreciation to meet the constant cost of wear and tear; but there are other cases where renewals and repairs are so involved and incurred at intervals so irregular that the fairest and most prudential method of treatment may be to charge all expenditure to the respective capital accounts, and rate the charge for depreciation proportionately high, so as to distribute the true cost truly over the whole term, and prevent irregularity of charge as between year and year in respect of expenditure made in the interest of a term.

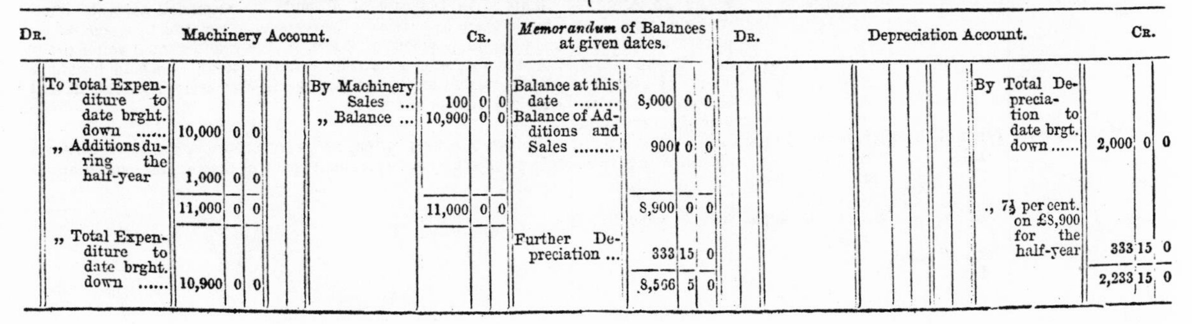

Dr. Machinery Account. Cr.

Dr.	£	s.	d.	Cr.	£	s.	d.
To Total Expenditure to date brght. down	10,000	0	0	By Machinery Sales ...	100	0	0
,, Additions during the half-year	1,000	0	0	,, Balance ...	10,900	0	0
	11,000	0	0		11,000	0	0
,, Total Expenditure to date brght. down	10,900	0	0				

Memorandum of Balances at given dates.

	£	s.	d.
Balance at this date	8,000	0	0
Balance of Additions and Sales	900	0	0
	8,900	0	0
Further Depreciation ...	333	15	0
	8,566	5	0

Dr. Depreciation Account. Cr.

Dr.	£	s.	d.	Cr.	£	s.	d.
				By Total Depreciation to date brgt. down......	2,000	0	0
				,, 7½ per cent. on £8,900 for the half-year	333	15	0
					2,233	15	0

The above particulars are capable of being exhibited in the following form among the assets in the balance sheet:—

	£	s.	d.
Machinery Account	10,000	0	0
Additions during the half-year	1,000	0	0
	11,000	0	3
Less Sales during the half-year	100	0	0
Total net expenditure	10,900	0	0
Depreciation Account........................	2,333	15	0
Balance	8,566	5	0

In all cases allow me again to urge the giving of the benefit of any doubt to the larger rather than to the smaller rate of charge. In the course of his career, it is on this point that an accountant practising in a manufacturing district has most frequently to take a stand. Private proprietors, managers, and directors of public companies, are too often prone to present the best possible aspect of the results of their efforts, and some of them will, if they may, dwell for years in a fool's paradise, holding their eyes shut to the inevitable day of reckoning, when it may be found that the lightening of the charge against earlier years has accumulated a crushing burden for some later unhappy day.

The same effect may happen not only by the short charging of expenditure, but by over-crediting in anticipation of profits, as, for instance, in the case of building societies, the practice of bringing in to the years in which they are received the premiums—paid by borrowing members upon mortgage loans—which should be distributed over the whole term of repayment, and in the case of insurance companies the treating of single premium receipts in like manner. I do no more than indicate this as an issue involving the same principle—the actuarial principle in its application to commercial accounts.

Now as to the modes of stating the accounts subject to depreciation, and the depreciation accounts themselves, there are three plans open.

(1.) To reduce the principal account itself by the amount of depreciation, and carry down the diminished value. This plan presents the advantage of simplicity in presenting the results, but by it are lost the total of the expenditure on the one hand, and the total of depreciation on the other, up to any given date and over any given period.

Another plan is to keep the principal account and its account for depreciation separate, and thus exhibit the total of each. But in this we lose sight of the balance representing the diminishing value, and this it is frequently necessary to know. But it is possible to keep a combined account exhibiting both totals and balances, and this is the form I suggest as the most comprehensive. (See p. 7.)

So far I have used for simplicity of illustration a single account as rated for depreciation. This is seldom, however, the whole case, a very general division being as follows:—(*a*) buildings, (*b*) engines, boilers, and gearing, (*c*) machinery, (*d*) loose appliances. There may also be (*e*) patterns, (*f*) patents, (*g*) goodwill, (*h*) leases. But by way of presenting something like a complete view of the range of capital items subject to annual or periodical reduction of value for depreciation, the following table is set out. Although each line has its special features, the same *principle* of treatment is capable of being applied to them all without exception.

The following is given as a general sketch showing the various tenures and modes of rating different property accounts.

Table of Capital Items subject to charge for Depreciation and Redemption, with general range of Rates and Remarks thereupon.

Object of requirement.	Tenure.	Matter.	Rates.	Remarks.
Location	Perpetual	Land (Freehold)		This may either appreciate or depreciate, according to location; but is seldom subject to rapid fluctuations, and often in the case of factories improvement of value is not realisable, except by costly structural changes or removals. If, in a case of appreciation of land, the tenement is a shop the trade of which is directly affected, the proper division and treatment of the profit and loss account will provide for an increased debit to the trading division and an increased credit to the proprietary division, and the capital value may be charged accordingly.
Location	Fixed Term	Leases		As an annuity having regard to interest, or at discretion, on equal division of original value by the number of years to run. There being no residue of value.
Habitation	Freehold	Buildings		
		Houses	2½ o/o @ 4 o/o on diminishing values	Having always a residue of value.
		Mills	2¼ o/o @ 5 o/o on diminishing values	Having always a residue of value.
Do.	Leasehold	Buildings	As an Annuity having regard to interest or at discretion, equal division of original value by the number of years to run.	This is in the case of absolute or presumed absolute term. Should there be provision for renewal or renewal by usage, as for instance, on payment of a fine of one year's annual value every twenty-one years, renewing a longer term, leasehold buildings may be treated for depreciation as if they were freehold, having always a residue of value.
Motive Power	Term of their Life	Engines, Boilers and Gearing (If treated together)	4 o/o @ 7 o/o on diminishing value	Boilers are very often, and very properly, treated separately, being subject to more frequent renewal than engines and gearing.
		Boilers if separately	10 o/o @ 12½ o/o	
Motive Power	Term of their Life			

Object of requirement.	Tenure.	Matter.	Rates.	Remarks.
Producing Appliances		Moving Machinery such as Fixed Tools in Engineering Works, Spinning and Weaving Machinery, &c.	5 o/o @ 10 o/o on diminishing values	Having always a residue of value.
Do.	Do.	Fixed Plant, as Blast Furnaces, Chemical Plant, &c., subject to rapid depreciation and constant repair, and of little ultimate value	Divide by the number of years upon the assumed life of the Business as if it were a lease, until reduced to ultimate break up value	In these cases no charge for re-erection should be capitalised except to the extent that such re-erection is an enlargement or improvement on the old plant.
Manipulating Appliances	Do.	Loose tools and utensils	Are subject to rating at the fullest possible range according to their nature.	They may even be treated as stock subject to valuation from balance to balance.
Do.	Do.	Furniture and Fixtures	7 o/o to 12½ o/o on diminishing values	They have always some residue of value.
Do.	Their brief term of Life	Patterns	15 o/o to 33⅓ o/o on diminishing values	Here, but for the fact that patterns constitute matter for a separate account, and the additions are numerous and constant, and the rate of depreciation high, it might be held that they be written off over a specified short term upon original cost, but amongst other reasons for not so doing, patterns have often a goodwill value.
Locomotion	The term of Life	Rolling Stock	7½ o/o @ 15 o/o on diminishing values as an annuity or at discretion	There being always a residue of value and generally a constant renewal and replacement.
Monopoly	The term of the grant	Patents and other monopolies	Divide upon the number of years of the full term of life or shorter estimated period of value	There is no residue of value except, perhaps, in the augmentation of the general goodwill of the concern.
Business connection	Uncertain	Goodwill	As an annuity or at discretion divide the purchase-money over the number of years of estimated period of value	It will often be found that proprietors who have paid for a goodwill desire to treat it of permanent value, but having regard to all the contingencies of business, it is never safe to assume it, and such premium value ought always to be written down.
Sowing Seed for future return		Opening of Mines and Quarries	As an annuity or at discretion in equal annual division over the estimated life of the Business, or estimated tonnage of mineral	In the opening of all mines and quarries, whether coal, metals, or stone, there is always a large—in most cases an immense—outlay and a long delay in preparing the way for a return of value. A normal tonnage should be estimated over a term of years taken to be the life of the undertaking. Thus, if there should be disappointment in respect of tonnage raised, the loss will be loss of capital in ultimate liquidation. Should there be a yield in excess of expectation, the rate may be reduced and discontinued altogether where break-up values have been reached.
Incidental	Immediate	Formation expenses	In equal portion on 3 to 5 years	At discretion this may be disposed of in first year, or the amount may be so small as to be thus properly dealt with; but where the amount is large, as may be the case in large transfers under deed, and where large commissions are paid, it is quite justifiable to spread the charges over a limited number of years, for the expenditure is incurred in the interest of the permanent working.

Thus underlying every illustration it will be seen that the actuarial principle, applied upon bases arbitrarily settled by the exercise of judgment founded on experience, settles the great guiding rule in the rating of depreciation.

There is one large class of expenditure which I have not yet specifically dealt with, although it is covered under the rules explained. I refer to the large sums raised from time to time on public works and for public purposes, such as dock and harbour works, county, city, and local board improvement purposes, and even national debts. The method of dealing with these is generally laid down under some special or general Act of Parliament. Such debts may be either permanent, or their redemption may be effected in two ways—(1) by equal annual instalments of the principal money and current interest upon the diminishing debt, or (2) on the annuity principle by equal annual payments over a fixed period.

Under the first-named plan the burden is a diminishing one, and ceases gradually. Under the latter the burden is equal upon every year of the period.

The former system has much in its favour. It is certainly more prudential than the latter, inasmuch as it takes the greater burden at the time when circumstances are sufficiently buoyant to determine the outlay, and in the event of any decay of prosperity the inheritance of responsibility from year to year is a diminished burden; and further, if prosperity continues, further expenditure and fresh loans become necessary, and there is the greater room for bearing the cost of them.

In favour of the latter course, it is often urged that certain expenditure is in the interest of a long period extending far into the future, say sixty years, and therefore it is not fair to the present to pay more than an equal annual share of principal and interest, but upon this ruling the whole principal money might be carried on as an undiminished quantity in perpetuity. It will readily be seen how in the event of any local depression or decay the burden of such indebtedness might be fatal to the corporate existence of any given community or trust.

I trust I have not too far enlarged upon my subject, so as take the mind from the solid apprehension of the main argument, but the subject is a large one, and it will be seen how without thoughtful applications of ascertained principles of account, and, I may add, of logic too, together with a wide-awake observation of the changing conditions arising from new processes and change of appliances and legal regulations, the experience of even the elders of the profession is never a superfluous quantity. Suffice now the further assurance, that the cultivation of the faculty of analysis will duly develop the power of construction in relation to any questions arising under this title, as indeed of any question of account.

PAYMENT OF DIVIDEND OUT OF CAPITAL

J. W. Best

SHEFFIELD CHARTERED ACCOUNTANTS' STUDENTS' SOCIETY.

PAYMENT OF DIVIDEND OUT OF CAPITAL.

By Mr. J. W. Best, A.C.A.

At an ordinary meeting of members held on Wednesday, the 4th November, A. T. Watson, Esq., F.C.A., the President, in the chair. The following paper was read by Mr. J. W. Best, A.C.A., on "Payment of Dividend out of Capital"—

This subject is, I think, one of the most difficult in the whole range of Company Law. It is one which an accountant has ever to bear in mind, for it involves a proper distribution of capital and revenue, and to be able to discriminate one from the other is one of the most essential qualifications for a good accountant.

I need hardly say that there is no difference of opinion that the payment of dividend to shareholders out of capital is illegal, but as to what constitutes a payment of dividend out of capital there is a difference of opinion and a good deal to be said on both sides of the question. Shareholders are very apt to take one point of view and creditors and the outside public another, but let us as unbiased parties take the independent ground, and see if we cannot come to some equitable and just conclusion.

First let us consider what are the admitted legal funds for the payment of dividends?

Clause 73 of table A says: "No dividend shall be payable except out of the profits arising from the business of the company," and, although table A applies only to those trading Companies registered under the Companies' Acts, where there are no special articles of association excluding or modifying these regulations, it is one of the fundamental principles of the Company Law, that the profits, and the profits alone, is the only fund out of which dividends may be paid.

Sec. 121 of the Companies' Clauses Consolidation Act, 1845, plainly enacts that dividend shall not be paid out of capital. It is as follows:—

"A Company shall not make any dividend whereby their capital stock shall in any way be reduced, provided always that the word "dividend" shall not be considered to apply to a return of any portion of the capital stock with the consent of all the mortgagees and bond creditors of the company, due notice being given for that purpose at an extraordinary meeting, to be convened for that object."

This Act applies to all Joint Stock Companies, whether registered under that or any future Act, where there is no provision to the contrary; and as there is no provision to the contrary in the Companies' Acts passed since, excepting as to the requirements necessary for effecting the return of any portion of the capital stock, it is still applicable to all existing Limited Companies.

In spite of this there have been several cases scarcely reconcilable with this enactment, the most notable being *Dent* v. *The London Tramways Company*, (16 Ch. Div., 344) where it was held that holders of preference shares whose "dividend was dependent upon the profits of a particular year only" were entitled to a dividend out of the profits of any year after providing for the depreciation of the tramway during that year, and without making good depreciation in preceding years. Although this seems to involve the payment of the dividend out of capital, you will notice that it was to *Preference* shareholders, whose dividend was dependent upon the profits of a particular year, and moreover, the right of these preference shareholders would have to have been acquired by the articles filed contemporaneously with the memorandum of association, and as both the memorandum and articles of association are public documents, no one need be deceived by it.

It could not in any way affect ordinary shareholders, and the broad principle remains that dividends are payable out of the profits arising from the business of a company, and that payment of dividends out of capital would be illegal.

Now the vital part of the question is this. What are profits arising from the business of the company?

I can't do better than quote the decision in *Stringer's* case (L.R. 4 Ch. 475) cited by Buckley in his work on the Companies' Acts. It was as follows:—

"The proper and legitimate way of arriving at a statement of profits is *to take the facts as they actually stand*, and after forming an estimate of the assets *as they actually exist*, to draw a balance so as to ascertain the result in the shape of profit and loss. If this be done *fairly and honestly*, without any fraudulent intention or purpose of deceiving anyone, it does not render the dividend fraudulent that there was not cash in hand to pay it, or that the company were even obliged to borrow money for that purpose, and the fact that an estimated value was put upon assets which were then in jeopardy, and were subsequently lost, does not render the balance-sheet delusive and fraudulent.

Now this clear and unmistakeable, and at the same time sensible decision, plainly indicates to my mind that the surplus of assets over liabilities and capital is the fund, and the only fund available for dividend. This might be considered by some to be an unprofessional way of stating what are profits, yet I think we, as accountants, should see that this is the result of all true and correct profit and loss accounts.

It may occur to you that sometimes there appears in the balance-sheet of a company items which are only fictitious assets, such as preliminary expenses, and that this definition of profits in that case would not apply. True, it is that preliminary expenses would have no realisable value, but it is necessary expenditure of capital for the purpose of earning, not merely one year's, but several years' revenue, and therefore it is one of those items of expenditure which, although not dealt with in the Companies' Acts themselves, was contemplated at the time, and specially provided for in table A, which says in cases where any item of expenditure may in fairness be distributed over several years which has been incurred in any one year, the whole amount of such item shall be stated, with the addition of the reasons why only a portion is charged against the income of the year.

Now, if the surplus of assets over liabilities and capital represents profit available for dividend, it follows that the excess of liabilities and capital over assets would represent loss, and therefore in such a case there would be no fund available for dividend. This seems plain and straightforward, but it is by no means certain. This loss may represent loss of capital and loss of revenue, or it may represent the difference between capital lost and revenue earned, and Buckley makes a distinction between the two. Here, I am confronted with an opinion far weightier than my own, and although it would be presumption on my part to submit that mine is worthy of consideration, still I cannot, for the life of me, see on what grounds he bases his views. I know I must be shortsighted, but perhaps the consideration of this complicated but very interesting question will elicit something that will give me a clearer view. If it does I shall be well repaid for my trouble.

Mr. Buckley says that the question is believed to be as yet entirely open whether a company, under the Companies Acts, which has lost part of its capital by loss on capital account, can continue to pay dividends until the lost capital has been made good.

Now what is the loss of capital, and what is a loss of revenue?

Buckley's illustration will best explain. He says:—

If a ship-owning company's capital be represented by ten ships with which it trades, and one is totally lost and un-insured, this loss is what is here called a loss on capital account.

The same company begins the year with ten ships, value say £100,000, and ends the year with the same ten ships, and the result of the trading, after allowing for depreciation of the ships, is a loss of £100. This would be what is here called a loss on revenue account.

Now, supposing that this company in the course of its business loses a ship valued at £10,000, but makes a profit in trading of £5,000. Can the company distribute the £5,000 profit as dividend before making good the £10,000 lost capital?

If the decision of this question were left to me, I should certainly say no. Such a distribution would be a payment of dividend out of capital.

Mr. Buckley says that he has always understood the true principle to be that capital account and revenue account are distinct.—Yes. And that for the purposes of determining profits, you must disregard accretions to or diminutions of capital.

If Mr. Buckley had used this broad statement without previously showing what he meant by a loss of capital, I should have agreed with him that this is fair and equitable and sound all round. Or again, if he had simply explained his meaning by the illustrations which follow, about 3% consuls purchased at 97 falling to 94, and a Tramway Company laying its line when materials and labour are both dear, at a cost of twice the amount the same line could be laid for now, I could not have done otherwise than coincide with his opinion that this particular kind of accretions to or diminutions of capital should be disregarded.

I should have said that the principle of valuing this particular class of assets at the market price would be, to say the least, a very imprudent basis of valuation.

I need only go back to what has been decided to be the proper and legitimate way of arriving at the profits of a company to find there that the proper mode of valuing assets is to estimate them fairly and honestly, as they actually exist, without any fraudulent intention of deceiving anyone; and what I consider to be the fair and honest basis of valuation, I will attempt to show.

There are two kinds of assets, the basis of valuation in each of which should be a different one.

There are *Assets, purchased or acquired in the interest of permanent working for the purpose of earning the revenue, such as buildings, plant, machinery, &c.*; and *Assets in which a Company deals in the ordinary course of business*; such as materials used in the manufacture of goods, or commodities manufactured or purchased for sale.

This latter class of assets (Stock-in-Trade) may always with safety, and at the same time honestly and fairly, be valued at the market price, though it is not always, in my opinion, prudent to do so. As a general rule, if market price exceeded the cost, I should myself treat them as being worth the cost, but if the cost exceeded the market price, I should take market price as the basis. I will here say that if the 3% consols referred to belonged to a person who speculated in stocks and shares for the purpose of his livelihood, I should value his stocks and shares at the market price, just in the same way as I should the stock-in-trade of a manufacturer.

Now it is the former class of assets, viz., those acquired in the interest of permanent working for the purpose of earning the revenue, where the difficulty of valuation is. What is the fair and honest way of estimating the value of these.

It would certainly be unreasonable for a company to take as the basis for valuation of buildings, plant and machinery, market price, or break-up value. If you purchase for a certain amount a lease, say for 20 years, and you find out five years afterwards that you could then have got the same lease for half the amount, the difference to you is not a loss of capital, but a heavier annual charge against your revenue during the whole term of the lease. You are providing out of revenue for the restoration of capital by writing off periodically such a sum as will extinguish the asset by the time the lease expires. Take the opposite view of the case. Supposing that you found five years' later that it would have cost you double the amount for the same lease, the difference would not be an increase of capital, but a smaller charge against your revenue than it otherwise would have been.

You are thinking of selling the lease, or realising it in any way. You have got it, if not for the full term of the lease, at any rate for a fixed period, and providing the asset is being written down, so by that time it will appear at realisable value, that is all that is necessary.

So it is with any item of Expenditure or Capital account, although you may have paid dearly for it, or the price has subsequently fallen, the price paid was in good faith for the benefit of the company. It was not like goods bought to be sold again. It was bought by the company to be used until worn out, for the purpose of carrying on its trade, and it is therefore revenue that would suffer.

Please note that I have been speaking of assets which exist.

The points to which I wish particularly to call your attention are, where the assets have ceased to exist, as in the case of the un-insured ship, and where the nature of the asset has entirely changed, as where a ship is realised and turned into money, at a loss say of £1,000.

These are losses which Mr. Buckley is of opinion a company could ignore, but for him to hold this view he must entirely disregard the law laid down in *Stringer's* case, which clearly defines what are profits available for dividend.

In an ordinary partnership, where partner's capitals are unequal but the profits and losses equal, would not such losses as these, where there is no special agreement to the contrary, be treated like any other loss, and be borne equally by the partners, and is there to be a difference in arriving at the profits of an *extraordinary* partnership in "a limited company."

Now, if profits is the only fund out of which a dividend can be paid, and the proper and legitimate way of arriving at a statement of profits available for dividends, is to have regard to the assets as they actually exist, it follows that a lost ship, or a loss in the realisation of a ship, must affect the value of a company's assets, and therefore the profits available for dividend.

And if profit on trading be distributed in the shape of dividend, regardless of the loss on capital account, it would not be a payment out of profits available for dividend, but out of capital, and there is no doubt that a payment of dividend out of capital is illegal.

And why is it illegal? Because it is in effect an unauthorised reduction of capital. It is equal to a return of paid-up capital, and you well know that a reduction of capital in any other way than with the authority, and under the order, of the court is a decided breach of the law.

A reduction of capital either by the cancellation of any lost capital, or by the return of any paid up capital, was only authorised by the legislature of 1877, under the most stringent conditions. Before the court will order a return of any paid-up capital or a reduction which involves the diminution of any liability in respect of unpaid capital, it will require to be satisfied that all creditors of the company have had notice of the proposed reduction. Any creditor may object at a time and place to be fixed by the court, and in the event of any objection, the court will require the company to set apart and appropriate the amount of the creditor's claim. For the protection of any other persons who may become creditors, the words "and reduced" must be added to the name of the company for such a period as the court thinks fit, and in the event of the company failing to give the requisite notice, any reduction shall be void as against the creditors who have not had such notice,

Now the whole tenor of the Companies' Acts is such as to imply that the paid-up capital of the company must not be interfered with. In Buckley's notes to sec. 12 of the 1862 Act a case is cited in which it was said, that "the statute contemplates the protection not only of shareholders for the time being of the company, but also those who may hereafter become shareholders, and further, the outside public, and in particular those who are, or may be, the companies' creditor."

In Buckley's notes to sec. 12 of the Act of 1862, there is a case given in which it is stated that "the actual capital of a company is to be a reality, and not a fiction, and a creditor is entitled to have it in his power to ascertain what is the actual amount of money or money's worth to which he can look."

A man about to deal with a private individual or firm knows, or is supposed to know, on what ground he stands, and with whom he is dealing. If the assets of a firm are insufficient to meet the liabilities, a creditor has his remedy against the private resources of each partner, but when dealing with a limited company the shareholders are only liable to the extent of their shares. What means has he of ascertaining the value of a company's credit, and of assuring himself to what amount he may safely trust them.

The commercial or social standing of the shareholders individually is no guide to him. All he can look to is the subscribed capital of the company, and what means have the public and creditors of ascertaining this?

The only official means provided for them is access to the public documents filed with the registrar of Joint Stock Companies, such as Memorandum and Articles of Association, yearly returns and lists of shareholders and capital subscribed, any special resolution which may have been passed by a company. A *creditor* may also inspect the register of mortgages.

But I ask what is the use, and where is the necessity of the Act of 1877 providing for a reduction of paid-up capital, if a company can disregard them, and do what is practically the same thing, pay dividends out of capital.

Of what value would the provisions for the protection of creditors and the outside public be, if a company could pay dividends and ignore losses of capital. Would it not be calculated to mislead and deceive any person who might wish to inspect or have copies of these documents. What guide to a man would it be to know the amount of the subscribed capital if a company could reduce it at will. When a company pays a dividend it gives notice to the public that it is a payment out of profits, and that the capital is left untouched, and the whole tenor of the Companies' Acts gives the public ample grounds for believing that such is the case.

Now I have tried to show you—

(1.) That profits is the only fund out of which a dividend can be paid.

(2.) That the proper and legitimate way of arriving at a statement of profits is to have regard to the value of the assets as *they actually exist*, or in other words, that the surplus of assets over liabilities and capital, is the profit available for dividend.

(3.) That if this be so, losses of capital must affect profits available for dividend.

(4.) That if profits on revenue account be distributed regardless of losses on capital account, it amounts to a payment of dividend out of capital.

(5.) That a payment of dividend out of capital is illegal, because it is in effect an unauthorised reduction of capital.

I say that a company which has made a loss of capital, must do one of two alternatives, either it must reduce the profits available for dividend, or it must reduce its capital by complying with the requirements of the Act of 1877, which specially provides for the cancellation of any lost capital, or capital which is not represented by available assets.

If such a point came before us, how ought we to deal with it as a matter of book-keeping ?

For my part I should consult the directors, and if they were of opinion that a loss of capital ought not to be charged to profit and loss account, I should, as it is an open question, see that a special account was opened in the ledger for it, and that it appeared separately in the balance-sheet.

As auditor, I should feel it my duty to draw the attention of the shareholders to it in my report, and there my responsibilities would cease.

Now, gentlemen, this is a subject worth consideration, and I hope we shall have it thrashed out.

I am open to conviction that my views are incorrect, but I am afraid it would be rather a tough piece of business to convince me that the contrary opinion would be in accordance with commercial morality, upon which all Acts affecting the commerce of this country are supposed to be based. We know it is stated that there never was an Act of Parliament that a coach and four could not be driven through, and I wouldn't like to say that the Companies' Acts are an exception to the rule. I do not think though that the majority of people would not conscientiously hold the view that these Acts intended that loss of capital by a limited company should be disregarded, but my observation has led me to believe that conscience is a very elastic thing sometimes.

A hearty discussion ensued, and the members present were unanimous in their opinion that a loss of capital by a limited company must either be written off under the Companies' Acts, or set off against the profits available for dividend.

A vote of thanks proposed by the President, and seconded by Mr. W. Holmes, A.C.A., closed the proceedings.

WHAT IS INCOME?

J. M. Wade

LIVERPOOL CHARTERED ACCOUNTANTS' STUDENTS' ASSOCIATION.

WHAT IS INCOME?

By Mr. J. M. Wade, F.C.A.

At the opening meeting of the Session, held on the 7th October, the following paper was read by Mr. J. M. Wade:—

Gentlemen,—I have in the first place to congratulate the Liverpool Chartered Accountants' Students' Association upon the commencement of another session, and to wish you all success.

Every year which passes by proves that owing to the growth of, and changes in, the commercial system of this country, accountants are becoming more and more useful and necessary to the community.

We have every reason to hope and expect, therefore, that our profession will also grow both in position and usefulness; will increase in numbers, and be more largely sought after as a means of earning an honourable living.

Not only for our own sakes, and for the sake of our own future, but also for the sake of our fellow labourers, for the sake of those who may come after us, and for the sake of the community at large, it is our duty to see that our profession is conducted in an honourable and trustworthy manner.

For this purpose the Institute was founded, and for this reason it should receive our hearty support.

This being our desire, the younger members of our profession cannot do anything more calculated to assist in the general welfare than to join together in the formation and support of associations such as this. They not only are a valuable assistance to you in your arduous endeavours to enter the portals of the Institute, but they enable you to learn a great deal about the habits of your fellow accountants, and a great deal about the details of your profession, which will be useful in after practice, and they bring us together, inspire us with an *esprit de corps*, and tend to promote unity of feeling and uniformity of practice, all of which will benefit us hereafter.

I cannot but feel that, to an outsider, the subjects selected for our consideration must appear somewhat uninteresting, and even to ourselves, if they were not the subjects out of which we have to gain our living, they would not be inviting.

After practicing accountancy all day, it would doubtless be more entertaining to go to a debating society and discuss politics; and to sit down and write an address on the subject is not, to me at least, an inviting task. But after all "life is real, life is earnest," and we have duties to perform as well pleasures to enjoy, and I do trust, as you have found accountants and students ready and willing to contribute to the best of their ability to the success of your association by addressing you upon various subjects connected with the profession, that the members of the association at large will, on their part, do their duty manfully by attending these meetings regularly, and taking a hearty part in the various discussions and debates.

I have often felt that one of the chief difficulties in preparing an address was the selection of a subject, and this being done, half the battle was won. For some days after I promised to address you I had to face this difficulty. Every portion of an accountant's duties seemed to me to have been pretty well thrashed out by you already, and I was almost giving up the task in despair, and preparing an address about everything in general, and nothing in particular, when it occurred to me that I could ask you the question "What is Income?" and perhaps make some observations thereon which might prove useful, and I decided to do so.

This question arises in some form or other in connection with nearly every branch of the profession, and whilst in many cases the answer is as easy and simple as the question itself, it is at other times surrounded with difficulties and doubt, and it is desirable that at all times an answer should be founded upon sound and well thought-out principles.

It arises in dealing with the investments of private individuals, with the accounts of partnerships, and constantly in the management of Trust Estates.

The same question arises under the head of Revenue or Profit and Loss, in dealing with the accounts of companies, and it has also got to be answered before we can form a correct opinion upon the question as to the desirability of paying interest out of capital during the construction of works.

It is constantly mixed up with questions of Apportionment and Depreciation, and has to be borne in mind when settling accounts for Income Tax.

Income may be described generally as the profit earned by capital invested, or derived from the labour of mind and body or from all these combined.

It may be likened to the fruit which a tree yields periodically, and which may be gathered and used without injury to the tree itself. But we must not be content to base our ideas of income upon a general illustration such as this without placing very careful limitations upon it. Let us consider the simile for a moment. If, when the fruit season arrives, we not only pluck the fruit, but break off a large portion of the branches as well and use them, our tree is reduced, and next season bears less fruit, and so on until in the course of time there is no tree left at all.

Capital often undergoes a very similar process, and it should be our care that our clients do not gradually exhaust their capital whilst under the impression that they are living upon their Income only.

Again, suppose a man who owns an orchard and depends upon it for his living. Each season he gathers the fruit, sells it, and lives upon the proceeds, and thinks he is living strictly within his means. What is the consequence? The trees languish for want of manure, and the crops grow smaller. The old trees die, and there are no new ones to replace them, and in the end there is no fruit at all to live upon.

It is obvious that if our friend wished truly to live within his income, it was necessary that out of the proceeds of the fruit he should first make ample provision for digging about and manuring his orchard, and for buying and planting young trees in place of old ones, and so maintain the fruitfulness of his orchard, and it was only what was left after making this provision, which could truly and safely be treated as Income.

Thus is illustrated the necessity for making due provision for depreciation and maintenance.

In advising private clients as to their investments, and the income thereon, I need suggest little beyond what will appear when I deal with Trust Estates.

There are two classes of investments.

One, such as railway shares, government investments, and the like, which may fairly be considered permanent investments, and the dividends thereon as Income.

There are other investments, such as shares in ships, or mines, the dividends upon which are partly a return of capital, because the ships grow old, and the mines get worked out, and it is folly to treat the whole of such dividends as Profit or Income.

How much should be treated as Capital, and how much Income, must be decided by a due consideration of the circumstances of the particular investment.

It is impossible to lay down any hard and fast line. Experience and judgment are the best guides, and it is always safest to err in favour of Capital.

There is another class of investments, which consist of shares in Limited Companies, formed for the purpose of owning ships or mines, or other similar investments. Some of these companies make due provision for depreciation themselves, and the dividends they declare may properly be treated as Income. Others make no such provision. This is especially the case in single ship companies, whose capital consists of the ship solely, and all the earnings are divided. Here the recipient of the dividend has got to make his own provision for depreciation out of the dividend he receives, and this should receive his full consideration.

The question as to what is Income arises in its most important aspects in the management of Trust Estates, and here we cannot be too careful.

The ordinary law only allows trustees to invest in securities such as consols and others of a similar permanent nature, and as long as trustees stick to these, they are pretty safe in treating the dividends as Income.

In many cases, however, trustees are authorised by the will, or other trust deeds under which they act, to hold investments of diverse sorts, freehold and leasehold land and houses, mortgages, shares in ships, mines, railways, &c. &c., and have large powers as to investment in similar securities.

Whilst in such cases trustees are justified in holding such securities when left in their care, I would strongly advise them not to invest trust funds in anything but first-class permanent securities, notwithstanding any powers conferred upon them, because if any losses occur upon such investments, the Court of Chancery might say to them "It is true you were authorised to make such investments, but you were not forced to do so." You were to exercise common sense and judgment, and if you were so foolish as to invest trust funds, which should be carefully husbanded, upon all sorts of foolish speculation for the sake of earning possible large dividends for life tenants, simply because the testator had such unlimited faith in your discretion as to give you almost unlimited power of investment, you must pay for your folly.

In some cases trustees not only have wide powers as to what class of investment they may hold, but the trust deed distinctly directs, that the rents, interest, dividends or other produce of such investments are to be treated as Income, and here of course it is all plain sailing, and I think deeds giving large powers to hold diverse securities should also give directions as to the Income thereon, because otherwise a very serious responsibility is thrown upon trustees, which it is unfair they should bear.

As a matter of fact. however, trustees are constantly authorised and directed to hold certain investments, whilst the deed is quite silent as to what is to be done with the produce.

Before referring to investments, the produce of which ought not to be assumed as a matter of course to be Income, I would say clearly that I am not going to lay down any rules as to dealing with the same. These are questions for solicitors to advise upon, or for the opinion of the Court to be taken upon. The duty of the accountant is to point out the difficulties to his client, and get him to obtain proper advice when any doubtful cases arise, and to see that he carries out the advice when obtained.

Seeing that in such cases as leaseholds, mortgages in possession, shares in ships, and the like, the Courts themselves do not seem to have laid down any well defined rules as to what proportion of the produce should be treated as Capital, if any, and what Income, it would be folly for an accountant to take upon himself the responsibility of doing so. He can only advise generally as to what he thinks would be a safe course, pointing out the dangers, a golden rule is ever to give Capital the benefit of the doubt. If you do this you are comparatively safe, because if a life-tenant claims a doubtful item as his, whereas you have placed it to the credit of Capital account, and he appeals to the Court, and the Court decides in his favour, the money is there safe, and you have only to transfer it from Capital account, where you had improperly placed it to the credit of the life-tenant, and the matter is rectified. But if you place a doubtful item to the credit of Income, it is paid over to the life tenant, and he spends it. Then if the person interested claims that it is Capital, and if he appeals to the Court, and the decision is in his favour, where are you? You might as well try to get butter out of a dog's mouth as to get it back again from the life tenant who has received, and spent it, and who, by the time this question is raised and decided, is probably dead and buried.

The produce of freehold land is Income, and with regard to buildings, although they do decay, yet the process is so slow, or is supposed to be so slow, that, subject to their being kept in repair, the produce may be considered Income.

The rents of leaseholds, after providing for repairs, are generally considered Income, and as leases are generally for long terms of 75 or 99 years, it does not matter much if they are only held for a short time. The proper course, however, is to create a fund by setting aside annual instalments sufficient to keep the property in full lease, or sufficient to keep the property in full lease, or sufficient to equal the original value of the investment at the expiration of the lease.

Sometimes buildings are left in the hands of trustees in an exceedingly old and dilapidated condition, so that before long ordinary repairs are useless, and the buildings must either be left to go to ruin, or partially or wholly re-built or re-constructed. If the latter course is pursued, as it ought to be, the buildings are made better than they were when they originally came to the hands of the trustees. In the course of re-construction considerable improvements are often introduced, and the result is that they become capable of producing an increased rental.

Now life tenants have no objection to the rents being improved, but they naturally object to being charged with the whole cost of re-construction—probably absorbing several years' income — when the benefit will be enjoyed by those who come after them as well as by themselves. It doesn't seem fair that they should pay the whole, and the equitable course seems to be for Income to contribute such a proportion as would represent ordinary repairs, and capital the rest. There is, however, frequently no power granted to trustees to expend capital upon re-construction or improvement, or the powers are vague, and possibly a trustee who did so expend capital might afterwards stand to be shot at. In all such cases, therefore, I would recommend trustees to obtain the sanction of the Court to any such capital outlay; and I have often had cases where the Court has sanctioned the outlay of capital for the whole or part of expenditure of this sort.

Interest upon mortgages is clearly Income, so long as the security remains good, but if the mortgage become deficient, and the mortgagees take possession of the property, it is not safe to apply the net rental towards the interest.

This is generally done, but it may be objected to.

I am not aware that any definite principle has been laid down as to dealing with deficient mortgage securities, though various plans have been adopted.

A fair suggestion is to take a moderate valuation of the property in possession, or say the proceeds of a sale when ultimately sold, and add to this the net rents during the time the property is in possession. Then find what sum with interest at 4 per cent. added for the same period will amount to the same total. This sum is Capital, and the interest, Income. For instance, suppose you have a mortgage for £1,500, and take possession. You ultimately sell for £1,000, and the rents received during the time you are in possession and up to the date of sale amount to £1,000, making a total of £2,000. Now it may be that the sum of £1,200 with interest at 4 per cent. for the same period, say £800, will amount to £2,000. In this case if you have paid the whole rents over to the life-tenant, you will have overpaid him £200. The difficulty in adopting this principle is that you have to wait until the property is disposed of, or otherwise dealt with, before knowing what is Income, and life-tenants cannot wait for ever for their income. Neither am I aware that the Courts have sanctioned this plan. It only illustrates the difficulties of the situation, and all an accountant can do is to point out the dangers, and let the solicitor advise.

Shares in ships provide another similar difficulty. The dividends are clearly not all Income, because depreciation is going on rapidly. One plan is to have a valuation made, and to pay the life tenant say 4 per cent. upon such valuation out of any dividends received, and to place the surplus, if any, to a reserve fund. This is not satisfactory to my mind, because I think depreciation ought *first* to be provided, and only the surplus remaining, if any, be treated as Income.

I don't know that any rules have yet been laid down as to dealing with ship's dividends, and I can only say that trustees should be very shy of holding such investments, and be carefully advised as to what portions of the dividends they treat as Income. I may, however, point out that there are two sorts of depreciation, one which arises from ordinary wear and tear, which should be provided for out of Income, and one which may arise from fluctuations in the market value of shipping. The latter is a natural shrinkage of capital, and the loss should therefore fall upon capital. In like manner any increase in the value of shipping, or other investments, is a growth of Capital, and has nothing to do with Income.

It is unnecessary to go through the numerous other sorts of investments we come across, even if time permitted, because I think in what I have already said I have so indicated the general principles which should actuate us in dealing with them all.

I now pass on to the question of Apportionment, which is a most important one affecting Income.

It arises in two ways. First, owing to deaths and changes of interest, and secondly, owing to the purchase and sale of investments.

The Apportionment Act was supposed to settle all questions of this sort, but according to some decisions it has left many points unsettled, and solicitors seem to me to have most diverse views upon the question.

As a rule all rents, interests, and dividends paid in respect of certain definite periods may be apportioned, and if a man dies in the middle of any such period, his estate takes the first half of such rent, interest, or dividends, and the successor the balance. But sometimes dividends are not paid in respect of any particular period. They are declared and paid at odd dates, just as there are profits in hand. In such cases it seems equitable that the proportion of profit earned up to the date of the death should be ascertained as nearly as possible, and credited to capital, and the successor should take the balance. But I have been told that the Apportionment Act does not apply to such cases, as they are not periodical payments, and the successor is entitled to all such dividends declared after he has succeeded to the property. It has been argued that if a shipowner dies during the voyage, the successor takes all the dividend, because the freight is not earned until the voyage is completed. I think every part of the voyage contributes to the earning of the freight, and the profit should be distributed over the whole period.

I have had a case of this sort. A voyage was completed and a dividend paid, and the managing owner retained a balance—say £500—towards the expenses of next voyage. In the middle of this voyage a shareholder dies. The u l-mate profit of the voyage is £800, which, added to the £500 brought forward, makes £1,300, out of which a dividend of £1,000 is paid, leaving £300 to be carried forward to the next voyage. What portion of the dividend of £1,000 goes to the estate of the shareholder who died in the middle of the voyage, and what proportion is Income of his estate?

Assume for the sake of convenience that he owned half the ship. The executors receive £500 dividend, and £150 of the £300 remaining in the managing owner's hands belongs to them. I hold that the £500 should be applied as follows:

£250 to Capital, representing half the £500 in hand when the voyage began.

£200 to Capital, representing the deceased's moiety of the profits earned during the first half of the voyage and whilst he was alive, and £50 to Income on account of the £200, moiety of the profits earned during the second half of the voyage, and after the death. The £150, the balance of the profits earned during the second half of the voyage, belongs to Income also, but it is represented by the moiety of the £300 remaining in the hands of the managing owner, and can only be credited to Income when actually received from him either as subsequent dividend or otherwise.

It may be argued that Capital ought to provide the fund which the managing owner requires to keep in hand for the working of the ship, and I do not see much objection to this in principle, but if this is done the accounts should be kept clearly showing the transaction, and so that Capital may ultimately get back any sum so advanced. I am afraid that this is not often done.

I have said enough to illustrate the difficulties which sometimes surround the Apportionment of dividends on a change of interest.

It is impossible to lay down hard and fast rules. One can only suggest general principles which ought to guide you, and remind you of the safety of erring—if you err at all—in favour of Capital.

The question of Apportionment arises in the second place in the case of sale and purchase of shares between the times the dividends are paid.

The Apportionment Act does not apply to these cases, and whilst it is clear if you sell stock in the middle of the half-year, you also sell three months' accrued dividend, yet a trustee would not be justified in paying over to a life-tenant out of the proceeds, a sum equal to three months' dividend. If he did, the owner of the capital might make him refund it. I confess it seems equitable that the principle of Apportionment should apply here, as elsewhere, for on the other hand a trustee may invest just before a dividend is earned, and a life tenant may claim the whole half-year's dividend upon such investment, although the money has not been there a month.

No doubt if a trustee were constantly buying just before dividend time so as to swell up Income—practically at the expense of Capital—or were constantly to sell out just before dividend time, so as to rob Income, the court would stop him, but as a rule trustees are supposed only to buy and sell for good and proper motives, and the court will not llow the proceeds of sales to be diminished, nor the cost of investments increased by any sums supposed to represent proportions of dividends.

I have known trustees reduce the cost of new investments by crediting the proportion of dividend up to date of purchase. It is for the life tenant to object to this if he likes.

As I said before, it is equitable, but I don't think it would hold water if attacked, but is one of those safe errors to make in favour of Capital.

I have also known a proportion of dividend to be taken out of the proceeds of sale, and credited to Income. This also is equitable, but unsafe, and should not be approved of by the accountant, without the risk of its being upset being pointed out.

In the case of allotments of new stock made in respect of holdings by trustees, sometimes they are taken up and paid for, and become a further investment of trust funds.

At other times there being, perhaps, no trust funds available for investment, the allotments are sold at a premium.

A few years since the London and North Western Railway allotted new stock at par. The original stock being at a considerable premium, these allotments were saleable at a premium also, and in some cases the proceeds were treated as a sort of bonus, and handed over to the life-tenants. This was wrong, the proceeds of sales of allotments of new stock being clearly Capital.

Various outside circumstances may, of course, affect the market values of original stocks, and allotments of new stocks, but I think it can be demonstrated logically that the intrinsic value of the original stock is reduced in proportion to the premium which the new stock should bring, and therefore the amount realised by the sale of a new allotment of stock represents a corresponding reduction of value in the original holding.

Law costs are often as a matter of course treated as being payable out of capital. Law bills should, however, be gone through carefully, and the items which relate to Income charged against Income, and those relating to Capital charged against it.

I won't trouble you with any remarks about Income Tax, nor about Partnership Accounts.

The same general principles apply, and no doubt a great deal might be said on these heads if time permitted.

Again, quite another branch of the same subject is brought before us in relation to profit and loss accounts.

This would form the subject of a paper itself, and I will only call your attention to one point in which there is perhaps a difference of principle in dealing with the capital and revenue accounts of companies, and the capital and income accounts of private trusts.

I have already pointed out that there are two sorts of depreciation of capital; one a shrinkage, arising from fluctuations in market value, owing to causes over which trustees have little or no control, and the other owing to ordinary wear and tear. Now in the former case trustees are in no way responsible. There is no obligation to maintain the trust fund at any specified value.

They take the trust funds as they find them, and are only bound to keep the investments, or other investments into which they may be changed for what they are worth, and if the investments fall in value to half their original amount, the trustees are not liable to make this up out of Income.

In the case of public companies, however, they have a fixed nominal capital, representing a certain value, and it is the duty of directors to maintain the investments on the asset side of their balance sheet at the full value of the capital on the other side.

If there is a great fall in values, so that these assets are no longer worth what they cost they should only be entered in the balance sheet at their present value, and the deficiency should, if possible, be charged to profit and loss. If this is impossible the deficiency should be charged to a suspense account of some sort, so that shareholders may see clearly how much of their capital has been lost.

It is not always necessary that subsequent profits should be entirely devoted to making up this deficiency, this may depend upon the wording of the articles, but it is desirable that some part at least of future profits should be devoted to this object, and directors should never be satisfied until they have entirely got rid of such an ugly item as a suspense account of the sort described, indeed, in some cases of this sort it is at once got rid of by special resolutions, and a corresponding reduction of the capital on the other side.

There is only one other matter upon which I would like to make a remark before closing, and that is perhaps only indirectly connected with my subject. It is about the desirability of paying interest out of capital during construction. This has been brought prominently before the public during the Manchester Ship Canal controversy.

So far as trustees are concerned, new undertakings, being always untried, and more or less speculative, are not the sort of securities in which they should invest, and as the appropriation of any part of Capital as interest, when no Revenue has been actually earned, is directly contrary to the principle of a trust, I could not approve of legislation sanctioning such a step. But with regard to individual investors, who are the absolute owners of their own money, the question is different. For them it is merely a question of convenience.

It is certain that many undertakings cannot possibly be completed under—say five years—however certain they may be to earn large dividends after that time. A man may be quite justified in putting his capital into an undertaking of this sort, and perhaps being uncertain as to how long it may be before the undertaking can be completed, he may not wish to have to make an uncertain calculation as to how much of his capital he should retain to live upon until that time, and may prefer to hand the whole over on the understanding that he is repaid a certain proportion annually until completion.

There is nothing necessarily improper in this, and, as I don't approve of too much grandmotherly legislation in a free country where people should learn from their own experience how to take care of themselves, I don't approve of the State preventing undertakings being floated with an inducement of this sort.

I do think, however, the state should insist upon two stipulations. First, that trustees should not be allowed to invest in such undertakings for the reasons stated, and secondly, that persons who are free agents should not be misled, but should have it clearly pointed out what it is they are doing when they invest, viz:—that they are living upon a portion of their own capital during construction, in the expectation of the undertaking—which will only represent the balance of such Capital—ultimately yielding such a return as they look forward to.

I now have only to thank you for your kind attention.

WEAR AND TEAR AND DEPRECIATION

A[dam] Murray

LIVERPOOL CHARTERED ACCOUNTANTS' STUDENTS' ASSOCIATION.

"WEAR AND TEAR AND DEPRECIATION."

Address by Mr. A. Murray, F.C.A. of Manchester.

At the opening meeting of the Session, held on the 6th October, 1887, the President, Mr. T. W. Read, F.C.A., in the chair, Mr. Murray delivered the following paper.

In submitting a short paper on the above subject it is intended only to offer some general remarks; to give a few cases in illustration; and to refer to others upon which a difference of opinion exists.

At the outset it will be convenient to make a distinction between Wear and Tear and Depreciation. Depreciation is a comprehensive term, including wear and tear; but the two are distinct elements and may be considered separately.

Wear and Tear may be defined as "diminished value arising from use," as in the Income Tax Act, 1878, 41 Vic. cap 15, Sec. 12, under which a deduction was for the first time allowed in the assessment of Profits under schedule D, such allowance being in respect of "diminished value by "reason of wear and tear." Although described in the act to be for "Wear and Tear," yet in the form of Income Tax Return No. 11a, under schedule D. the word "Depreciation" has been adopted, still the income tax commissioners and surveyors, limit the allowance to wear and tear.

The word "Depreciation" is almost universally used in the deduction from property, plant and machinery accounts, and the corresponding charge made to Profit and Loss account, but in the case of most ordinary trading concerns "wear and tear" might properly be substituted for "Depreciation."

Under the head of "wear and tear" it is proposed to deal with the ordinary charges made in trading accounts for the use of buildings, machinery and plant. It is equally an item in calculating the cost of production as is the payment for labour and for materials consumed.

In ascertaining the cost of materials and stores used, the stock is taken at the end of the period against the stock at the beginning, and purchases during the period, the difference being the consumption.

In the case of buildings and machinery a deduction is made, but the effect is the same as taking the property and plant into stock at a reduced amount, or at an increased amount if the additions during the period have been in excess of the deduction for wear and tear.

Although the process differs, yet the result attained is the same, the cost of materials used being *ascertained*, the charge for the use of buildings and machinery being *estimated* without reference to change in value from other causes than use. It would not be a safe basis to take the value as there is a fluctuation in the value of buildings and machinery irrespective of use.

In order that the cost of production should be approximately correct for the purpose of fixing the selling price, or for comparison with the market price, it is important that wear and tear should neither be over nor under-estimated. For instance the cost of building a cotton mill and furnishing it with machinery, may some years ago have been equal to 30s. per spindle. Such a mill may now be built fully equipped with machinery having all the latest improvements, at about 20s. per spindle.

In the case of an old mill it would be misleading to charge more for wear and tear than would be sufficient in the case of a new mill, consequently an old mill, unless it had been written down in the books at a high rate for wear and tear, might stand at a sum relatively higher than that of a mill built in more recent years. On the other hand, in the times of large profits (now passed away) it was not unusual to write off altogether the cost of the mill and machinery, or to reduce it to an amount much below the value. In such case the element of wear and tear might be lost sight of, or under estimated, and thus the spinner would be deceiving himself as to the cost of production.

In the present days of bare profits it is of the utmost importance that the cost should be fairly estimated, and the mill proprietor should look at the question of wear and tear between himself as a landlord on one hand and as a tenant on the other.

It is not unusual in the cotton manufacturing districts for a manufacturer to rent a weaving shed with looms and power at an annual rent of so much per loom, and an owner occupying his mill, should in like manner charge his business with a rent equal to interest on the value of the buildings and machinery, together with a charge for wear and tear beyond the cost of repairs, renewals, and maintenance, the outlay in respect of which should be debited to the trade account as part of the ordinary expenses.

Much confusion and uncertainty exists in the property and machinery accounts of many manufacturing businesses, by reason of the way in which wear and tear and renewals are treated. It is not unusual to make a deduction from the property accounts for wear and tear, and then to add to those accounts the outlay, not only in the nature of additions and extensions, but also for renewals, the result not unfrequently being that the property account is upheld at a sum far beyond its real working value, and as a consequence the profits are apparently more than the actual profits. A safer course, in my opinion, is to make a deduction from the property for wear and tear, charging such deduction to the Profit and Loss Account, as well as the entire cost of maintenance, thus increasing property, machinery and plant accounts only by the actual additions thereto.

The accounts of railway companies, and gas companies, are kept on this principle, with this difference, that there is not any charge for wear and tear beyond maintenance, it not being required in the statutory form of accounts for those companies that there should be any such charge, and consequently, in the Revenue Account actual maintenance is included only.

In the case of railway companies owning steamships there is a charge which is called "depreciation," but it would be more correctly described as "provision for renewal of steamships."

Some municipal corporations owning gas works, have exceeded their powers in charging the Profit and Loss Account with wear and tear where there is not any such requirement in the special acts conferring borrowing powers for gas works purposes, and the ratepayers are thus placed in a less advantageous position than that of shareholders of a gas company, in addition to which a sinking fund has also to be provided out of the gas profits of a municipal corporation.

In making a deduction for wear and tear it is the practice with the majority of companies to follow the course usual with private trading concerns. Some, however, do not take wear and tear into account, beyond the actual outlay.

If it is objected that the cost of maintenance and renewals over a number of years may be unequal, this difficulty is met by estimating what amount annually is likely to be required for such purposes, and by charging the Profit and Loss Account with such amount, carrying the same to the credit of a "Renewals and Repairs Account," debiting the outlay from time to time to such account.

It is not proposed to suggest what the rates for wear and tear should be in various businesses. These must be estimated by those conversant with and able to judge from practical knowledge of each particular business. It is sufficient to lay down what is believed to be a sound general principle *i.e.*, to maintain existing works and plant out of revenue, and in addition to charge profit and loss with a deduction from property, machinery and plant in respect of wear and tear.

It is customary to make the deduction by a percentage rate from the cost *as reduced from time to time*, and not from the original cost. There is thus a larger amount for wear and tear charged in the early years, but the practice is preferred, seeing that in the later years when the charge for wear and tear is less there will be an increased expenditure for repairs and renewals as the unexpired term becomes shorter.

If the life of an article, subject to wear and tear, was a known quantity, then the question of charge would be simplified. In such case interest would have to be added to the cost and balance of cost, from year to year, writing off an annual sum to the trading account, by which, cost and interest would be either extinguished altogether, or reduced to the value of old material at the end of the term.

Let us now look at depreciation as distinguished from wear and tear; as the converse of appreciation; and as a separate element.

Numerous and varied cases will suggest themselves.

In addition to ordinary wear and tear, manufactories and works are subject to depreciation arising from (*a*) improvements by which machinery may become of little more value than that of old material. (*b*) The less profitable state of trade. (*c*) The reduced cost of labour and materials.

Where a manufacturer occupies his own property (as is almost invariably the case) as a prudent man he ought to have a reserve taken out of profits for these contingencies.

It is an excellent plan to have an inventory of principal machines, tools, &c., kept in such a way as to show wear and tear deducted, as well as the reduced cost, in detail. By this means if part of the machinery becomes superceded and has to be realised, the loss is readily ascertained and can be charged to contingent fund. This is not a merely theoretical system, but is in actual practice; of course in such a case the loss or difference having been written off, any substitution would be chargeable to plant account, as in the case of an addition. Such an inventory would be of great use, as affording the means of making a comparison between the reduced cost of machinery as in the books, and the then working value.

The proprietor of a mill or works built 20 years ago, would find that as between himself as landlord and as a tenant, he would now have to charge himself with rent only on the reduced value, and the difference between the present value and the cost, would be a loss of capital, and not loss as a trader.

It may be considered refining too much to make this distinction, still it is a convenient rule to apply, and assists in arriving at the correct principle in cases which frequently arise.

Another case which properly comes under the description of depreciation is that of a leasehold property. If land is held under lease for 21 years to be surrendered at the end of the term with the property upon it, the amount paid to the lessor and the cost of buildings erected by a lessee with interest thereon, can be dealt with without any doubt as to the correct principle in such case, the term being fixed and not uncertain as in the case of machinery.

Let us suppose that the land for the term of lease

cost	£1,000
and the buildings erected by the lessee..	2,500
	£3,500

If the lessee occupies the property for the purpose of his business, he has to charge his trading with an annual rent, which he will ascertain in the following manner, the value of money being taken at 5 per cent. We find from one of Inwood's tables that the amount of £1 with interest at 5 per cent. for 21 years, would be £2·786, therefore the amount for £3,500 would be £9,751. Then we see from another of the tables that £1 per annum at 5 per cent. would in 21 years amount to £35·7193, then as £35·7193 : £9751 : : £1 : £273, thus giving the annual rent or instalment as £273.

If the land had been leased at £50 per annum, then the charge to the business would be the rent, and the annual instalment to write off the £2,500, (the cost of the buildings) and interest. In either case the annual charge is equal to the rent, between the proprietor as a landlord, and as a tenant. A ledger account of the cost, interest and instalments with annual rests would, of course, be closed by the last instalment.

Another case which comes within the experience of many of us, is that of a colliery.

A field of coal is leased, say for 30 years subject to royalty on coal as it is won. The lessee expends on "sunk capital account" £100,000, in opening up and sinking pits. The charge to the Profit and Loss Account in addition to the royalty on the coal, will be the annual instalment to be written off in the same way as in the previous case.

Taking money at 5 per cent. the £100,000 would in 30 years amount to £432,190, £1 per annum at the same rate would amount to £66·4388 : then as £66·4388 : £432,190 : : £1 : £6505·08, this being the annual charge to be made by the lessee in his Profit and Loss Account as the annual rent which would be charged to him had the outlay been made by the lessor, he being content to have his expenditure back in 30 annual instalments, including principal and interest.

The effect of wear and tear or depreciation taken out of the profits of a business is of course to increase the balance of floating assets over liabilities, or to reduce the excess of liabilities over floating assets, and it may not be unsuitable to refer to the proper application of money arising therefrom.

In the case of works mortgaged, or advances by bankers or others it would of course be wise to reduce any such liability. If there were not any such claims to meet then it would be well to take the money out of the business rather than expend it in additions or extensions.

A common error has been to use available funds of this kind for the purpose of building additional works or factories instead of investing the money to meet the cost of substitutions. When such time arrived there had been years of bad trade, and thus the means were not forthcoming, the consequence being embarrassment, if not ruin.

And now a few observations as to accounts and balance sheets in relation to the subject under consideration.

As a means of affording information to those interested it is desirable that wear and tear and depreciation should be shown as a deduction from time to time in the balance sheets of all trading concerns in the same way that additions to property and plant are usually set forth. In exceptional cases the error is made of having a depreciation account as a *fund* on the debit side of a balance sheet, the usual practice however being to charge wear and tear and depreciation against profits and to reduce the property or machinery accounts correspondingly. It is misleading and erroneous to look upon such an entry in the balance sheet as a *fund* represented by assets. The property and machinery being of less value ought to be written down. The amount of wear and tear or depreciation is no doubt represented by money if taken out of profits, but it is only a change between fixed and floating assets, the latter being correspondingly increased.

It is not usual to charge Profit and Loss Account, in anticipation of wear and tear or depreciation, and so create an actual fund, but if such be the case it would be more intelligible if any transfer of the kind was made to the credit of such an account as "renewals and repairs account."

It has from time to time been suggested that there should not be any deduction made from profits for depreciation, but that it should be left to partners and proprietors to decide for themselves how much of the profits or dividends is in respect of interest, and how much principal.

There appear to be several objections to such a mode of dealing with the accounts of trading concerns, although in some cases it is the practice.

In the case of property, machinery, or plant subject to depreciation such as:—

Manufacturing concerns.
Leasehold colliery.
Steamship company, &c.

the balance sheet would be misleading, inasmuch as the capital of the company would apparently be represented by property and assets, when in fact they had greatly depreciated, and in some cases would cease to be of any value whatever.

In a company, the shares of which had not any stock exchange quotation, and where sellers and buyers, had to arrange prices between themselves, intending purchasers would not have the means of satisfying themselves as to the value of the shares.

It is not sufficient to say that existing shareholders are aware that part of the share capital is being repaid while outsiders would be in ignorance thereof. Dividends in such cases (consisting of both principal and interest in uncertain amounts) would not be any criterion of value.

Directors generally would not approve of such an anomalous and objectionable mode of making up the accounts of their company.

Accountants would hesitate, or indeed refuse, to sign such a balance sheet, inasmuch as it did not "represent the true position of the company."

Having had experience of wear and tear and depreciation in various forms, their influence should be used to secure adequate deductions in order that balance sheets may be accurate, so that objection could not be taken to them.

It would be most unsatisfactory and dangerous if property and assets were not written down, money arising from depreciation being applied in discharge of liabilities, or in reduction of share capital.

It is greatly to be feared that in many cases where machinery (from the speed at which it is run) is subject to a high rate of wear and tear, sufficient allowance is not being made, and that consequently dividends include some portion of the capital where the shareholders are under the belief that they consist of profits only.

Such a theory as has been suggested would, if recognised, lead to much inconvenience in the case of trust estates where there were life interests. Trustees could not be expected to take the responsibility of making a division of dividends between life-tenants and those entitled in remainder, and it would be most unsuitable to leave them in a position of having to decide how much should be considered income, and what portion a repayment of principal.

We now come to the conclusion of a paper, in which the intention has been to deal with a few leading features of the subject under consideration including the following :—

The distinction between wear and tear and depreciation,
The deduction from buildings, machinery and plant, for

wear and tear to be in addition to the cost of maintenance, chargeable to the trading account,

A renewals and repairs account, to equalise the charge to trading account,

Inventory of plant and machinery,

Accuracy of balance sheets.

The illustrations given are few in number, but the principle suggested if approved, may be applied in any variety of circumstances. The subject is an important one, and sufficient may have been said to create a desire to follow it out in more complete detail.

WHAT IS PROFIT OF A COMPANY?

Ernest Cooper

CHARTERED ACCOUNTANTS STUDENTS' SOCIETY OF LONDON.

WHAT IS PROFIT OF A COMPANY?

By Mr. Ernest Cooper, F.C.A.

A meeting of the members of the above society was held at Winchester House, Old Broad Street, E.C., on the 6th inst, and the meeting was also open to all members of the Institute. Mr. Frederick Whinney, F.C.A., occupied the chair, and there were present, Messrs. J. W. Blackburn, J. C. Bolton, Arthur Cooper, W. C. Jackson, G. W. Knox, G. B. Monkhouse, Adam Murray, F. W. Pixley, J. J. Saffery, (Vice-President of the Institute), T. G. Shuttleworth, G. van de Linde, T. A. Welton, and many others. Mr. Ernest Cooper on being called upon read the following paper:—

The questions of what is profit of a Company and how profit is to be ascertained are of exceptional interest to Chartered Accountants. It is our business as experts in bookkeeping and accounts to draw up Balance Sheets and Profit and Loss Accounts, showing what are profits of every description of Company, and as we have been reminded by the recent decision of *The Leeds Building and Investment Society* (36 Ch. D. 787) our responsibility as auditors is hardly less than that of the directors, for correctly disclosing the position of a Company whose accounts we certify.

Mr. Buckley, Q.C., in the preface to the fifth edition of his work on the Companies Acts, writing in November last year, says:—

"We are little nearer to knowing what profit is, than we were five years ago," and Mr. F. B. Palmer, in the still more recent fourth edition of his work, "Company Precedents" commences his remarks on "what are profits," by saying, "There is a difference of opinion as to how profits should be ascertained."

And, further, accountants must often have found in the course of their practice, that this state of uncertainty in regard to profits is not unusual with lawyers.

When we find eminent legal authorities to whom we habitually look for guidance upon a matter so closely concerning our profession as the Company law, owning to difference of opinion in relation to accounts, we are driven to look into the matter for ourselves. In attempting to do so, I wish to be understood as not expressing final opinions, but, as the title I have adopted indicates, I shall assume the position of an enquirer, expressing only my own present views.

I will first endeavour to state Mr. Buckley's view. He says, "The writer has always understood the true principle to be that Capital Account and Revenue Account "are distinct accounts, and that for the purpose of "determining profits you must disregard accretions to or "diminutions of capital;

and again, "Capital may be lost in either one of two "ways, which may be distinguished as loss on Capital Account "and loss on Revenue Account. If a Shipowning Company's "capital be represented by ten ships with which it trades and "one is totally lost and is uninsured, such a loss would be "what is here called a loss on Capital Account. But if the "same Company begins the year with ten ships, value say "£100,000, and ends the year with the same ten ships, and the "result of the trading after allowing for depreciation of the "ships is a loss of £1,000, this would be what is here called "a loss on Revenue Account."

Again, "The creditors of the Company are entitled to have "the Capital Account fairly and properly kept; but *quære* "whether they are entitled to have losses of capital on "Capital Account made good out of Revenue."

Again, "But when all proper allowances have thus been "made in favour of capital, the balance, it is submitted, is "Revenue applicable for payment of dividend."

Mr. Buckley also says, "But the question is believed to "be as yet entirely open whether a Company under the "Companies Acts, which has lost part of its capital by loss "on Capital Account, can continue to pay dividends until "the lost capital has been made good."

From these extracts it is seen that Mr. Buckley adopts as applicable to Companies registered under the Companies Acts, 1862 to 1886, what is known as the "Double Account" system as distinguished from the "Single Account" system, and further—in adopting the double account view—he bases upon the supposed separation of Capital and Revenue the very important doctrine, that although Capital may have been lost as he describes it on Capital Account, Dividends may perhaps still be paid. In his third edition, he said "This view is advanced with great diffidence," but in the fifth edition the double account view is adopted without hesitation.

Mr. F. B. Palmer, on the other hand after describing what he calls the double account view, adopts the Single Account view, which he states thus:—

"Profit is to be ascertained as in an ordinary partnership "namely by a Balance Sheet, showing the general result of "the Company's operations to date. That is to say, the "Capital Account and Revenue Account are to be treated as "one continuous account, on the debit side of which must "appear the paid-up Capital, the Reserve Fund, if any, the "debts and liabilities, and the balance to the credit of the "Profit and Loss Account; and on the other side the assets a "their ascertained or estimated value, and if there is a "deficiency, the debit balance of Profit and Loss."

Mr. Palmer adds, "Ninety-nine companies out of a hundred "under the Act of 1862, ascertain, or purport to ascertain, "their profits in accordance with this view."

Further Mr. Palmer says, "It has generally been "assumed that the Double Account system can only be "adopted where the adoption of that system is specially "prescribed by the Legislature, as in the case of Railway "and Tramway Companies." That "the Single Account "view is in accordance with the practice adopted by the "commercial world in ascertaining the profit or loss of an "ordinary partnership; and it may, no doubt, be asked with "some reason, How can that which in the case of an "ordinary partnership would not be profit be profit in the "a case of a limited company seeing that the creditors have "only a limited fund to look to."

Before examining these conflicting views, it will be convenient to state, as clearly as possible, what I understand to be the meaning of various terms.

First, by the words in my title *Profit of a Company*, I mean profit of a limited company registered under the Companies Acts, 1862 to 1886.

I shall refrain from referring otherwise than incidentally to chartered companies, or companies under deeds of settlement, or to insurance or cost book mining companies, or industrial and provident societies, as no important points of principle seem to arise in connection with my subject out of these classes of companies.

But it will be necessary to consider companies for public works formed by Act of Parliament, and governed by the Companies Clauses Act, 1845, such as railway, gas, water and dock companies, and to compare rather carefully the constitution of this class of companies with companies registered under the Companies Acts, 1862 to 1886. It will be convenient, before entering upon the main subject, to consider, not only what is the constitution of each of these two classes of companies, but also what is meant by the terms "Capital," "Profit and Loss," and "Revenue," and the "Double Account" and "Single Account," as applied to them.

We are not concerned with the various definitions of *Capital* adopted by political economists, but with the commercial meaning, and either of the following definitions seems sufficient, viz: "The aggregate of the sums contributed by its "members [to a partnership] for the purpose of commencing "or carrying on business, and intended to be risked by them "in the business;" or the following from Mozley & Whiteley's Law Dictionary "The net amount of property belonging to a merchant after deducting the debts he is owing."

Lord Justice Lindley, from whose work I take the first definition, says, his "observations apply as much to com- "panies as to partnerships."

I understand the capital in a business, equally of a company, a partnership, or of an individual to be, *the sum by which the assets exceed in value the liabilities.* Such difference or surplus I understand to be the *real* capital of a Companies Act Company, and whether this surplus appears in the balance sheet under separate heads of Capital, Reserve Fund, and Profit and Loss Account, *all represent equally capital in fact*, although, of course, Reserve Fund and undivided profits, are not in a Company capital in the terms of the Companies Acts, and are, in some respects, subject to different conditions in a Company to a partnership.

But the word "Capital" has come by usage to have other meanings as applied to Companies, and although confusion is caused by the application of the same name to things essentially different, we must accept the meanings of the word as they stand.

In Companies Act Companies the word "Capital" is used:

(1) To describe the money paid up or deemed to be paid up on shares or stock by proprietors without regard on the one hand to the fact that the whole or part of the amount may have been lost and on the other hand that the Company may have acquired additional surplus funds in the shape of undivided profits, and reserve funds;

(2) The uncalled portion of subscribed shares;

(3) The nominal capital of a Company, that is to say the amount agreed to be the capital as originally stated in the memorandum or articles of Association, or as subsequently increased or reduced;

(4) The word "capital" is applied (inaccurately I think) to describe the amount owing on debentures, which is sometimes spoken of as debenture capital;

(5) It is used (I think also inaccurately) to describe as capital, outlay assets of the Company of a special nature, such as a factory or ships, or outlay on a mine.

But although we must accept these applications of the word "capital" it is well to bear in mind that the *real* capital is the surplus of assets. It is also worth while to remember that Capital Account, Reserve Funds and Profit and Loss are nominal accounts, representing in the case of a Companies Act Company no real debt of the Company, and as I shall contend not representing specified assets, but included by means of double entry in the books and in the balance sheet, and indicating the amount of the surplus of assets over liabilities, and creating the balance. The Capital Account (including reserves and profits) indicates the amount of that undivided, and in a sense undivisible, portion of the assets which belongs to the proprietors of the Company. I say "in a sense undivisible," because an agreement between the partners for division of assets would not constitute a real separation, in fact, as all assets would remain parts of one fund charged with payment of the creditors and all collectively (but subject to payment of creditors) are property or capital of the partners.

I consider equally of an individual, or of a partnership, or of a Companies Act Company, that every increment to capital is profit, and every diminution, loss, or adopting in a different sense, Mr. Buckley's words, every "accretion to or diminution of Capital" is Profit or Loss, and inversely I consider every profit is an increase, and every loss a diminution of the real capital. But this view is not universally held by lawyers.

I do not consider the word "Profit" as synonymous with "net revenue."

Revenue, I understand to be "the product of lands, works, or other property," When the expense of collection is deducted; the remainder is net revenue. It is, I think, essential to arrive at what is in the strict sense called profit, that loss also should be contemplated, or in other words that there should be trading and the materials for a Profit and Loss Account.

Although in a limited sense the operations of Parliamentary Companies involve loss in carrying on the business, as for instance from bad debts, still Parliamentary Companies for public works do not in their constitution, speaking broadly contemplate loss, but only expense of collection as a deduction from the income derived from the work, and they have not in practice a Profit and Loss Account.

By the term "double account system" I understand the necessary condition to be that the assets of a Company are kept in two separate parts or funds. The one the Capital Account comprising the capital raised and the assets to which the capital raised has been applied, and any outstanding liabilities in this account.

The other Revenue Account in which the assets representing the earnings of the Company, and any Liabilities incurred in connection with the earnings are contained. In order to constitute the two accounts, the assets must be capable of being individually earmarked as respectively either on Capital Account or Revenue Account, and the two accounts can be separated only to such extent as the assets are capable of being so separately earmarked.

By "single account system" I understand that the whole of the Assets and Liabilities of the Company, both those representing the Capital and the earnings are taken together and form one fund in one account, stated in practice in the form of a Balance Sheet.

Companies for public works formed by special Act of Parliament, I will for shortness call "Parliamentary Companies" and Companies registered under the Companies Acts, 1862 to 1886, "Companies Act Companies." The Companies Acts, 1862 to 1886, for the same reason I will describe as the "Companies Acts" or the "Company Law."

I will examine first the constitution of Companies Act Companies.

The Company Law as we at present understand it, that is to say statutes enabling a number of persons by registration, without the intervention of a Royal Charter or Special Act of Parliament, to create and carry on a Corporation distinct from themselves, and to select their own objects, is of very recent origin.

Incorporation by registration was first sanctioned in 1844, and limited liability was only granted in 1855 to Companies incorporated by registration.

The Company Law is an extension or development by statute of the ancient Law of Partnership.

As Sir G. Jessel said in "*Griffith* v. *Paget* (6 C.D. 511,) "these Companies are commercial Partnerships, and are, in "the absence of express provisions, statutory or otherwise, "subject to the same considerations" as partnerships, and he defines Articles of Association as in effect Articles of Partnership.

We are especially thrown upon the Law of Partnership in regard to accounts. There is an almost complete absence of provisions relating to accounts in the Companies Acts.

The form of Articles of Association, Table A., Scheduled to the Companies Act, 1862, is optional, and does little more than sketch an ordinary commercial Balance Sheet for adoption by Companies allowing themselves to be governed by Table A.

The Act of 1880 relating to Banks merely provides for audit.

We must therefore when considering the accounts of Companies Act Companies bear in mind that the principles which guide us are mainly derived, not from the Companies Acts, but from the practice in regard to Partnerships, and also from general commercial usuage.

The Company Law does not place any restrictions upon the objects or operations of companies.

The Law in one respect is far more favourable to companies than to partnerships for it allows the members to limit their liability to such amount as they desire. But when doing so the law very naturally imposes for the protection of creditors the condition that (as has recently been clearly decided by the House of Lords, in *Trevor* v. *Whitworth*, 12 App. Cas. 409) to the extent that the capital of a limited company is subscribed it shall be incapable of withdrawal or repayment, but shall remain as security for the creditors, unless it be lost in the course of the company's operations. This condition has been defined by V. C. Wood in *McDougall* v. *Jersey, Imperial Hotel Company*, (2 Hem. & M. 528) as "the contract entered into with the legislature on behalf of the public," as the basis of the grant of limited liability.

The statutory obligation to keep the capital intact does not apparently extend to unlimited Companies Act Companies. The Act of 1862 does not require an unlimited company to state its capital on registration in the memorandum but only in the articles of asssociation, which may be altered by special resolution, so that it seems to be open to an unlimited company by its regulations to determine from time to time the amount of the capital.

Lord Justice Lindley says the capital of a Company not limited by shares may apparently be reduced. The same learned author points out that the Banking Companies Act of 7, George IV., and the Letters Patent Act (relating to Companies formed although not incorporated under letters patent) contain no statutory provisions relating to the capital.

The freedom from statutory control of the capital is an important consideration in comparing parliamentary companies with other kinds of Companies.

Companies Act Companies have the same power of choosing the manner of dealing with their capital in the course of their operations as a partnership, and it is clear that in the case of those classes of companies which give or receive credit, borrow, lend, or deal in money, or trade in goods, the capital brought in by the shareholders becomes inextricably mixed with the other funds, and incapable of being traced or separated. A glance at the Balance Sheet of a partnership or Company of any of the classes mentioned will show this.

But to make the matter clear, take the Balance Sheet of the London and Westminster Bank of 30th June, 1888. We find its capital including reserves and undivided profits is,

using round figures, say	4,700,000
and that there is owing to customers on deposits, &c	25.300,000
	£30,000,000.
The Assets are Cash.......................	7,000,000
Premises say	500,000
the Advances	17,000,000
and the Investments	5,500,000
	£30,000,000

Now assume, although I think incorrectly, the premises to be acquired by outlay of capital, and to be on Capital Account, and of the capital, £4,200,000 remain. How can we say which or what part of the cash and advances and investments are composed of the money received as capital, and which or what part are composed of money received on deposit and current accounts. Then, if these are inseparable or undistinguishable, as they evidently are in fact, how can they be separated by an account, We can only take the undivided whole, and show by an account what the fact is, that capital and deposits and current accounts have contributed in given proportions to the composition of the whole of the assets. But when an amount is lost we cannot distinguish the loss, as either the loss of an asset composed of capital or of a deposit. We can only say that as the liability to customers for their deposits is not reduced by the loss, the effect of every loss must be to reduce capital, or the property of the proprietors. And if we cannot separate the assets representing capital from those representing deposits, for the same reasons we clearly cannot separate the assets which represent the share capital from the assets representing the Reserve Fund or the Balance of Profit and Loss.

But to follow out Mr. Buckley's example of a Shipping Company take the Balance Sheet of the Cunard Steamship Company of 31st December, 1886. We find the Share

Capital is about..........................	1,600,000
the Reserve Fund say	100,000
and the Liabilities say	600,000
	£2,300.000
The ships and wharves deducting provision accounts stand at say	2,000,000
The cash and stores and debts owing to the Company amount to..................	300,000
	£2,300.000

It is seen that as to £400,000, the ships represent more than the share capital, or in effect have been paid for out of the Reserve Fund of undivided profits and money obtained on credit. How can we say which or what part of the ships represents share capital, which part reserve, and which part borrowed money.

Clearly there is not a distinction in fact, and how can an account alter the fact.

Consider now, the nature and constitution of Parliamentary Companies under the Companies Clauses Acts. These are usually formed for the construction of Railways, Waterworks, Gasworks, Canals, and Docks.

A number of capitalists seeking to construct a public work apply to Parliament for power for two principal objects:—

1.—To construct the work.

2.—To raise a given fund or capital for the purpose.

Merely incidental to these objects are the incorporation of a Company, the acquisition of land, and the carrying on of the work for the benefit of the proprietors.

And it is also incidental to the carrying on of the work, that it be maintained in working order out of the revenue derived from it.

The Company incorporated acquires no powers beyond the two main ones, and such as arise out of, or are incidental, thereto.

The authority to raise money for the work implies:

(1) The limitation of the capital to the amount authorised to be raised under the powers, and

(2) The limitation of the application of all money raised to the work and equipment thereof, and the retention in the work of all money expended upon it, so that debentures of a parliamentary Company acquire the nature and most of its incidents of capital, and only in a limited sense can the debenture holders be considered as creditors.

The creation of a corporation for the purposes of the work, implies a limitation of its powers to the construction and carrying on of the work.

A Parliamentary Company cannot sell or pledge, or even abandon, any part of its work; and it cannot apply its capital to payment of creditors, debentures or other.

I may, perhaps, describe these limitations as part of the contract entered into by the corporation with the Legislature in the case of Parliamentary Companies.

Parliament accords limited liability to the members of Parliamentary Companies (not expressly, but by refraining from imposing liability), and in these companies the stipulation that capital may not be withdrawn, is in effect imposed as in Companies Act Companies, but in a different form, viz., by requiring the maintenance of the work.

But bear in mind the actual cost or value of the work of a Parliamentary Company, or the actual amount of money raised, are not necessarily the same as the debit and credit sides of the Capital Account. The money value may be either more or less than the total to the credit and debit of the Capital Account of a parliamentary company in proportion as the stock or debentures have been issued at a premium or at a discount. Real value is immaterial. All that is essential is that the whole of the capital raised shall go solely to the work, and that the work, regardless of its value, shall be maintained. When maintenance is provided for, the whole of the Revenue must be applied first to interest on debentures and then to dividend.

It is natural that Parliament should require that before the proprietors are allowed to divide the revenue of the work, it should be ascertained on behalf of the public, which has an interest in the work, that the conditions on which the power (usually in effect partial monopoly) was granted have been complied with; and as a consequence Parliamentary Companies, with unimportant exceptions, are required to prepare and publish and furnish to the Government, accounts showing what capital has been raised, and that it has been applied to the work, or awaits such application, or in other words that the capital raised has been kept separate and intact. The accounts show whether the contract entered into with the Legislature, if I may so describe it, has been carried out.

Out of this necessity of keeping the Capital Funds distinct from the Revenue in Parliamentary Companies, arises necessarily what is known as the double account system.

The keeping of Capital and Revenue as distinct accounts, constitutes neither a privilege nor a restriction, but is merely he recording of facts, which Parliament in the public interest requires, shall exist in the case of Parliamentary Companies. In Companies Act Companies the public is not interested any more than in partnerships, and Parliament does not require that any particular state of facts shall exist, nor do such state of facts usually exist in the circumstances of Companies Act Companies, and if the facts to support the double account do not exist, the account cannot be prepared.

Accounts are a record of facts, and that which is incapable of separation in fact, cannot be separated by accounts. I have shown that in a Parliamentary Company the capital is in fact, required to be kept distinct from the Revenue, but I think that in describing a Companies Act Company, I have said enough to show that in such Companies this is rarely so in fact, nor is it usually possible that it can be so, nor does Mr. Buckley show any reason why it should be so.

But the capital may be, and sometimes is, kept separate in a Companies Act Company. Assume a Company, by its regulations or by contract, determines that the capital raised shall be kept distinct from other funds. Take for example, an Indian Railway Company formed as a Limited Company under the Companies Acts. The accounts are by contract with the Indian Govenment kept in a form very similar to that prescribed by the regulation of Railways Acts, 1868, and so the Indian Government insures the application of the capital to, and the maintenance of, the work, and constitutes something in the nature of a charge in favour of the public on the railway, in the same way as Parliament has done in the case of railways in the United Kingdom. But can it be seriously contended that the Company by the contract with the Indian Government can evade its legal obligation under the Companies Acts to ascertain, before paying dividends, that it has "the value of its capital intact?"

Take again Tramway Companies registered under the Companies Acts, in regard to which I may point out in passing a strange state of affairs exists, for although the Regulation of Railways Act, 1868, expressly includes tramways, and Mr. Sutton, in his treatise on the Tramway Acts, says, they are no doubt included in the provisions of that Act, I have ascertained by enquiry that only in very rare instances do the Companies adopt the prescribed form of accounts for railways, and in only a few cases is the Capital Account kept distinct, and no Tramway Companies, I believe, make the required return to the Board of Trade; and, moreover, the Board of Trade does not enforce the Act against tramways.

But assuming, as in some instances is the case, that a Tramway Company chooses to keep its Capital Account distinct, can it thereby obtain any advantage over other Tramway Companies which do not, in regard to the obligation of maintaining the value of its capital intact under the Companies Acts. I shall refer to the question of the modes of valuing tramways in the accounts of Companies Acts Companies. My present purpose is to suggest that a Company cannot by its regulations or by contract evade the obligation to take into account the value of all liabilities and assets in ascertaining profits available for distribution.

It is remarkable that Mr. Buckley cites no authority in support of the double account view. Moreover, he seems, elsewhere in his remarks, to contradict himself, and to dispel the double account view by a quotation from *Stringer's* case, (4 Ch. 475), viz: "The proper and legitimate way of "arriving at a statement of profits is to take the facts as "they actually stand, and after forming an estimate of the "assets as they actually exist to draw a balance so as to "ascertain the result in the shape of profit or loss." Apply this case to Mr. Buckley's example of the ship totally lost and uninsured. How, if the facts are taken as they stand, can a balance be drawn until the loss of the ship has been made good. But why "totally lost." If the boats and rigging are lost and uninsured are they to be made good out of income? and why one ship? Supposing nine of the ten ships are lost, is the Company still to be allowed to pay dividends out of the income of the remaining one ship.

But Mr. Buckley not only cites no cases in support, but he does not refer to several decisions which seem opposed to the double account view, and to the payment of dividends until capital is intact.

The following among other cases are cited by Mr. Palmer, in support of his views: In *Robinson v. Ashton* (20 Eq. 28), Sir G. Jessel, said "the rise or fall in value of fixed plant or real "estate belonging to a *partnership*, was as much profit or "loss of the partnership as anything else." V. C. Kindersley, in *Helby's* case (2 Eq. 167.) "A balance sheet or summary of "accounts would show on the one hand all the assets, and on "the other hand all the liabilities of the Company (including, "of course, the capital paid up) and it was only from that sort "of statement that any safe conclusion could be drawn as to "the question whether there had been any profit for the half "year or not, and whether any, and what, dividend should "be declared."

Sir G. Jessel, in sanctioning the writing off of the lost capital of the *Ebbw Vale Company* (*Times*, 20th Jan., 1873), remarked, that "but for the power (to write off") no dividend would be possible."

Mr. Justice Chitty, in the *Midland Land and Investment Companies'* case (8th Nov., 1886) said, "in declaring a dividend, "in my opinion, in a trading concern, the Directors are entitled "to put an estimate on the value of their assets from time to "time in order to ascertain, whether there is, or is not, a surplus "remaining after providing for liabilities (including, of course, "paid up capital), and where they make those valuations from "time to time on a just and fair basis, and take all the pre- "cautions which ordinary prudent men of business engaged "in a similar business would do, they are entitled to treat "the surplus thus ascertained as profit."

And in the *Oxford Building Society's* case (35 Ch. D. 502) Mr. Justice Kay said, "but they (the Directors) must not "shut their eyes or abstain from the exercise of ordinary "prudence, or violate the regulations" of the Company.

The origin of views similar to those held by Mr. Buckley, seems to lie in considering that the Share Capital is represented by certain specified assets, such as works, and that these assets are capital whilst the other assets are not. It seems to be assumed that Companies Act Companies have, like Companies for public works, a restricted destination for the capital raised. This is, of course, usually not so. The capital of a Companies Act Company like that of a partnership is destined, and is applied to any or all of the objects of the Company indiscriminately; among which objects is usually the giving credit, and obtaining money on credit, and employing such money, in conjunction with the capital and profits, in any or all of the objects indiscriminately. It is sometimes assumed that a distinction may be drawn between that in which a Company deals and other assets, that whereas book debts and stock-in-trade are not capital, investments and plant are; but this view does not seem capable of being supported, as all assets of a Companies Act Company are interchangeable, and what is invested in plant may at any time change to stock-in-trade or debts.

I have dealt, I fear, at wearisome length with the double account system, and the distinction between Parliamentary and Companies Act Companies, because, I think, these questions are the basis of the difference of opinion, not only of Mr. Buckley and Mr. Palmer, but of many lawyers as to what is profit.

I need not refer to Mr. Palmer's views further than to say that so far as they go, I consider that they state accurately the way in which profits should be, and are by general usage, ascertained.

I have now to consider some of the questions which arise in ascertaining profit.

In regard to the liabilities I need say little. I may suggest merely for consideration that the Balance Sheet should, so far as practicable, be a Statement of Liabilities and Assets, and whether the common practice of including on the liability side of the Balance Sheet, so called Reserve and Provision Accounts, which in fact represent deductions from assets, such as Bad Debt, Reserves and Depreciation Funds is not open to objection; and whether the better plan is not to deduct these accounts from the assets.

Numerous questions arise upon the valuation of assets. I shall confine myself to pointing to a few of these questions, and commenting briefly upon them. One matter I think it is of great importance for auditors as well as directors to bear carefully in mind that the law itself or knowledge of the law in regard to accounts of Companies, is (as I think Mr. Buckley's remarks in regard to profits suggests) in an extremely imperfect state. Many practices of Companies in regard to their accounts, I think we may assume, will in course of time, come up for consideration by the Judges, with whom, of course, and not with accountants, must rest the ultimate decision of doubtful points arising upon accounts.

First, in regard to under-valuation of property, it is a common practice of Companies to value certain assets at less than their real value. The Bank of England for many years has excluded the premises in Threadneedle Street, which were estimated in 1832 as worth a million sterling, altogether from its accounts. The premises of many banks are believed to be undervalued, owing to periodical amounts having been in prosperous years written off premises, when it has been known the premises have been in fact not diminishing in value. Similarly many Companies include investments in their Balance Sheet at sums very largely below their real market value, owing to their having refrained from re-valuing the investments from time to time, as the value increased. Companies owning factories built upon sites which have largely increased in value, refrain from revaluing their property, and so allow the factory to remain in the Balance Sheet at only a portion of the real value.

In some cases Companies create out of profits large secret contingency funds, which cause the Balance Sheet to misrepresent the position. The effect of this is that a large amount of profit (assuming it to be such) is concealed, and thereby retiring shareholders are losers.

So far as I am aware, these proceedings have not been directly challenged in the Law Courts as regards Companies Act Companies, and a custom may, perhaps, be said to have grown up, which will be found to resist attack; but upon what principles it will hereafter be held that a Company may misrepresent its position in the direction of understating its assets, I cannot pretend to say. In any event, no doubt the Courts will insist that the misrepresentations shall be free from *mala fides* or any attempt to serve the interests of one class of shareholders at the expense of another. Although the practice may be wrong, the danger to directors and auditors of understating value, seems remote. Still it is not easy to see why if an incoming shareholder who is misled by over valuation, is entitled to damages against directors to whom he was a stranger, an outgoing shareholder whose paid agent in a sense the directors are, is not entitled to recover the loss occasioned by having sold his shares below their real value, owing to under representation of the Company's position.

In regard to the annual re-valuation of works and plant I need not say that in practice this is unusual. I have contended that there is no distinction as regards Capital Account between this and any other class of assets. The question then suggests itself are works and plant subject to different principles as regards valuation for a balance sheet, and if so, why? Mr. Buckley suggests that if capital and revenue are to be treated as one we must re-value the tramway of a Tramway Company for the Balance Sheet and take into consideration in doing so the market price of the iron used in the construction of the tramway. A Land Company, it is seen in the *Leeds Building Society's* case, must re-value its land. A Shipping Company must provide for depreciation of its ships. But the land of a Land Company is not analagous to plant as regards such a Company, but is stock-in-trade, *i.e.*, the article it deals in and provision for depreciation of plant although including loss of value from change of fashion, or growing obselete, is not usually understood to include re-valuation. Is a tramway or a Factory Company required to do more than maintain and keep its tramway or factory up to date. That is to say is it to consider for what the factory could be replaced, if destroyed, and then to value no higher than the cost of replacement. Again, when shipping is depressed and ships equal in every respect can be bought at 30 per cent. less than the Company's fleet stands in the books, must the Company write off the 30 per cent. to profit and loss.

First, a fall in value that is fairly believed to be temporary need not, I think, be taken into account in reference to an asset if a permanent and non-marketable nature, and it would doubtless be contrary to commercial usage in regard to partnerships from time immemorial to do so.

It is not, I think, necessary for a Company in valuing any of its assets to consider the effect of liquidation of the Company if, as is usual, the permanent continuance of the business is what is contemplated in its constitution. If a temporary fall were loss to be provided for, a temporary rise would seem to be profit to be taken credit for. Nor is it necessary to consider for what the property will sell, for a buyer of an unmarketable asset is not usually forthcoming, and the Company is not a seller.

But if the depreciation is on a fair estimate of the asset, and surrounding circumstances considered of a permanent nature, I see no means by which the directors of a Tramway or Shipping Company can justify showing profits, or sanctioning the payment of dividends, until the loss in value is provided for.

The justification for valuing works and plant on different principles to stock-in-trade is not, I think, as is often said, because these assets are so called capital outlay, but is derived from commercial usage or custom, which custom in turn is based on reason and common sense. The principles are identical with those applicable in a partnership. In a partnership, temporary fluctuations, whether in value of materials or otherwise, are ignored, not because works are capital outlay, but because, among other reasons, revalution up and down would lead to confusion in the accounts, and to misrepresentation of the trading profits. I know of no reason for applying different reasoning to Companies.

But when the asset is of a marketable nature, and can be readily sold and replaced by purchase, the fall in value, although temporary, should, I think, appear in the account, and be charged to Profit and Loss. Mr. Buckley discusses the fall of £3 in the market value of £100 of Consols, as a loss on Capital Account, but in this he will not, I think, be followed by business men, and Mr. Palmer distinctly dissents from this view.

Preliminary expenses are usually included with the assets of the Company. The decision in *Bale* v. *Cleland*, (4 Fos. & F. 117) that if done openly they may be spread over years, dividends being paid in the meantime removes any difficulty, but introduces an important principle in regard to the valuation of assets. The reference in Table A. clause 80, to items of expenditure which "may in fairness be distributed over several years" is sometimes spoken of as justifying the inclusion of preliminary expenses as an asset. The question is, I think, open whether the cost of constructing the Company may not be deemed to be represented by the created Company itself, and so justify the amount being treated permanently as an asset, as it undoubtedly often is. In Railway Companies the preliminary expenses are deemed part of the cost of the railway.

Whether brokerage on the issue of shares in a Companies Act Company and cost of underwriting the Capital (which seems to be a reduction of the Capital) can properly be treated as preliminary expenses, or otherwise included as an asset, is also, as far as I am aware, not yet clearly settled, and the recent decision that shares cannot be issued at a discount, may throw new light upon the question of Brokerage.

The recent conversion of numerous private partnerships into public Companies brings the question of the valuation of goodwill into prominence; doubtless goodwill is property, but peculiar questions arise upon valuing it from year to year in the Balance Sheet. The connection with a given number of customers is the property purchased, but if those customers fall away, or if in the case of a newspaper the circulation falls off, the value of the goodwill would seem to fall with them. Lord Justice Lindley says, it is only so far as goodwill has a saleable value that it can be regarded as an asset of any partnership.

To what extent the outlay of a Company formed for prospecting or exploring can be treated as an asset is sometimes a difficult question.

The question does not usually assume importance until the Company commences to earn income, and a Profit and Loss Account can be drawn up. But the question then arises, what part of the outlay is an asset and how the result is to be valued in ascertaining profits. It would seem to be necessary to form a *bonâ fide* estimate of the value of what has been acquired by the outlay, and if this value is less than the amount expended the difference must be written off.

The addition to outlay of interest during construction or what I think, equivalent in effect, the payment of dividends during construction has been held by Mr. Justice Fry in the *Alexandra Palace* case to be illegal in a Companies Act Company, and Directors have been held liable to refund the amount paid. It would, therefore, be presumption to discuss the question in a contrary view, but it is well to bear in mind where this decision leaves us. When the asset constructed comes to be valued for the Balance Sheet, interest on the outlay during its construction will, as in the case of assets purchased form, an element of value, so in effect interest will be included and will go to swell the profit available for dividend. In *Bardwell* v. *The Sheffield Waterworks*, (14 Eq. 517) it was held that "The Company were "entitled to add to the capital required for the construction "of the works, the amount of the interest or dividends on "the loans or shares by means of which it was raised until "the completion of the works," on the ground that if the Company, instead of themselves constructing the works had employed a contractor, he would have included interest in his estimates. It is difficult for an accountant to reconcile the principles in which the two decisions are based.

An important point arising on valuation, is that of assets purchased with foreign currency which has depreciated or increased in value. Advances represented say, in Rupees are usually taken at the exchange of the day, but the same need not be said of investments in property. Property ought, I think, to be subjected to valuation in sterling apart from the value of the currency. The value of land for instance, in a foreign country by no means necessarily, nor usually, follows the rise or fall of the currency. Attempts have been made, to induce the Courts to sanction the valuation of assets acquired by a Company in exchange for shares issued as paid up, on different pinciples from those applied to other assets, but it does not seem that this has been established, and the decision in regard to the issue of shares at a discount, seems to remove any doubt that value must exist for the whole of the capital credited.

Various other questions suggested themselves, but I have, I am afraid, attempted already too much. I have avoided questions relating to valuation of stock-in-trade as they have been already discussed at your meetings.

I should have liked, had time allowed, to consider what are realized profits, as distinguished from profits earned. Realized profits were held by Mr. Justice Kay, in the *Oxford Building Society*, case (35 Ch.D. 502), to mean "Profits tangible for the purpose of division." If my view, that no specific assets represent the profit, this definition does not give us much assistance. But I must leave this question in the hope, that some one, at one of your future meetings, will endeavour to make clear what is the distinction between the terms; I should also have liked to enquire, what distinction there is, between such terms as "realized profits," "profits earned," "profits of the business," and net profits."

I have said, that it is not the view generally of lawyers that every accretion to capital is profit.

In a recent case, the property of a mining Company, in the course of a few years, was found to have increased fourfold in value. A proportion of all profits had been reserved and made payable to the persons, from whom the Company acquired the mine. The Company decided to wind up and sell its mine for four times the cost to a new Company mainly composed of the same shareholders as the old Company. Several eminent counsel were consulted, but were unable to agree, whether the increase of value was profit, or what was called accretion to capital, but eventually the increase was treated as profit and divided accordingly. The *Bridgwater Navigation Company's* case (39 Ch. D. 1) seems to have been decided in an opposite sense, but this case is, I believe, under appeal, and the circumstances are peculiar, and Lord Justice Cotton, speaks of the increased value as profit, but its application was held to depend upon the Articles of Association. The *Scinde Railway* case was decided upon the terms of a special Act of Parliament. I am not aware of any instance, in which an accretion to capital of a Companies Act Company has been held to be other than profit.

I have endeavoured to show that the double account system is inapplicable to Companies under the Companies Acts.

That every accretion to the capital of a Companies Act Company is profit, and that profit is the surplus of assets over the liabilities, including with the liabilities the paid up capital, and that the amount of profit is arrived at by ascertaining this surplus, after fairly estimating the value of all assets and liabilities.

I do not expect to have convinced those who agree with Mr. Buckley's views; but I shall be satisfied if anything I have said leads students to examine the subject more carefully for themselves. I have said, I do not pretend to express final opinions. On the contrary, I shall gladly modify any opinions I have expressed, if they are shewn to be unsound.

LEE *Versus* NEUCHATEL ASPHALTE COMPANY

CASES

DETERMINED BY THE

CHANCERY DIVISION

AND IN

LUNACY

AND ON APPEAL THEREFROM IN THE

COURT OF APPEAL.

LEE *v.* NEUCHATEL ASPHALTE COMPANY.

C. A.

1887

STIRLING, J.

Dec. 7, 8, 13.

1888

Feb. 22.

C. A.

1889

Feb. 5, 6, 9.

[1886. L. 630.]

Company—Dividends—Payment of Dividend out of Capital—Wasting Property.

Where the shares of a limited company have, under a duly registered contract, been allotted as fully paid-up shares in consideration of assets handed over to the company, it is under no obligation to keep the value of its assets up to the nominal amount of its capital, and the payment of a dividend is not to be considered a return of capital, merely on the ground that no provision has been made for keeping the assets up to the nominal amount of capital.

There is nothing in the *Companies Acts* to prohibit a company formed to work a wasting property, as *e.g.*, a mine or a patent, from distributing, as dividend, the excess of the proceeds of working above the expenses of working, nor to impose on the company any obligation to set apart a sinking fund to meet the depreciation in the value of the wasting property. If the expenses of working exceed the receipts, the accounts must not be made out so as to shew an apparent profit, and so enable the company to pay a dividend out of capital, but the division of the profits without providing a sinking fund is not such a payment of dividends out of capital as is forbidden by law.

Decision of *Stirling*, J., affirmed.

THIS company was incorporated in July, 1873, as a limited company with a nominal capital of £1,150,000 divided into shares of £10, of which 35,000 were preference and 80,000 ordinary shares.

C. A.
1889
LEE
v.
NEUCHATEL
ASPHALTE
COMPANY.

One of the objects of the company as defined by the memorandum of association was to acquire as from the 1st of July, 1873, and on the terms expressed in an agreement dated the 17th of July, 1873, and made between the *Neuchatel Rock Paving Company* and five other companies of the first six parts, and *H. A. Bradbury* contracting on behalf of this company of the sixth part, or on such other terms as might be mutually agreed, the concession granted by the Government of *Neuchatel* and held by the *Neuchatel Rock Paving Company,* and the exclusive right thereunder of getting the bituminous rock and mineral products from the *Val de Travers,* and all the mines, works, business, property, and assets of the last-mentioned company, and also all the sub-concessions held by the other five companies, and all the business properties and assets of those companies. Another object mentioned in the memorandum was to work, dig, win, quarry, and get bituminous rock and other products under the above concession or any other concession to be acquired by the company, and the products of any mines acquired by the company, and to sell and dispose of the same on such terms as the directors might think fit, and to acquire, erect, and set up any new buildings or machinery for developing and carrying on the operations of the company, and to carry on the business of manufacturers of asphalte and bituminous rock pavement in every branch, and (subject to any exclusive concessions for the time being in force, whereby the area of the company's operations might be restricted) to lay down in all places wheresoever the pavement manufactured by or for the company.

By the agreement of the 17th of July, 1873, referred to above, the *Neuchatel Rock Paving Company* agreed to sell and transfer to the new company when formed, the above concession and all their mines, works, business, property, and assets; and the other five companies respectively agreed to sell and transfer to the new company their sub-concessions, business properties, and assets. The consideration was that there should be allotted to the *Neuchatel Rock Paving Company* 20,000 preference shares and the 80,000 ordinary shares in the intended company, and to the other five companies the number of preference shares therein mentioned, all such shares to be allotted as fully paid up. The total number of preference shares thus to be allotted was 33,700 out of the 35,000.

The agreement was carried into effect, and on the formation of the company the shares were allotted in pursuance of it, and it will be seen that the company therefore was in substance an amalgamation of the six previous companies, no money passing.

The articles of association contained the following clauses :—

"97. The net profits of the company shall be applied and divided as follows. First, a dividend at the rate of £7 per cent. per annum shall be paid on the preferred shares in proportion to the amount for the time being paid up or deemed to have been paid up thereon. And subject to the payment of such dividend as aforesaid a like dividend shall be paid on the ordinary shares. And after payment of such dividend as aforesaid on all the shares the surplus of the net profits shall be divided by way of dividend rateably amongst all the shareholders in such proportion as aforesaid, but without preference or distinction.

"98. No such distribution of profits shall be made without the consent of a general meeting. It shall, however, be competent for the directors, without such sanction, in the interval between two meetings to declare an interim dividend on the preferred shares at any rate not exceeding 7 per cent., and on the ordinary shares not exceeding 4 per cent. per annum.

"99. In case of any dispute as to the amount of net profits the decision of the company in general meeting shall be final.

"100. The directors may, before recommending any dividend on any of the shares, set aside out of the net profits of the company such sum as they think proper as a reserved fund to meet contingencies or for equalizing dividends, or for repairing and maintaining the works connected with the business of the company, or any part thereof, and the directors may invest the sum so set apart as a reserved fund, or any part thereof, upon such securities as they may select; but they shall not be bound to form a fund, or otherwise reserve moneys, for the renewal or replacing of any lease, or of the company's interest in any property or concession.

"126. In case of a winding-up or distribution of the assets of the company, the holders of the ordinary shares shall be entitled

C. A.
1889
LEE
v.
NEUCHATEL
ASPHALTE
COMPANY.

to participate in such assets rateably with the holders of the preferred shares, the intention of these presents being that the priority hereby conferred on the preferred shares shall be confined to dividend, subject to any exceptional claims which may be maintained by the holders of fully paid-up shares."

The original concession was of a right to get bituminous rock within a defined area in the *Val de Travers* for a period of twenty years from the 15th of December, 1867, to the 15th of December, 1887, and the consideration for it was a royalty of 19¾ francs per ton, with a minimum rent of 40,000 francs. In 1870 this was modified for the period between the 16th of December, 1870, and the 16th of December, 1881, the dead rent being raised to 100,000 francs, and the royalty varying according to a complicated scheme depending on the quantity got, but being at a rate much less than 19¾ francs if more than 5000 tons were got in a year.

The company found the terms of the concession burdensome, and negotiated for a fresh one. On the 22nd of January, 1878, the *Neuchatel* Government extended the term of the concession to the 15th of December, 1907, and extended the concession over a wider area. The state made the concession an exclusive one, reserving only the right of working asphalte for its own use. The royalty was fixed at 6 francs per ton, and the minimum rent at 150,000 francs. The company paid down a sum of 200,000 francs (£8000) to the *Neuchatel* government for this concession. The result of the modification was that in seven years, from December, 1878, to December, 1885, the *Neuchatel* Government received from the company for rent and royalties nearly £40,000 less on the whole than they would have received if the same quantity had been worked on the old terms.

The result of the company's operations was as follows:—From the 1st of July, 1874, to the 30th of June, 1875, there was a loss of above £6000, but in each of the subsequent years down to December, 1878, the receipts considerably exceeded the outlay, and the loss was made up within three years. No part of the excess was distributed until 1880, when, the surplus for the year ending the 31st of December, 1879, being £8165, a dividend of 4s. per share was paid on the preference shares. No dividend was declared for the following year, but dividends of 5*s.*, 3*s.* 6*d.*, and 5*s.* per share were paid on the preference shares for the years 1881, 1882, and 1883. No dividend was declared for 1884, but out of the surplus for that year £21,060, together with a considerable sum held over from the preceding year, was applied in reduction of capital expenditure.

The accounts for the year ending the 31st of December, 1885, shewing a surplus of £17,140, the directors proposed (after setting apart £1000, which they had previously determined to set apart yearly towards repayment of the £8000 which they had paid for the second concession) to pay a dividend of 9*s.* per share on the preference shares, which would amount to £15,369. A general meeting approved of this proposal.

The Plaintiff, who was a holder of 628 ordinary shares and 16 preference shares in the company, brought his action on behalf of himself and all other the shareholders, except the Defendants, against the company and the directors, alleging that the value of the concession had become depreciated, and a large part of the capital of the company lost, and that there could not be any profits applicable to payment of a dividend until such loss and depreciation had been made good; and the Plaintiff claimed, on behalf of himself and all other the shareholders of the company, or (as the case might be) on behalf of himself and all other holders of ordinary shares, a declaration that the company did not in 1885 earn a profit of £17,140, or any profit available for payment of a dividend, and an injunction to restrain the company and the directors from paying a dividend. One of the directors, who was a large preference shareholder, was appointed to represent the preference shareholders.

The case was argued before Mr. Justice *Stirling* on December 7, 8, and 13, 1887.

Rigby, Q.C., and *Upjohn*, for the Plaintiff:—

The directors are in effect proposing to pay dividends out of the capital of the company. The property of the company is of a wasting nature. Its concession has depreciated in value by reason of the quantity of rock extracted and sold, the lapse of time, and the loss of capital to the extent of £32,736. Neither

C. A.
1889
LEE
v.
NEUCHATEL
ASPHALTE
COMPANY.

in the accounts for 1885, nor in any previous account, has the company been properly debited with this depreciation, but nearly the whole of the moneys received for asphalte sold have been treated as available for distribution, so that the company is in effect returning to its shareholders in the shape of dividends a portion of the capital they have subscribed. No net profits were made in 1885, and before any dividend is paid the amount of the previous losses of the company ought to be made good. The moneys paid for the concession must be treated as paid for the purchase of all the asphalte comprised therein, if it can be gotten during the term, and, if it cannot all be gotten, then for the purchase of so much as can be gotten during the term. The amount which can be so gotten should be ascertained, and the prime cost of each ton of asphalte should figure on the debit side of the account as something to be deducted before any profit is arrived at. This has never been done: *Bloxam* v. *Metropolitan Railway Company* (1); *Mills* v. *Northern Railway of Buenos Ayres Company* (2). The case of *Knowles* v. *McAdam* (3) was overruled in *Coltness Iron Company* v. *Black* (4), upon the question of income tax; but if that question is eliminated, the judgments of *Kelly*, C.B., and *Cleasby*, B., in the former, and of Lord *Cairns* and Lord *Penzance* in the latter case, are all in our favour upon our contention as to the deductions which ought properly to be made from trade profits. It has been held in the case of tramways that, before net profits can be ascertained, a sum of money ought to be set aside as representing depreciation by wear and tear: *Dent* v. *London Tramways Company* (5); *Davison* v. *Gillies* (6), and the principle is applicable more strongly here, where the mine becomes less valuable every year. The loss should be made good out of the profits: *Upton* v. *Brown* (7). It is clearly *ultrà vires* in a company to pay away or return the capital to which its creditors have a right to look: *Guinness* v. *Land Corporation of Ireland* (8); *Trevor* v. *Whitworth* (9); *In re National Funds Assurance Company* (10); *In re Ebbw Vale*

(1) Law Rep. 3 Ch. 337.
(2) Ibid. 5 Ch. 621.
(3) 3 Ex. D. 23.
(4) 6 App. Cas. 315, 324.
(5) 16 Ch. D. 344.
(6) 16 Ch. D. 347, n.
(7) 26 Ch. D. 588.
(8) 22 Ch. D. 349.
(9) 12 App. Cas. 409.
(10) 10 Ch. D. 118.

Steel, Iron, and Coal Company (1); *In re Kirkstall Brewery Company* (2).

Robinson, Q.C., Sir *Horace Davey*, Q.C., and *W. P. Beale*, for the Company and four of the Directors:—

The gist of the argument for the Plaintiff is that there has been a loss of capital to the company. There not only has been no such loss, but the company is now richer in assets than when it was formed; and the Plaintiff has failed to show that the company has not carried on its business in a prudent manner. The concession is now for a longer period, and it embraces a larger area. This is not the case of the purchase of property by a company for cash. The company purchased six undertakings for a nominal sum, which was paid entirely in shares; and took over the debts and assets of the selling companies. So that the subject of the purchase was partly corporeal and partly incorporeal, and the cost is the amount paid, less the value of the corporeal subject-matter, which is now greater than it was at the time of the purchase. The evidence is that there is more asphalte than can be got during the concession, and the Plaintiff has entirely failed to shew the loss or depreciation on which he relies. There is a distinction, which has been lost sight of in the argument for the other side, between fixed capital, or the amount sunk in the purchase of the undertaking, which cannot be paid away, and circulating capital, which stands upon a different footing. The question here is merely one of prudence or imprudence, and the Court cannot interfere with the decision of the shareholders upon the point. All that was decided in *Davison* v. *Gillies* (3) and *Dent* v. *London Tramways Company* (4) is that, before distributing profits as dividends, allowance must be made for maintaining the undertaking in a proper state of efficiency, and in this case the property of the company is in that state.

W. Pearson, Q.C., *Buckley*, Q.C., and *Methold*, for the other three Directors:—

A company is not bound to make a valuation year by year of

(1) 4 Ch. D. 827.
(2) 5 Ch. D. 535.
(3) 16 Ch. D. 347, n.
(4) Ibid. 344.

C. A.
1889
LEE
v.
NEUCHATEL
ASPHALTE
COMPANY.

its fixed capital before declaring a dividend; and it is illusory to say in a case like this that, whether the mine is inexhaustible or not, you must each year deduct a given sum for prime cost. Here, after all the extraction of asphalte, and the lapse of years, the concession is worth more now than it originally was.

[STIRLING, J., referred to *In re Ambrose Lake Tin and Copper Mining Company* (1).]

Upjohn, in reply.

1888. Feb. 22. STIRLING, J. (after stating the facts of the case, continued):—

It appears by the report of 1884 that the directors had resolved that the sum paid for the renewal of the concession should be written off at the rate of £1000 a year. The accounts for the year ending 1885 shew an excess of receipts over expenditure to the amount of £17,140 13s. 2d., out of which, after setting aside £1000 in reduction of the amount paid in 1877 for the renewal of the concession, it was recommended by the directors, and resolved by a majority of the shareholders, that a dividend on the preferred shares at the rate of 9s. a share should be paid. This action has been brought to restrain the payment of that dividend.

Now the Court only interferes in an action constituted as the present is, where the acts proposed to be done by the directors are beyond the powers of the company. In order, therefore, to justify the interference of the Court in this action, the Plaintiff has to shew that it is beyond the powers of the company to pay the proposed dividend, and for this purpose he must establish that the dividend is intended to be paid, not out of profits, but out of the capital of the company. Accordingly, the allegations on which the Plaintiff's title to relief is founded are shortly these: that a large portion of the capital of the company has been lost, and that no profits were in fact made by the company in 1885, or, at all events, none sufficient for the payment of the proposed dividend.

The evidence adduced at the trial in support of these allega-

(1) 14 Ch. D. 390.

tions by the Plaintiff (and none was adduced by the Defendants) was directed to two points—first, to establish that the concession held by the company was a wasting asset which had during 1885 and the preceding years become depreciated both by effluxion of time and by the exhaustion of the subject-matter; and that neither in the year ending the 31st of December, 1885, nor in any preceding year, had adequate allowance been made for such depreciation; and, secondly, to shew that in addition there had occurred in the realization of the assets taken over by the company on its formation, a serious loss of £32,000 and upwards. Now, the capital of the company is nominally £1,150,000, but actually it has never existed in the form of cash, or otherwise than in the shape of the assets taken over at the formation of the company, or subsequently, from time to time, belonging to it. There is no evidence before me of the value either of the assets transferred to the Defendant company, or of the shares issued by it at the time of its formation; and in the absence of evidence it cannot be assumed that the value of the assets transferred to the Defendant company amounted to the par value of the shares, or that the value of the assets was £1,150,000, or any other sum.

In my opinion, the capital of the company at the time of its formation really consisted of the aggregate of the assets taken over from the various selling companies under the agreement of July, 1873. That agreement was merely a scheme for ascertaining and declaring the interests of those companies in that aggregate in accordance with the agreed value of their several contributions thereto, and unless it can be shewn that, after payment of the dividend, the assets now belonging to the Defendant company will fall short of those belonging to the company at the time of its formation, it cannot, in my judgment, be said that the dividend is being paid out of capital. Whether it would be necessary for the Plaintiff to establish more than this, I need not at present consider.

Has then the Plaintiff established such a deterioration in the value of the assets? I shall first deal with the value of the concession; and as regards the exhaustion of the subject-matter, I think not much weight can be attached to the Plaintiff's allega-

C. A.
1889
LEE
v.
NEUCHATEL
ASPHALTE
COMPANY.
Stirling, J.

tion. It is true that 230,000 tons have been extracted from the mine; but the amount remaining available for extraction is, according to the Plaintiff's own witnesses, no less than 1,340,000 tons. There is no probability that that amount can or will be got during the existence of the present concession. Then, as to effluxion of time, the question is, is the present concession at the present time of less value than was the concession taken over by the Defendant company on the 17th of July, 1873? The present concession is for a longer period, extends over a wider area, and is held on more favourable terms than the former.

What then do the Plaintiff's witnesses say as to its value? Two only have dealt with this—Mr. *Bauerman* and Mr. *Elder*.

[His Lordship then considered their evidence at some length. That of Mr. *Bauerman* was to the effect that the concession was of greater value now than the former one was in 1873. The evidence of Mr. *Elder* went to shew depreciation, but his Lordship considered his evidence to fall far short of what was necessary to establish the Plaintiff's case.]

Again, it was contended that if the company were to do in every year down to the expiration of the concession, as was proposed to be done in 1885, the concession would expire, and no fund would exist to represent its value; but it cannot, as I think, be assumed that the company will do in every year as was proposed to be done in 1885. They have not done so in the past. For 1884, as well as for some previous years, they paid no dividend. It may be that in some future year, the company will have to set apart a substantial sum to represent depreciation in the value of the concession; but so long as the capital remains intact, and the current receipts exceed the current expenditure, both according to the general law and under the provisions of these particular articles of association, it rests entirely with the shareholders to decide whether the excess shall be divided among them or set apart as a reserve fund for replacing wasting assets, and the Court has no power to interfere with their decision however foolish or imprudent it may seem to be.

The remaining point, as to the alleged loss on realization of certain assets, may be more shortly dealt with. It was based on a statement contained in one of the admitted documents.

No evidence was adduced by the Defendants, and the precise nature of this loss has not been made perfectly clear. It may possibly be nothing more than a matter of book entry. Assuming, however, that the loss actually occurred to the extent of £32,736 1*s.* 10*d.*, which is the statement referred to, nevertheless it appears that profits to a greater extent have been made and retained in the coffers of the company, and are, in the balance-sheet for the year ending the 31st of December, 1885, represented by investments to the amount of £36,000 and upwards, and the company are entitled, as I think, to set-off these investments as against the alleged loss.

I am therefore of opinion that the Plaintiff has failed to establish a case for the interference of the Court, and that the action must be dismissed. If there is no arrangement as to the costs, they must follow the event.

W. W. K.

C. A.

The Plaintiff appealed, and the appeal was argued on the 5th and 6th of February, 1889.

Rigby, Q.C., and *Upjohn*, for the Appellant :—

The preference shareholders are only entitled to dividends out of the net profits. There can be no profits unless the capital is kept up to the original amount. It appears by the books that there has been an actual loss of capital to the amount of £32,000 since the first concession, which ought to be replaced. But independently of this, the property is itself wasting. It consists of nothing but the concession, which only lasts till the year 1907, and the machinery. The capital therefore diminishes in value every year, and when the concession expires the shareholders will have nothing to represent their capital. The company ought therefore to set aside a sufficient sum to replace the capital at the end of the concession before they declare a dividend. It is said that the 100th article permits the directors to declare a dividend without providing such a fund; but if so, the article is *ultrà vires*, and void. It is in effect a permission to the company to reduce its capital, which cannot be done except in the method provided by the Act of Parliament: *In re Almada and Tirito*

C. A.
1889
LEE
v.
NEUCHATEL
ASPHALTE
COMPANY.

Company (1); *Trevor* v. *Whitworth* (2). The nominal amount of the share capital must be taken as the value of the capital when the company was formed, and the value ought to be kept up to that amount. There is no distinct authority relating to a company for working a wasting property, but *Coltness Iron Company* v. *Black* (3) is in our favour. There Lord *Blackburn* (4) adopts the definition of "profits" given by *McCulloch* in his book on Political Economy, who says: "Profits really consist of the produce or its value remaining to those who employ their capital in an industrial undertaking after all their necessary payments have been deducted, and after the capital wasted and used in the undertaking has been replaced." Although the declaration of dividends is generally a matter of internal management, yet the Court will interfere if a company is improperly employing capital in the place of income for that purpose: *Bloxam* v. *Metropolitan Railway Company* (5).

[LOPES, L.J.:—All the shareholders knew that it was a wasting property.]

They had no power to agree to let it waste. It is not like the case of an ordinary partnership. They must keep within the Acts of Parliament. This is an attempt to make a return of capital to the shareholders, which is beyond their power.

Sir *Horace Davey*, Q.C., and *W. P. Beale*, Q.C., for the company and the directors:—

We contend that this is a question of internal management, with which the Court cannot interfere. The Plaintiff has no case unless he can shew that the act intended to be done is *ultrà vires.* He contends—(1) that there has been an actual loss of capital, and that there cannot be profits until the loss has been made up; (2) that before the company can declare a dividend it must have capital assets not less in value than its nominal capital; (3) that where property belonging to a company is of a wasting character, the company is bound to set apart a sinking

(1) 38 Ch. D. 415.
(2) 12 App. Cas. 409.
(3) 6 App. Cas. 315.
(4) Ibid. 329.
(5) Law Rep. 3 Ch. 337.

fund to make up the depreciation, and that any provision in the articles dispensing with this obligation is *ultrà vires*.

As to the first point, we say on the evidence that there has not been a loss of capital. But suppose there had; it would be a bold proposition to say that a company cannot pay a dividend unless its assets are worth as much as they were at first. Can it be contended that before a railway company can pay a dividend it must revalue its undertaking? Suppose, owing to a fall in the price of iron, a railway is not worth nearly so much as it was at first, can it be urged that the company can declare no dividend until it has laid by enough to make up the difference? The Appellant forgets the distinction drawn by economists, which is a very substantial one, between fixed capital, the money expended in purchasing which is sunk once for all, and circulating capital, capital circulating like stock-in-trade, which in the ordinary course of business is parted with and replaced by other. Then on the evidence the assets of the company are worth a great deal more than they were when the company started, so there is no loss.

Then as to the second point, that the company must keep up its assets to a value equal to the nominal amount of its capital, there is no authority that shews a company to be under such an obligation. *Davison* v. *Gillies* (1) goes no further than to decide that the directors must keep the concern in a state of efficiency, so as to be capable of earning profits. *Dent* v. *London Tramways Company* (2) shews that Sir *G. Jessel* did not decide so much as he had been supposed to decide in the earlier case. Both cases go on the articles of the companies, and are quite consistent with each other, and neither of them supports the contention of the Appellant.

The third contention of the Appellant is that because the property is a wasting property, the company is bound to set apart a sinking fund. No doubt it may be considered prudent for a company, the principal part of whose assets is of a wasting character, to set apart such a fund; but whether it is under a legal obligation to do so is quite another matter. *Lambert* v. *Neuchatel Asphalte Company* (3), if it does not support a

(1) 16 Ch. D. 347, n. (2) 16 Ch. D. 344. (3) 30 W. R. 913.

C. A.
1889
Lee
v.
Neuchatel
Asphalte
Company.

plea of *res judicata*, which we submit it does, is at all events an authority in our favour.

[*Rigby*, Q.C.:—The question whether the article was *ultrà vires* was not raised there.]

We contend that the decision in *Lambert's Case* (1) concludes the matter; an appeal was abandoned. The declaration of a dividend is eminently a matter of internal management, and unless the Plaintiff can make out that there is an obligation on the company, paramount to anything in the articles, to set apart a sinking fund, the Court cannot interfere.

Robinson, Q.C., and *Methold*, for the preference shareholders:—

This concession is only a part of the company's business. It has power to take other concessions, and it has long ago replaced the purchase-money of this concession. An acceptance of the principles contended for by the Appellant would be ruinous to companies, for it would make it impossible for directors ever to recommend a dividend without going into elaborate calculations as to the value of their assets.

Rigby, in reply.

1889. Feb. 9. Cotton, L.J.:—

This is an appeal from a decision of Mr. Justice *Stirling*, who dismissed the action. The action is brought by one ordinary shareholder, on behalf of himself and all other the ordinary shareholders against the company and the directors, one of whom has been appointed to represent the preference shareholders.

In order to understand the nature of the case, it is necessary to state shortly the nature of the formation of the company. There were six companies, which were in various ways entitled to the benefit of, and were working a concession for carrying on mines near *Neuchatel*, which produced the asphalte. The present company was formed by the amalgamation of these six companies. The nominal capital of the company is £1,150,000, divided into £10 shares. No money was paid when the present company was formed, but the assets of the previous companies

(1) 30 W. R. 913.

were taken over by the present company, and out of the 115,000 shares in that company 113,700, representing a nominal capital of £1,137,000, were given to the six old companies, and the concession and other rights which were made over were taken as being the assets to answer that share capital.

The object of the action is, on behalf of the ordinary shareholders, to prevent a dividend from being paid out of the excess of the receipts of the company above its expenditure for the year 1885. On what ground is that put? The articles justify the declaration of a dividend by a general meeting without making any reserve for the renewal or replacing of any lease or of the company's interest in any property or concession, but that is said to be *ultrà vires*. The Plaintiff puts his case in three ways. The first point I understand to be this, that a great part of the capital of the company has been lost. Now, what is meant by "capital"? If it is meant that any part of the assets has been lost, in my opinion that is wrong. I do not say that no part of the assets has ever been lost, but on the evidence before us the assets of this company are of greater value than at the time of the formation of the company in 1873. They then had, it is true, a concession, but for a shorter period than the one they have now got, and the royalty was very heavy. Now they have a longer time for the concession to run than they had in 1873, and they have got very much more profitable terms than they had at the first. In my opinion, so far from there being any loss of assets, the company has now in its possession a larger amount of assets than it had at the time it was first formed. Of course the present case is very different from that of a company where money has been paid on all the shares. That case is open to very different considerations. Here all that was taken by this company from the first companies was their assets, and in my opinion those assets have increased in value, so that as a matter of fact that first point entirely fails.

The Plaintiff's second point is that the property of the company is not now sufficient to make good the share capital; that assets to provide for that share capital must be made up before any dividend can be declared; and that if dividends are declared without that being done, that is to be treated as a return and a

C. A.
1889
LEE v. NEUCHATEL ASPHALTE COMPANY.
Cotton, L.J.

division of capital amongst the shareholders, and therefore illegal. In my opinion that is entirely wrong. It is a misapplication of the term "return of capital."

The word "capital" is used in many senses: one sense is the nominal capital, or, as I prefer calling it, the share capital, that capital which in the case of a company limited by shares is to be defined by the memorandum of association. Mr. *Rigby* relied on the provision (*Companies Act*, 1862, s. 12), that no alteration can be made in that capital but by adding to it except in the case of a reduction under the Act of 1867. It is impossible that the assets can be stated in the memorandum of association, but the share capital has to be stated. Then it is no doubt the law that the capital, in the sense of the assets of the company obtained for the shares, must not be applied except for the purposes of the company. That we shall have to consider both in this and in other parts of the present case. In my opinion there is no obligation in any way imposed upon the company or its shareholders to make up the assets of the company so as to meet the share capital, where the shares have been taken under a duly registered contract, which binds the company to give its shares for certain property without payment in cash. Shares must be paid up in cash, unless under an agreement duly registered there is a contract to allot or give the shares for something different. If there is an arrangement of that kind, which is obviously delusive, it may be that, although it has been duly registered, the shareholders who have taken the shares under it may, on proper proceedings being taken, be obliged to pay up in cash the difference between the value of their property and the nominal amount of their shares. But there is no suggestion that that ought to be done here, and in my opinion it would be wrong to say that a division among the shareholders of money which the company are not bound to apply in making up the nominal amount of their share capital is a return of capital. In my opinion this second point fails as well as the first.

The third point was to my mind the only one which occasioned any difficulty. It is said that the concession is a wasting property, and as it is a wasting property, that dividing its annual proceeds is dividing part of the capital assets of the company, which are represented by this concession. That was pressed upon us, and that is a difficulty, because it is established, and well established, that you must not apply the assets of the company in returning to the shareholders what they have paid up on their shares, or in paying what they ought to have paid up on their shares. But we must consider exactly how the case stands. There is nothing in the Act which says that dividends are only to be paid out of profits. There is a provision to that effect in Table A, and that rather favours the view that the matter of how profits are to be divided and dealt with, and out of what fund dividends are to be declared, is a matter of internal regulation. But still there is this firmly fixed, that capital assets of the company are not to be applied for any purpose not within the objects of the company, and paying dividend is not the object of the company, the carrying on the business of the company is its object. If this property was property of another nature, property which would not be reasonably or properly consumed in providing profit, the case would stand in a very different position. If there was a permanent property which would not be reasonably or properly so consumed, but the fruit of which only would be used in providing profit, then if the directors were to sell, or the shareholders were to authorize a sale of that, and then to declare a dividend out of the proceeds, that would clearly come within the case of *Guinness* v. *Land Corporation of Ireland* (1), for it would be applying the capital of the company to a purpose which was not authorized. But here, for the purpose of getting the profit, there is necessarily a consumption year by year of part of the capital of the company.

Then what is to be the result? I think that in such a case as this, even without reference to the particular provision of art. 100, the question whether what has been done is really a division of capital by way of dividend must be considered in a reasonable and sensible way. If it is made to appear, as was said in *Stringer's Case* (2), "That for the purposes of fraud, or for any other improper motive, a company has declared and paid a wholly delusive and improper dividend, and has thereby in effect taken away from its creditors a portion of the capital which was available for

(1) 22 Ch. D. 349. (2) Law Rep. 4 Ch. 475, 488.

C. A.
1889
LEE
v.
NEUCHATEL
ASPHALTE
COMPANY.
Cotton, L.J.

the debts of those creditors, I entertain no doubt the Court would have full jurisdiction, and would exercise it by ordering the repayment of the money so improperly paid." If here it could be shewn that this dividend had been declared from improper motives, fraudulent motives, or with the intention not of dividing profit, but of dividing and returning capital, I think the Court ought to interfere; as it ought, in my opinion, to do in any case where there is any such improper dealing, either by directors or by the majority of the shareholders of the company. But if the Court sees that the directors and the company have acted fairly and reasonably in ascertaining whether this is a division of profit and not of capital, and then in what is really a matter of internal arrangement (if it is done honestly, and does not violate any of the provisions of the articles) the Court is very unwilling to interfere, and in my opinion ought not to interfere, with the discretion exercised by the directors, who have the management of the company, or with the powers exercised by the company within the articles. Of course, if a power given by the articles goes beyond what can be given to the company or to the directors, then the Court must interfere; but in my opinion the only thing here to be considered is—is this really a division of the capital assets of the company under the guise of making and declaring a dividend? In my opinion, in this company, as in other companies, the directors and others who have the control, ought to consider whether in a fair, reasonable way what they are going to divide is to be considered as profits, but, in considering that, they may well have regard to the articles. There is no such necessity as was contended for by Mr. *Rigby*, to set apart every year a sum to answer the supposed annual diminution in the value of this property from the lapse of time. Reference was made to two decisions of the Master of the Rolls, which I think are to be explained so as in no way to conflict with the decision of Mr. Justice *Stirling* in this action, *Davison* v. *Gillies* (1) and *Dent* v. *London Tramways Company* (2). Those two decisions are entirely consistent with one another, and entirely depend on the directions contained in the articles of association, not on the general law. In *Davison* v. *Gillies* there was in the articles a direction that profits should be ascertained after making

(1) 16 Ch. D. 347, n. (2) 16 Ch. D. 344.

provision for the reparation of the tramway, and the Master of the Rolls said, when profits are to be divided by the directors it must mean the net profits, and that no dividend could be declared until provision had been made for the depreciation in the tramway and in the plant of the company. In *Dent* v. *London Tramways Company* (1), which was a case where preference shareholders were to have their dividend for each year paid to them out of the profits of that year only, what he held was: that they were entitled to be paid out of the profits of the year after setting aside sufficient for the maintenance of the tramway during that year only; and, therefore, he directed that provision should be made out of the profits of the year, not for the entire depreciation from the neglect to repair the tramway, but for the depreciation attributable to that year. That, in my opinion, entirely explains how those two decisions were come to, which Mr. *Rigby* contended were not consistent with one another. They favour the view which I entertain, that in considering whether this is to be treated as an honest division of profit, or as a division of capital under the guise of declaring a dividend, the Court will have regard to the directions of the articles, although, of course, if those articles authorize not a mere division of profit but a division of capital (using "capital" in the proper sense of the word—by which I mean permanent assets, and assets not to be expended in providing for the profit earned by the company), such a provision will be *ultrà vires* and void. Here there was not a division of capital under the form of a declaration of dividend by a scheme or plan for dividing assets of the company, the declaration of dividend was in accordance with the articles, and not contrary to the general law, and the Court ought not to interfere. In my opinion, therefore, the appeal fails.

LINDLEY, L.J.:—

I have come to the same conclusion. The actual point to be decided appears to me to be comparatively easy. The difficulty in the case arises from the invitation made to us by Mr. *Rigby* to lay down certain principles, the adoption of which would, in my judgment, paralyze the trade of the country.

(1) 16 Ch. D. 344.

C. A.
1889
LEE
v.
NEUCHATEL
ASPHALTE
COMPANY.
Lindley, L.J.

This company was formed in 1873, and, it may be stated shortly, was formed for the purpose of working a concession, which may be called a lease, of some asphalte mines or mineral property in *Switzerland*. The original lease was afterwards extended, and the company may be treated as having been formed for the purpose of acquiring a lease which will run out in 1907. It is obvious with respect to such property, as with respect to various other properties of a like kind, mines and quarries and so on, every ton of stuff which you get out of that which you have bought with your capital may, from one point of view, be considered as embodying and containing a small portion of your capital, and that if you sell it and divide the proceeds you divide some portion of that which you have spent your capital in acquiring. It may be represented that that is a return of capital. All I can say is, if that is a return of capital it appears to me not to be such a return of capital as is prohibited by law.

In order to make this out it is necessary to look through the *Companies Acts*. I have done so, and that not for the first time, and I cannot find any provision in the Acts which prohibits anything of the kind. The sections referring expressly to capital are very few. The two most important are the 8th and the 12th sections of the Act of 1862. The 8th section says that, when a company is registered as a company limited by shares, the memorandum of association must state the amount of capital with which the company proposes to be registered, divided into shares of a certain fixed amount. Then the 12th section says that the capital so referred to in the memorandum may be increased or converted into stock, but the conditions contained in the memorandum shall not be otherwise altered. That prohibits what is called a reduction of capital. Then under sect. 26, certain returns are to be made, and in the returns so to be made must be specified among other things the amount of the capital and the number of shares into which it is divided, and the number of shares which have been issued and the number which have been forfeited, and the amount of calls made on each share and the total amount of calls received. In sects. 28 and 34 there is further provision that any alterations made in the capital pursuant to the Act are to be notified to the Registrar. Then in the

Act of 1867 provision is made for reducing the capital, and that was amended in 1877 by being applied to a reduction of capital when part of the capital was lost.

What I have stated is the whole of the enactments relating to capital which are to be found in the *Companies Acts*. If you look further you find next to nothing about profits or dividends. There is nothing at all in the Acts about how dividends are to be paid, nor how profits are to be reckoned; all that is left, and very judiciously and properly left, to the commercial world. It is not a subject for an Act of Parliament to say how accounts are to be kept; what is to be put into a capital account, what into an income account, is left to men of business. Mr. *Rigby*, with the courage which was necessary, asked us to say there was in these articles a provision as to division of profits which was contrary to law. If he can make that out he wins, but if he cannot make it out he loses. He saw that plainly enough. Now that raises a curious question, because, putting it into plain language, he is asking us, at the instance of the ordinary shareholders, to break faith with the preference shareholders. He invites us to do it because, he says, the bargain into which the two classes of shareholders have entered cannot be upheld in point of law. But he admits that if the bargain is to stand as entered into he is in the wrong. We must be careful before we say that a contract is illegal or invalid in point of law, and I now propose to address myself to that question.

This company having been formed for the purposes to which I have alluded, the articles contain clauses about distribution of profits. Art. 97 says: "The net profits of the company shall be applied and divided as follows: First, a dividend at the rate of 7 per cent. per annum shall be paid on the preferred shares in proportion to the amount for the time being paid up, or deemed to have been paid up thereon," and then it goes on as to payment of dividends on the ordinary shares. Art. 98 says: "No such distribution of profits shall be made without the consent of a general meeting." Art. 99: "In case of any dispute as to the amount of net profits the decision of the company in general meeting shall be final." Then sect. 100 contains a provision which carries the case against Mr. *Rigby* unless it is illegal. It

C. A.
1889
LEE
v.
NEUCHATEL
ASPHALTE
COMPANY.
Lindley, L.J.

says: "The directors may, before recommending any dividend on any of the shares, set aside out of the net profits of the company such sum as they think proper as a reserve fund to meet contingencies, or for equalizing dividends, or for repairing or maintaining the works connected with the business of the company or any part thereof, and the directors may invest the sum so set apart as a reserve fund, or any part thereof, upon such securities as they may select; but they shall not be bound to form a fund or otherwise reserve moneys for the renewal or replacing of any lease, or of the company's interest in any property or concession."

First of all let us see what that means. We are dealing with a lease for a limited number of years, which is a wasting property, and while it is wasting the capital spent in acquiring it is wasting. The article says in so many words that although in every year the capital may be wasted by working out the mine so that at the end there may be nothing left, yet this company is formed on the principle that it shall not be obliged to replace year by year that which is so wasted. Mr. *Rigby* says that is contrary to law. Let us see whether that is made out.

Having stated shortly what are the provisions of the Acts of Parliament relating to this matter, I may safely say that the *Companies Acts* do not require the capital to be made up if lost. They contain no provision of the kind. There is not even any provision that if the capital is lost the company shall be wound up, and I think this omission is quite reasonable. The capital may be lost and yet the company may be a very thriving concern. As I pointed out in the course of the argument, and I repeat now, suppose a company is formed to start a daily newspaper; supposing it sinks £250,000 before the receipts from sales and advertisements equal the current expenses, and supposing it then goes on, is it to be said that the company must come to a stop, or that it cannot divide profits until it has replaced its £250,000, which has been sunk in building up a property which if put up for sale would perhaps not yield £10,000? That is a business matter left to business men. If they think their prospects of success are considerable, so long as they pay their creditors, there is no reason why they should not go on and divide profits, so far as I can see, although every shilling of the capital may be lost. It may be a perfectly flourishing concern, and the contrary view I think is to be traced to this, that there is a sort of notion that the company is debtor to capital. In an accountant's point of view, it is quite right, in order to see how you stand, to put down company debtor to capital. But the company do not owe the capital. What it means is simply this: that if you want to find out how you stand, whether you have lost your money or not, you must bring your capital into account somehow or other. But supposing at the winding-up of the concern the capital is all gone, and the creditors are paid, and there is nothing to divide, who is the debtor? No one is debtor to any one. If there is any surplus to divide, then, and not before, is the company debtor to the shareholders for their aliquot portions of that surplus. But the notion that a company is debtor to capital, although it is a convenient notion, and does not deceive mercantile men, is apt to lead one astray. The company is not debtor to capital; the capital is not a debt of the company.

Having shewn from the Acts (negatively, of course, because this is a negative proposition, and can only be proved by looking through the Acts) that the Acts do not require the capital to be made up if lost, I cannot find anything in them which precludes payment of dividends so long as the assets are of less value than the original capital. If they are so, it becomes a question of prudence for mercantile men whether they will wind up or not. I have already pointed out that the Act says nothing to make the loss of the capital a ground for winding up, and I have already pointed out that it says nothing about profits. The Act does not say that dividends are not to be paid out of capital, but there are general principles of law according to which the capital of a company can only be applied for the purposes mentioned in the memorandum of association. That is a fundamental principle of law, and if any of those purposes are expressly or impliedly forbidden by the statutes, the capital cannot be applied for those purposes even though there may be a clause in the memorandum that it shall. That was pointed out by the House of Lords in *Trevor* v. *Whitworth* (1), and particularly in the elaborate judgment of Lord *Macnaghten*, in which he expressed

(1) 12 App. Cas. 409.

C. A.
1889
LEE
v.
NEUCHATEL
ASPHALTE
COMPANY.
Lindley, L.J.

an opinion, although the point was not before him for decision, that if a company put into the memorandum of association a clause authorizing it to spend its capital in buying up its own shares, such a contract would be *ultrà vires*. That was only an expression of opinion by the learned Lord, but no one who has carefully studied the Acts of Parliament can entertain any doubt of the soundness of the opinion.

Now we come to consider how the *Companies Act* is to be applied to the case of a wasting property. If a company is formed to acquire and work a property of a wasting nature, for example, a mine, a quarry, or a patent, the capital expended in acquiring the property may be regarded as sunk and gone, and if the company retains assets sufficient to pay its debts, it appears to me that there is nothing whatever in the Act to prevent any excess of money obtained by working the property over the cost of working it, from being divided amongst the shareholders, and this in my opinion is true, although some portion of the property itself is sold, and in some sense the capital is thereby diminished. If it is said that such a course involves payment of dividend out of capital, the answer is that the Act nowhere forbids such a payment as is here supposed. The fact is, you cannot get out of the Act any prohibition against paying dividends out of capital except by having reference to the general principles to which I have alluded, and which general principles cannot be stretched, to my mind, to such a length as Mr. *Rigby* invites the Court to stretch them.

It appears to me that the proposition that it is *ultrà vires* to pay dividend out of capital is very apt to mislead, and must not be understood in such a way as to prohibit honest trading. If you treat it as an abstract proposition that no dividend can be properly paid out of moneys arising from the sale of property bought by capital, you find yourself landed in consequences which the common sense of mankind would shrink from accepting. On the other hand, if the working expenses exceed the current gains, you cannot divide your capital under the head of profits when there are no profits in any sense of the term, as was done, for example, in *Rance's Case* (1), *In re Oxford Benefit Building and Investment Society* (2), and *Leeds Estate, Building and Invest-*

(1) Law Rep. 6 Ch. 104. (2) 35 Ch. D. 502.

ment Company v. *Shepherd* (1). If those cases are studied, it would be seen, I think, with sufficient clearness that that is really what is meant. You must not have fictitious accounts. If your earnings are less than your current expenses, you must not cook your accounts so as to make it appear that you are earning a profit, and you must not lay your hands on your capital to pay dividend. But it is, I think, a misapprehension to say that dividing the surplus after payment of expenses of the produce of your wasting property is a return of capital in any such sense, as is forbidden by the Act. *Stringer's Case* (2) may be usefully referred to on this subject.

As regards the mode of keeping accounts, there is no law prescribing how they shall be kept. There is nothing in the Acts to shew what is to go to capital account or what is to go to revenue account. We know perfectly well that business men very often differ in opinion about such things. It does not matter to the creditor out of what fund he gets paid, whether he gets paid out of capital or out of profit net or gross. All he cares about is that there is money to pay him with, and it is a mere matter of bookkeeping and internal arrangement out of what particular fund he shall be paid. Therefore you cannot say that the question of what ought to go into capital or revenue account is a matter that concerns the creditor. The Act does not say what expenses are to be charged to capital and what to revenue. Such matters are left to the shareholders. They may or may not have a sinking fund or a deterioration fund, and the articles of association may or may not contain regulations on those matters. If they do, the regulations must be observed; if they do not, the shareholders can do as they like, so long as they do not misapply their capital and cheat their creditors. In this case the articles say there need be no such fund, consequently the capital need not be replaced; nor, having regard to these articles, need any loss of capital by removal of bituminous earth appear in the profit and loss account.

It appears to me that our decision is perfectly consistent with the view taken by the Master of the Rolls in *Davison* v. *Gillies* (3)

(1) 36 Ch. D. 787. (2) Law Rep. 4 Ch. 475.
(3) 16 Ch. D. 347, n.

C. A.
1889
LEE
v.
NEUCHATEL ASPHALTE COMPANY.
Lindley, L.J.

and *Dent* v. *London Tramways Company* (1). They both turned on the articles which he had to deal with. I feel there is a little difficulty in reconciling the two, but they do not touch this case.

I hope I am not inadvertently, certainly I am not intentionally, laying down any rule which would lead people to do anything dishonest either to shareholders or creditors.

In my opinion the appeal fails entirely, and the judgment of the Court below must be affirmed with costs.

LOPES, L.J.:—

After the very full and exhaustive judgments that have been delivered I shall content myself with expressing my views very shortly; indeed I should think it unnecessary to do more than express my concurrence, except that the questions raised in this case are very important.

It is said by the Appellant that a company is not at liberty to pay a dividend unless they can shew that their available property at the time of declaring the dividend is equivalent to their nominal or share capital.

In my opinion such a contention is untenable. Where nominal or share capital is diminished in value, not by means of any improper dealing with it by the company, but by reason of causes over which the company has no control, or by reason of its inherent nature, that diminution need not, in my opinion, be made good out of revenue. In such a case a dividend may be paid out of current annual profits, out of profits arising from the excess of ordinary receipts over expenses properly chargeable to the revenue account, provided there is nothing in the articles of association prohibiting such an application, and provided it is done honestly. It appears to me that if a contrary view were adopted it might be successfully contended that where, owing to extraneous circumstances, the capital is increased in value, that increase might be dealt with as revenue or profits, and go to increase the dividend. This is contrary to all practice, and I think contrary to principle. The capital and the revenue accounts appear to me to be distinct and separate accounts, and,

(1) 16 Ch. D. 344.

for the purpose of determining profits, accretions to and diminutions of the capital are to be disregarded.

But it is said that where the capital is in its nature of a wasting character, depreciated by efflux of time or exhaustion of materials, as in the case of mines or leaseholds, then a sum must be laid aside to meet the gradual depreciation, and that until such sum is laid aside there is nothing in the nature of profits divisible amongst the shareholders.

In the case now before the Court one of the articles provides that the directors may, before recommending any dividend, set aside and invest out of the profits such sums as they may think fit as a reserve fund; but the article goes on to say that they are not obliged to reserve moneys for the renewal or replacing of any lease, or of the company's interest in any property or concession.

Unless this article is *ultrà vires* no question arises, for the article expressly exonerates the directors from creating a reserve.

Is then this article *ultrà vires?* I think not. I know of no obligation imposed by law or statute to create a reserve fund out of revenue to recoup the wasting nature of capital. Subject to any provision to the contrary contained in the articles, I believe the disposition of the revenue is entirely in the hands and under the control of the company. Provided there is by the company no infraction of the capital, and nothing in the articles to the contrary, the disposition of the revenue is a matter of internal arrangement.

The capital in an undertaking like this is in its inherent nature wasting. The scheme of this undertaking is that there should be a gradual exhaustion of material; the wasting is the business of the company, and without such gradual exhaustion there would be no revenue. I am unable to see in this case that either capital or the produce of capital has been dealt with in a way which is not authorized.

With regard to the cases of *Davison* v. *Gillies* (1) and *Dent* v. *London Tramways Company* (2) it appears to me that the Master of the Rolls decided those cases with regard to the articles of association of the companies.

(1) 16 Ch. D. 347, n. (2) 16 Ch. D. 344.

C. A.
1889
LEE
v.
NEUCHATEL
ASPHALTE
COMPANY.

I think, therefore, that this appeal should be dismissed with costs.

Solicitors for the Plaintiffs: *Clarke, Woodcock & Ryland.*

Solicitors for the preference shareholders: *Makinson, Carpenter & Son.*

Solicitors for the company: *Bompas, Bischoff, Dodgson & Coxe.*

H. C. J.

THE WRITING OFF OF DEPRECIATION ON THE WASTING ASSETS OF A JOINT STOCK COMPANY

J. D. S. Bogle

THE WRITING OFF OF DEPRECIATION ON THE WASTING ASSETS OF A JOINT STOCK COMPANY.

PRIZE ESSAY.

By Mr. J. D. S. Bogle.

In the Autumn Session of the London Students' Society the committee offered a prize for the best Essay on this subject. Seven members of the society competed; and the Essays were submitted to a committee consisting of the President, (Mr. Griffiths), the Vice-President (Mr. Waterhouse), and one of the past Presidents of the Society (Mr. Welton). The prize was awarded to Mr. J. D. S. Bogle, and his essay was read and discussed at a Meeting held on the 20th November, 1889. Mr. T. A. Welton, F.C.A., presiding.

The following is the text of the Essay:—

Before proceeding to lay down rules as to the various modes of providing for Depreciation, it will be well in the first instance to consider the general principles involved in this important subject.

Depreciation may be defined as "the actual loss upon assets "which are diminishing in value (or 'wasting') from various "causes."

This diminution in value being an unavoidable feature in almost all commercial undertakings, the next question is; on what principle is it to be provided for in their accounts, so that a correct view of the profits may be arrived at?

The broad line to be taken is that profits only consist of the produce on the value of Capital (after all necessary expenses have been deducted, and after the Capital wasted and used in the undertaking has been replaced), remaining to those who employ it in an industrial undertaking. If the produce derived after defraying the necessary outgoings be insufficient to replace the Capital exhausted, a loss has been incurred.

That this is also the opinion of the most eminent accountants may be gathered from the following extracts:—

Mr. T. A. Welton considers that "Where there is a term "fixed, after which a company must cease to be a going con- "cern, the loss to be apprehended upon winding up its affairs "should no doubt be covered by a Sinking Fund," and again—

"Where the benefit of the outlay in the nature of things "must some day come to an end, as in the case of the cost of "opening a Colliery or Quarry, the value is less considerable "than that of the goodwill of a permanent business, and "ought to be sunk in the same manner as the value of a "Leasehold."

Mr. Ernest Cooper holds that "Every diminution of Capital is Loss," and thinks "it is necessary for a Company "in valuing any of its assets to consider the effect of liquida- "tion of the company if the permanent continuance of the "business is not contemplated in its constitution."

Mr. F. W. Pixley is of opinion that "If the Capital of a "company, or even part of it, has been invested in the pur- "chase of a business for a term of years only, a Sinking Fund "should be raised sufficient to redeem the Capital at the "expiration of this term."

Mr. van de Linde says "Provision is to be made to recoup, "during the course of years a colliery has to live, and coal is "being got, the *Capital expended upon* it."

But the legal decisions and the opinions of lawyers upon the subject are most contradictory, confused, and unsatisfactory.

Mr. H. B. Buckley says that "For the purpose of deter- "mining profits, you must disregard diminution of Capital."

Mr. F. B. Palmer holds exactly the opposite view.

Mr. Buckley also says "The proper way to arrive at "profits is to take the facts as they actually stand, and after "forming an estimate of the assets as they actually exist, "to draw a balance so as to ascertain the result in the shape of "profit or loss," which seems to contradict his previous remark.

Mr. Justice Chitty thinks "The directors must provide "for liabilities, including, of course, paid up Capital, before "they treat the ascertained surplus as profit."

Mr. Justice Kekewich says "A proper provision for "Depreciation should be made before any profits can be "arrived at." (*Glasier* v. *Rolls.*)

In the recent important case of *Lee* v. *Neuchâtel*, it was held that though the property of the company (a bituminous mine in Switzerland) was of a wasting nature, and had become depreciated, both by efflux\on of time, and in consequence of the rock dug out, the company was not bound to provide a Reserve Fund to meet the Depreciation; and, therefore, the payment of dividend appealed against was not a payment of dividend out of Capital.

This remarkable decision leaves it open to the directors of a company, if they obtain authority from the Shareholders, to distribute the whole of the surplus assets (or Capital) of the company in the shape of dividend.

In such a case the creditors' safeguard is gone—and the principle of limited liability surely implied that the capital should be preserved intact for the safety of the creditor, in consideration of the counter-balancing disadvantages that he has only a *limited* fund to look to. And the preference shareholders (if their preferential rights apply to capital as well as to dividend) stand to some extent on the same footing as creditors in relation to the ordinary shareholders, and would be equally entitled to object to dividends being paid to ordinary shareholders until adequate Depreciation had been provided for, on the ground that their Capital is actually being distributed in violation of the terms of issue. The proper mode of meeting the case would be to write down the lost Capital by reducing the nominal value of the shares.

In his judgment in *Lee* v. *Neuchâtel* Lord Justice Lindley remarked that "The capital spent in acquiring the property may be regarded as spent and gone," (the effect of which dictum would be that the whole cost of a mine should at once be written off to the debit of Profit and Loss, and the result of this would of course be to prevent dividends being paid until the whole outlay had been recouped), and instances the case of a daily newspaper, where a large sum may be sunk before the receipts equal the current expenses. With all due deference to the opinion of so eminent a judge, this comparison of a newspaper with a wasting mine is surely an unfortunate one. Although a large amount of Capital has been expended on the former, it is a *going concern of a permanent nature*, so that the outlay will always be of some value, and if the earnings in course of time much exceed the expenses, it may even appreciate in value, and with the goodwill fetch more than was originally expended in establishing it. On the other hand, as regards a mine, at the end of the lease *no value remains whatever.*

If, bearing in mind these inconsistent opinions, we turn to the statutes for guidance as to what provision is to be made for Depreciation, the only regulations bearing upon the matter are contained in Table A of the Companies Acts 1862, where in Article 73—"No dividend shall be payable except out of the "profits arising from the business of the Company," and in Article 80, in making up annual accounts "Every item of "expenditure fairly chargeable against the year's income shall "be brought into account."

As Table A is optional, however, this does not afford us very great assistance as a precedent, but gives an indication of what was the intention of the framers, and this is emphasised by the form af a balance sheet given in the Table, where on the Assets' side it says "The cost is to be stated, with deductions "for Deterioration in value as charged to the Reserve Fund "or Profit and Loss."

Under these circumstances, a heavy responsibility is thrown upon Accountants, who must be guided by principles based upon common sense and experience, in assessing the circumstances in each case that comes before them. It must not be forgotten that too heavy a charge for depreciation may affect a business as unfavorably as too small an allowance, for by doing this, the selling price of the article produced may be fixed at too high rate, and the sales be consequently greatly reduced in volume, when, if the manufacturer only knew it, he could afford to sell much more cheaply. And in the case of a Company injustice may be done to the outgoing shareholders if by excessive Depreciation the profits have been unduly decreased, for he will probably have to sell his shares at a lower price than they are really worth; and conversely, if the Depreciation is insufficient, the incoming shareholder suffers, for he will no doubt have paid more for the shares than their real value.

Having now discussed the general question of Depreciation, we may proceed to consider in detail the various classes of wasting assets and lay down some rules for writing off the diminution in value in each case, but it must be noted that Railways, Gasworks, Waterworks, and similar concerns have forms of account specified by Act of Parliament, in which either no charge is allowed for Depreciation and wear and tear beyond maintenance; or if depreciation is allowed certain fixed rules are laid down which must be adhered to, so that this class of accounts does not fall to be considered.

The various Assets susceptible of Depreciation may be broadly classed as follows:—

1. Machinery and Plant.
2. Rolling Stock.
3. Shipping.
4. Mines, Collieries, and similar undertakings.
5. Patents, Copyrights, and Leases.
6. Buildings (Freehold).
7. Land (Freehold).
8. Goodwill.

1. Machinery and Plant.—The "life" or term of useful existence of Machinery differs from the "life" of a building which is given up at the end of the lease, inasmuch as while the latter has absolutely no value left, the former has always a residue of value. Moreover, while a building requires more extensive repairs the nearer the end of its term of life approaches, machinery depreciates more rapidly in value in its earlier than in its latter stages. In many instances a fixed deduction is made for wear and tear, and the whole of the expenditure both for additions, renewals, and repairs added to the property account, but it is submitted that this practice is very apt to lead to the Plant and other property appearing in the books at a figure much above their real value. The safest and most scientific mode in all, save exceptional cases, would appear to be to keep up the existing Plant, &c., out of Revenue and charge Profit and Loss with a certain amount of Depreciation.

The best method of fixing the amount of deterioration is to find out as nearly as possible the average life of the particular class of machinery in question, and what it will be worth at the end of the "life," and then calculate what rate of discount upon the diminishing annual value will suffice to write the item down to its residual value in the period.

There are many other circumstances which may affect the value of machinery besides actual wear and tear, such as—new inventions and improvements outside, which may render the existing machinery of very little saleable value; greater cheapness of labour and materials, and depression of trade; but it would not be safe to take these matters too much into account, for generally a business is conducted on the principle of being a continuous and permanent concern, and should be exposed to such fluctuating conditions of value as little as possible.

In practice it is not easy to differentiate between Depreciation through wear and tear proper, and other causes, but it is advisable to endeavour to do so for Income Tax purposes, as under the Income Tax Act of 1878 (section 12), an item described as "Diminished value by reason of wear and tear" is allowed to be deducted, but not other kinds of depreciation.

2. Rolling Stock.—If the rolling stock belongs to the parties using it, the approved method is to write off a small percentage on the diminishing values, as there is always a residue of value left.

But as a general rule, wagons are hired on the "Purchase Lease" system, which means that principal and interest are paid every year during the continuance of the lease, until the whole amount is paid off, and the replacements and renewals, which are very frequent, are placed to Revenue Account. The ultimate value when the Instalments are all paid should be ascertained, and divided by the number of instalments, the product being placed to capital account each time, and the remainder of the instalments (after first deducting the interest charged, and dealing with it separately) debited to Profit and Loss as Depreciation.

3. SHIPPING.—The chief elements of Depreciation in this class of property are wear and tear, decay from age, and modern improvements.

In theory, the mode to be followed is to charge Repairs and Renewals to Revenue, and form a Depreciation fund sufficient to make up the difference between the cost of the Asset and its value as old material when no longer fit for use.

There are two classes of Shipping Companies, however; what are called "Single Ship Companies," and the Companies formed to work a fleet of ships, and intended to be permanent concerns.

Single Ship Companies are formed to work one ship only, and the general practice is for the net earnings to be paid away as made, after deducting maintenance and some reserve for contingencies. Having regard to the fact that such Companies are not of a permanent nature, and that when the ship is worn out, the *raison dêtre* of the Company is gone, this practice has a good deal to recommend it, for the effect of reserving for depreciation in this case would simply mean that the sum reserved would be locked up in securities and yielding a small rate of interest, for it could not be employed (as in the case of a general shipping company) in purchasing fresh ships, &c. The shareholders should be plainly given to understand, however, that their capital is being gradually returned to them, and it would be well (though possibly unattainable in practice), if some indication could be given to them of the rate of depreciation, so that they could form for themselves an idea of the value of their shares, and thus avoid the unfortunate results that often arise from the value being enormously over-estimated from a want of knowledge of the true position.

As for general shipping companies, the formation of an adequate reserve is absolutely necessary, otherwise the consequences would be disastrous, and in such companies this is almost invariably done, though in many cases it is questionable, if, especially in bad years, a sufficient reserve has been provided.

As a rule it may be taken that the life of a steamer averages about 20 years, and frequently the rate of depreciation is fixed by the articles of association, or in general meeting.

Sometimes 6 and 7 per cent. is allowed for, which in most cases may be considered a fair rate.

4. MINES AND COLLIERIES. — In all enterprises of this description, a large amount of capital, which can never be recovered, is expended at the outset in opening the mines or quarries, sinking shafts, &c., which represents the capital cost of bringing to the surface the quantity of mineral estimated to be contained in the property comprised in the lease. This might be written off by instalments calculated on a division of the amount by the term of the lease, or might be written down in the term of the lease by the annuity system. But in a coal mine, for instance, many unforeseen contingencies may happen—a fault may occur in the seam, a mine may be flooded, the coal may become thinner, and the whole of it be worked out in 30 instead of 40 years, and then the calculations upon the *term* of the lease would be entirely thrown out. The true theoretical system would appear to be a calculation based upon the estimated *tonnage* of the mine. Thus, if the area comprised in a lease was estimated to contain 10,000,000 tons of coal, and a sum of £150,000 had been expended in opening the mine, and the value of the plant, &c., at the end of the lease was expected to be £10,000, the net cost of making the coal available has been £140,000. If this amount is now divided by the estimated tonnage, it gives 3.36d. per ton as the rate to be taken in reserving for the estimated exhaustion of the mine. In actual practice, however, this plan is not perfect, nor is it strictly adhered to, for it is impossible to estimate the yield of a mine except approximately. The depreciation allowed for should not be simply deducted from the figure at which the capital sunk in the mine is stated in the balance sheet on the assets' side, but should preferably be stated on the liabilities side as a reserve or sinking fund account, the reason being the absence of any certainty that the sum reserved accurately represents the diminution of value. Care should be taken that the amount reserved is not used in extending the works etc., unduly, which would defeat its own object. The disadvantage attending the reserving large sums for depreciation, which would necessitate corresponding investments of a low dividend-earning power applies equally here as in the case of shipping companies, under which head this point is also referred to.

5. LEASES, PATENTS AND COPYRIGHTS.—The purchase money for a lease is often divided by the number of years the lease has to run, the amount thus ascertained being written off each year. This rule may be adopted if it is specially desired that the chief burden should be borne during the first years of the lease, but the true actuarial method is to find the annual value of the purchase money based upon the recognized rate of interest, say 5%, and after charging the interest to the cost of purchase, writing off the instalment thus ascertained on the other side.

If money has been spent in structural alterations of the property comprised in the lease, which is absolutely irrecoverable outlay, the better plan is to divide the outlay by the number of years in the lease, for it is almost certain that additional repairs will be required during the latter period of the lease, which will fully counterbalance the heavier burden of interest incurred during the earlier years.

A Patent or Copyright should be written off over the number of years for which it was granted, or as an annuity, as when the term has expired it is no longer of any value, unless that derived to a certain extent from reputation, and the custom created by the previous monopoly.

6. BUILDINGS (FREEHOLD).—Buildings undoubtedly diminish in value in the course of time, which should be provided for by fixing a rate varying according to circumstances, but seldom exceeding 3 per cent., to be written off the diminishing value. Many Banks write down their premises systematically, until they now appear at a figure far below their real value, so that their balance-sheets do not exhibit a correct view of the state of affairs in this direction.

7. LAND (FREEHOLD).—The value of land seldom fluctuates with any rapidity, but to meet a continuous and steady fall in value, a moderate rate of Depreciation on diminishing value should be taken. On the other hand it is not advisable to make any alterations in value in respect of land which is *appreciating*, for the improved value is rarely realisable.

8. GOODWILL.—If in the purchase of a business goodwill has been paid for, and the profits are large, then there would seem to be no need to write off any part of the goodwill, for it is a reality, which, so far from diminishing, may even grow in value. But if it is found, from actual experience of dividends earned, that too high a price has been paid for it, allowance for Depreciation shoul be made down to the real value, *i.e.*, the value upon which dividend at a fair rate can be realised. Theoretically this would be the correct method to adopt, but as a matter of fact it is seldom resorted to in such circumstances, for the very time when such Depreciation would be most desirable, is the period when the concern is least able to bear it. Keeping this view of the case before us, the practice of writing down Goodwill may be commended as being an error on the safe side.

PRELIMINARY AND FORMATION EXPENSES do not perhaps come strictly under the head of "wasting assets," although they have to be provided for by writing them off, for they never were of any real value; unless in some cases they may have been considered as an equivalent for goodwill. They represent exceptional expenses incurred in acquiring the business, which it would be manifestly unjust to charge against the profits of the first year, and may *be spread over a course of years*, according to circumstances.

Such are some of the considerations which present themselves in discussing the important question of writing off depreciation, but within the brief limits of this paper, it has of course only been possible to deal with them in a somewhat cursory way.

MR. ARTHUR WHINNEY desired to congratulate Mr. Bogle upon the essay which he had read, but there was one point to which he would like to draw attention, namely the case of *Lee* v. *Neuchâtel Company*. He could not agree with the remarks which Mr. BOGLE had made regarding the case, which were to the effect that it was held that the property of the company was of a wasting nature and had become depreciated, and that the Directors were not bound to provide a Reserve Fund, and therefore that the directors of a company could, with the authority of the shareholders distribute the capital in dividends. He did not agree with that statement as a general principle, applicable to the majority of companies registered under the Companies Acts, and would, with the consent of the meeting, go carefully into the points of the case. LEE was a shareholder holding 628 ordinary shares and 16 preference shares in the Company. He particularly wished to draw attention to the fact that LEE was a shareholder and not a creditor. The Company was formed to acquire from five other companies some rights and concessions which had been granted to them by the Government of Switzerland to dig out bituminous rock and generally to manufacture asphalte, and really was an amalgamation of these six companies, this company taking over the above assets and giving in exchange for them its own shares. No money passing. Article of Association No. 100, was as follows:—

"The directors may, before recommending any dividend "on any of the shares, set aside out of the net profits of the "company, such sum as they think proper as a reserved "fund, to meet contingencies or for equalizing dividends, or "for repairing and maintaining the works connected with the "business of the Company, or any part thereof, and the "directors may invest the sum so set apart as a reserve "fund or any part thereof, upon such securities as they may "select; but they shall not be bound to form a fund or other- "wise reserve moneys, for the renewal or replacing of any "lease, or of the Company's interest in any property or "concession."

It would appear from this, that this case which was so often quoted as one laying down a general principle on the subject of depreciation, was not the case of an ordinary company as in the first place no money ever passed on the shares, and secondly there was this article. Now, unless the article could be upset by its being proved to be *ultrâ vires*, he thought LEE must lose, as in fact Lord Justice Lindley remarked. The question whether the article was *ultrâ vires* was gone into very fully on the appeal, and was answered very fully by Lord Justice Lindley. He would not therefore trouble the meeting on this point, suffice it to say that it was held that the article was not *ultrâ vires*. He thought therefore that the general statement that directors are not bound to form a reserve fund against depreciation was incorrect. Then as to the alleged depreciation. The depreciation must have occurred by either the rock being dug out or by effluxion of time. As to the former that was dealt with by Lord Justice Cotton who said "On the evidence before us, the assets of this company are of "greater value than at the time of the formation of the "company in 1873." It was stated on the appeal that there was more rock than could be dug out during the time the concession would last. The other way in which the property could depreciate was by effluxion of time. The evidence showed that instead of the property being depreciated in this way, they had got a new concession on much more favourable terms, so the case failed there.

Mr. WHINNEY hoped that he had been able to show that this case laid down no hard and fast rule such as would apply to ordinary companies, viz., where the shares had been paid for in cash, so he thought the statement that the directors of a company could distribute the capital in dividends was erroneous. In order to show that this case was inapplicable to ordinary Joint Stock Companies registered under the Companies Acts, he quoted the following extracts from the judgments delivered.

LORD Justice COTTON said, "Of course the present case is "very different from that of a company where money has been "paid on all the shares. That case is open to very different "considerations," and again "It is established, and well "established, that you must not apply the assets of the com- "pany in returning to the shareholders what they have paid "up on their shares, or in paying what they ought to have "paid up on their shares. But we must consider exactly how "the case stands. There is nothing in the Act which says "that dividends are only to be paid out of profits. There is a "provision to that effect in Table A, and that rather favours "the view that the matter of how profits are to be divided and "dealt with, and out of what fund dividends are to be "declared is a matter of internal regulation. But still there "is this firmly fixed, that capital assets of the Company are "not to be applied for any purpose not within the objects of "the company, and paying dividend is not the object of the "company, the carrying on the business of the company is its "object."

LORD Justice LINDLEY said, "This company is formed on "the principle that it shall not be obliged to replace year by "year that which is so wasted" ("By working out the "mine.")

Again "The Act does not say what expenses are to be "charged to capital and and what to revenue. Such matters "are left to the shareholders. They may or may not have a "sinking fund or a deterioration fund, and the articles of "association may or may not contain regulations on those "matters. If they do, the regulations must be observed, if "they do not, the shareholders can do as they like, so long as "they do not misapply their capital and cheat their creditors." In concluding his judgment Lord Justice Lindley said "I "hope I am not inadvertently, certainly I am not intention- "ally, laying down any rule which would lead people to do "anything dishonest either to shareholders or creditors."

Mr. G. W. KNOX, F.C.A., said he must also congratulate Mr. BOGLE on his most valuable contribution to their professional literature.

The question of depreciation on various kinds of property, had given rise to a great deal of anxious thought, not only to accountants but also to valuers for many years. Of course, the case of *Lee* v. *Neuchâtel* was a chief point in the paper, but its prominence he hoped would not prevent other points in the essay being discussed. A report of the Judge's summing up had appeared in *The Accountant* which he had read, and he certainly gathered from that, that the judges then laid down certain principles with regard to companies generally, which seemed to him (the speaker), to be in accordance with the remarks made by Mr. BOGLE in his paper. These principles he conceived to be utterly at variance with the views of accountants on the subject.

In this particular case, there might have been reasons why the judges' decision could have been in no other direction than it was, but he thought that the feeling amongst accountants had been brought about by the general statements to which he had just alluded.

Referring to the question of the valuation of machinery and plant, he might say that in the North of England it was a very general practice to call in practical valuers every few years to value the property for the purpose of check, so that the rate of depreciation could be proved to be adequate.

He thought that it became them as accountants to see that the greatest possible care was used, both in the certificates they gave, and in their balance sheets. In this respect they could not exercise too much care. He thought, looking at the essay as a whole, they could not but congratulate Mr. BOGLE upon the way which he had drawn it up and presented it to them.

Mr. T. A. WELTON (the chairman) said, that being one of the Committee who had examined the various essays sent in, he had been able to read all of them, and was glad to say that the general level of merit was very satisfactory. He thought that the points touched upon in Mr. BOGLE'S essay were, many of them, full of interest and he had shown great ability in treating them. There was one important deduction to be drawn from the decision in *Lee* v. *Neuchâtel Asphalte Co.*, which had not been discussed very fully and that was, that there had been amongst lawyers a too definite view that capital must be maintained intact, and that there must be realisable sovereigns for the whole of the assets, which appeared in a company's balance sheet. If that were the case, and that principle had to be applied to all kinds of companies, then such a company as the London, Chatham and Dover Railway would be quite unable to go on paying dividends until the capital had been made up out of the profits.

In the *Neuchâtel* case all that the judges appeared to him to have done was that they had laid it down that there was no absolute sanctity in the obligation to keep capital intact in the sense mentioned. All railways and similar undertakings have to be considered in connection with the circumstances under which they were formed. Whatever the interest earned might be, that interest the proprietors were entitled to receive, subject to the due and efficient maintainence of the railway. In the *Neuchâtel* case, no money was paid for the shares. A certain undertaking was taken over, and the undertaking such as it was, being adequately maintained, the judges held that that was sufficient. In the course of their respective judgments, perhaps more was said than need have been said. He was glad, however, of the decision they had come to, because he much preferred that the Court should show a certain liberality in dealing with the administration of a company, rather than that they should lay down a hard and fast line. This doctrine about capital being maintained intact, might do great mischief if it were rigidly enforced. The cost of a concession or of a goodwill would be a very doubtful asset if you wanted to sell the concern.

If it were held that there must invariably be actual value on the "assets" side, and that the undertaking must be saleable at the figures mentioned in the balance sheet, it would injure and cripple a very great part of our joint-stock enterprise. He considered that the great distinction they had to make was the distinction between the proper earnings after due deductions that can be ascertained, and fluctuations in the values of capital assets. Assets which are not held for realisation.

There was another point in the essay to which he wished to refer and that was with regard to patents. He considered that the writer, if he had referred to the history of some of the recent companies founded to work patents, would perhaps have found reason to vary what he had said, as to writing off the cost of patents regularly in the same manner as that of a lease unless they are workable at a steady profit from the first, which was not often the case. Sometimes the first year or two must be occupied in maturing and rendering the invention workable and the profits might grow slowly, until towards the end of the term, when they might become very large. If an excessive price had been paid, the proper way of dealing with it, whether the thing purchased were a patent or goodwill, was to apply to the Court to reduce the capital.

With regard to preliminary expenses, if the company had been judiciously founded he thought the preliminary costs were a proper charge on capital. If the preliminary expenses were not a proper outlay the company ought never to be founded. The practice of writing off such expenses had arisen because of their smallness, and because there was no tangible asset to represent them, and such practice was unobjectionable in itself, but the clearing off of such an item ought never to be a matter of anxiety. He thought there had been some little confusion in what had been said about the actual payment back of capital. You can pay it back in the case of a single ship company without saying so, in the shape of returning everything earned to the shareholder, without providing a reserve, but you cannot openly describe the dividend as a return of capital. Even if the market value of ships had gone up, he considered that depreciation must be provided for at the same rate as in ordinary times, otherwise the profit made by a shipping company might be represented as being something more than the true earnings of the year. He would be very glad if the law were altered, so that a company could not only return without leave any portion of the shareholders' capital, which could be returned out of the earnings, and not out of the realisation of assets (as in the case of a single ship company or of a mine), but might also if capital was lost, deduct from the paid up capital the amount lost, without asking the permission of the court. A private firm's losses went in reduction of its capital as a matter of necessity, and he was generally in favour of equalising the conditions affecting joint-stock companies and private firms, so far as this might be practicable.

With regard to leases, he thought an interest bearing sinking fund should be formed, and considered it preferable, that it should be so arranged as to accumulate to the full value of the asset some years before the end of the lease. The same principle would apply to buildings upon a freehold which at a measureable distance of time, might require to be rebuilt.

Messrs. Wingfield, Comins, Ford and Wells, also congratulated Mr. BOGLE upon the excellence of his essay, and at the same time invited an expression of his opinion on several points which they raised.

MR. BOGLE thanked the meeting for the attention which had been given to the reading of his essay, and also for the very flattering terms in which it had been referred to by the various speakers, and said he would endeavour to reply to the criticisms upon one or two points in the essay in the order in which they were made.

In reply to Mr. Whinney's criticisms, the short summary given of the case of *Lee* v. *Neuchâtel* was taken from the "head note" of the law report on the subject perused by the speaker, and according to his reading of the case it was perfectly accurate. The conclusion which he had drawn to the effect that "This decision left it open to the directors of "a company, if they obtained authority from the shareholders "to distribute the whole of the surplus assets (or capital) of "the Company in the shape of dividend," as applied to companies of the kind dealt with in the paper, viz., companies possessing wasting assets, he considered was amply justified. He would endeavour to prove this to his hearers by quoting extracts from the judgment, which would show that the remark of the judges were undoubtedly intended to apply as a general principle to the cases of *all* Joint Stock Companies, where wasting assets were concerned.

In Mr. Whinney's opinion, it was *not* stated in general terms in this decision that "Directors are not bound to form "a Reserve Fund to provide against Depreciation." It seemed to him (the speaker) that the judge said so plainly, in so many words, as witness the following extracts:—

Mr. Justice STIRLING.—"*Both according to the general law,* "and under the provisions of the particular articles of association, it rests entirely with the shareholders to decide whether "the excess (of receipts over expenditure) shall be divided "among them, or set apart as a reserve fund for replacing "wasting assets, and the court has no power to interfere with "this decision, however foolish or imprudent it may be," and, as quoted by Mr. Whinney himself, Lord Justice Lindley says

"Shareholders may or may not have a deterioration fund. If "the articles contain regulations on these matters, they must "be observed; if they do not *the shareholders may do as they* "*like*, so long as they do not misapply their capital, and cheat "their creditors."

Lord Justice LOPES is even more emphatic.—"I know of no "obligation imposed by law or statue to create a reserve fund "out of revenue to recoup the wasting nature of capital."

These opinions prove that, not only was Article 100 *intra vires*, but that even if there had been no such article, the Directors need not form any Reserve fund whether in a similar case.

Generally, these dicta appear plainly to authorise the paying away of Capital practically, though not ostensibly, in the shape of dividend by any company, (and not merely in this individual case), there being in the opinion of the judges nothing in law to prevent this being done, and the two following extracts show very clearly what the judges consider is repayment of capital, and what is not:—

"If this was a *permanent* property which would not be "reasonably consumed in providing profit, if the share-"holders were to authorise a sale of that, and then to declare "a dividend out of the proceeds, that would be applying the "capital of the company to an unauthorised purpose."

"It is obvious with respect to *Mines and Quarries and so* "*on*, every ton of stuff which you get out of that which you "have bought with your capital may from one point of view "be considered as embodying and containing a small portion "of your capital, and that if you sell it and divide the pro-"ceeds, you divide some portion of that which you have spent "your capital in acquiring. It may be represented that that "is a return of capital. All I can say is, if that is a return "of capital, it appears to me *not to be such a return of* "*capital as is prohibited by law*."

He would now deal with one or two particular points raised connected with this case.

For one thing, the speaker did not see the force of the objection that no money passed. A thing must be taken to be worth what is given for it (in the absence of evidence to the contrary), and presumably these shareholders parted with their property for the amount (and whether they accepted cash or shares was immaterial) which it was *worth to the company taking it over*.

Then as to the depreciation of this mine, it had been held that the asset was of greater value than at the time the company was formed. In the speaker's opinion the question here was not what the mine was worth, looking upon it as a property in fee simple, but what was its value each year *to the company*, for to them it was only a *leasehold* property, and it could not be denied that at the end of the lease no value would remain to the company.

The fact that the concession was in one way more valuable than it was before, should only modify the rate of depreciation. If more valuable than it originally was, this would appear in the shape of increased dividends.

He hoped his hearers would not think that he approved of the decision, far from it; but it was the latest decision of importance, and until it was overruled by some fresh case, (which he trusted might be soon), they had no alternative but to look to this case for guidance.

Replying to various other remarks, he might remind Mr. Wingfield that the essay dealt with *wasting* assets only, and it was in view of this fact that this definition given ot depreciation was based, and he did not think it could be made more comprehensive. There was a great difference between the gradual diminution in value of an asset, and a sudden fall in value from some accidental cause, such as the burning of part of a building. The latter would not be depreciation in the proper sense of the term at all.

Goodwill was always a difficult question to deal with, but while he considered it must be brought into the accounts of the company if the goodwill existed and had been paid for, yet the value should be estimated on a prudential basis.

As regarded single ship companies, mentioned by Mr. WELLS though he did not look with unqualified approval upon the practice of dividing the net earnings as made, yet custom had made this procedure so universal that it would be hard to alter it. As he had mentioned in his paper, he thought in such cases the shareholders should be furnished with such information as would show them the true position in which the company stood. He had seen lately with pleasure a case where such a company had been sensible enough to go to the court and reduce its capital to make up for the depreciation of the vessel.

A vote of thanks to the author of the essay and to the Chairman terminated the proceedings.

COMMERCIAL FAILURES.

The number of Failures in England and Wales gazetted during the week ending Dec. 13th, was 107. The number in the corresponding week of last year was 101, showing an increase of 6, being a net decrease in 1889, to date, of 282.

	1889	1888	1887
Building & Timber Trades	6	14	11
Chemists and Druggists	2	2	1
Coal and Mining Trades	1	6	1
Corn, Cattle. and Seed Trades ..	8	5	2
Drapery, Silk, & Woollen Trades ..	8	8	10
Earthenware and Glass Trades ..	—	1	1
Farmers	7	7	6
Furniture and Upholstery Trades ..	1	1	2
Grocery and Provision Trades ..	23	22	20
Hardware and Metal Trades ..	3	—	4
Iron and Steel Trades	1	2	3
Jewellery and Fancy Trades	2	1	2
Leather and Coach Trades	4	3	4
Merchants, Brokers, and Agents ..	12	6	8
Printing and Stationery Trades ..	1	1	1
Wine, Spirit, and Beer Trades ..	9	12	11
Miscellaneous	19	10	20
Totals for England and Wales—	107	101	107

The number of Deeds of Arrangement filed at the Bills of Sale Office during the same week was 68. The number in the corresponding week of last year was 64, showing an increase of 4, being a net decrease in 1889, to date, of 55.

The number of Bills of Sale filed in England and Wales for the week ending Dec. 13th, was 202. The number in the corresponding week of last year was 234, showing a decrease of 32, being a net decrease in 1889, to date, of 2,023.—*Kemp's Mercantile Gazette.*

New Books.

The Christmas number of *The Century* is unusually attractive. It contains *inter alia* an interesting collection of private letters of the great Duke of Wellington, showing the gentle side of the character of

"He that gaind a hundred fights
Nor ever lost an English gun;"

The autobiography of JOSEPH JEFFERSON; an exceedingly interesting article on the New Croton Aqueduct which is to safeguard New York against the possibility of a future water famine; a very pretty sketch "Captain Joe;" "The Nature and People of Japan;" A description of that colossal painting on view during the Paris Exhibition this year—"The Paris Panorama of the 19th Century;" "The Taming of Tarias," a charming little tale of the French Canadian Frontiersmen, &c., &c., while it goes without saying that it is magnificently illustrated.

Messrs. FIELD and TUER, *The Leadenhall Press*, haev brought out a very pretty little story with a dash of tragedy in it, "In Chains of Fate" by JOHN MAX that is well worth the reading. Also a reprint of the first book issued by the Religious Tract Society "The Christmas Box or New Year's Gift" date 1825, which is illustrated in that quaint old—world style with which our parents were acquainted and which this firm has done so much to make the present generation familiar with.

OBLIGATION OF COMPANY TO PROVIDE FOR DEPRECIATION OF WASTING ASSETS BEFORE DECLARING DIVIDENDS

Glasgow Institute of Accountants Debating Society

GLASGOW INSTITUTE OF ACCOUNTANTS DEBATING SOCIETY.

OBLIGATION OF COMPANY TO PROVIDE FOR DEPRECIATION OF WASTING ASSETS BEFORE DECLARING DIVIDENDS.

A meeting of this Society was held on the 28th ult., when a discussion took place on the above point with special reference to the case, *Lee v. Neuchâtel Asphalte Company*, which decision will be fresh in the minds of our readers.

The chair was occupied by Mr. Robert A. Mair, C.A.

Mr. W. D. Cairney, C.A., in opening the debate, said:—The Neuchâtel Asphalte Company was formed in 1873 to take over a concession granted by the Swiss Government to the Neuchâtel Rock Paving Company, along with all the mines and other assets of that company, and to acquire the concessions, mines, and all other assets of five other companies, so that the Neuchâtel Asphalte Company is really an incorporation of six companies. It may be noticed that the purchase price of all these concessions and assets was agreed to be paid not in cash but in shares; these shares were divided into 35,000 preferred and 80,000 ordinary of £10 each, representing a capital of £1,150,000, and with the exception of 1,300 preferred shares, these were duly allotted to the owners of the six selling companies as in full payment of the purchase price. The articles of association provided that an interim dividend might be declared by the directors of not more than seven per cent. on the preference shares and four per cent. on the ordinary shares, but that any larger division of profits should receive the consent of a general meeting of the shareholders. The directors were also empowered by the articles to write off from the profits a sum for depreciation of the mines and for expiration of the concessions, but the articles did not bind the directors to write off any sum, leaving it in their option to do so or not as they thought best. I understand that the distinction between the preference and the ordinary shares in this company is simply the common one of the preference shareholders having a prior right to share in the profits, and that to a greater extent than the ordinary shareholders, but in a liquidation of the company both sets of shareholders participate equally in a distribution of the assets. Now, in these circumstances it is manifest that the interests of the preference and the ordinary shareholders are not alike, indeed they are conflicting, the former benefitting by no depreciation being written off (provided, of course, that the company retains sufficient funds to carry on its business), while the latter derive an advantage correspondingly greater as the provision made for depreciation is increased.

The original concession purchased was for 20 years from 1867 to 1887. In the course of a few years the Neuchâtel Asphalte Company found the annual rent and royalty payable to the Government too heavy, and upon an application to the Government the duration was increased ten years and the terms very considerably modified, so much so that the company began to divide profits. From 1879 to 1883 dividends were paid, no allowance, however, having been made for depreciation. In 1884 a profit of £22,060 was made, making with balance from last year £33,359, and in this year the directors resolved that a sum of £1,000 annually should be written off in respect of the sum paid in 1877 for the renewal of the concession, and the balance of £38,359 it was resolved should be set aside to form the nucleus of a sinking fund to meet the expiration of the original concession and the general depreciation of the mines. This was accordingly done, and as a consequence no dividend was paid for that year. Next year, 1885, a profit of £17,140 was made, £1,000 of this profit was written off in respect of the renewal of the concession, as formerly agreed upon, and on the recommendation of the directors the shareholders in general meeting by a majority, resolved that the balance of £16,140 be applied in payment of a dividend of nine shillings per share on the preferred shares of the company alone. The ordinary shareholders contended that this balance should have been written off to a sinking fund as in the previous year, holding that in an accounting, depreciation must be provided for, and that upon making a fair allowance for such depreciation no profits existed out of which a dividend could be paid, consequently that the dividend declared must be paid by the company out of capital, which they held was illegal. I think it necessary to give these particulars in order that we may discuss this question with a full knowledge of the facts of this case, but the main interest lies not so much in the case itself as in the judgment of the Court, which goes very much further than the case under consideration, and so far as I have been able to ascertain, deals for the first time on clear and defined principles with the question of wasting assets.

I will now proceed to state in a necessarily greatly condensed form the grounds upon which the Court based its dismissal of the appeal.

Lord Justice Cotton said, it had been contended, (1) that a large part of the capital had been lost, but this was not the case for it had been proved that the assets were now larger, and the terms of the concession more advantageous to the Company than when the Company was formed. (2) That the assets of the Company were insufficient to make good its Share Capital, and that the deficiency should be made up before any dividend is declared. To this the Lord Justice answered that there was no obligation in the Companies Acts to this effect, "where the Share Capital has been issued under a duly registered contract enabling allotment for something different from cash." The qualification is, I think, unnecessary and may be disregarded. (3) That "this concession being a wasting property, the payment of this dividend was dividing part of the capital of the Company represented by this concession." The Lord Justice held that there was here no such thing as a sale of a "permanent property" the distribution of the proceeds of which among shareholders would be equivalent to a return of capital as laid down in *Guinness v. Land Corporation of Ireland*. Besides "he was not satisfied that a proper provision had not been made for depreciation by the establishment of a reserve fund," but in any case it was not incumbent upon the directors to write off each year a sum to meet supposed depreciation.

Lord Justice Lindley said, that if it were a return of capital to divide among the shareholders the proceeds accruing from the sale of the minerals, it was not such a return as is struck at by the Act. The question of depreciation is a matter of internal management with which the Acts have nothing to do. "The Companies Act of 1862 does not require the capital to be made up if lost, and it does not prohibit payment of dividends so long as the assets are of less value than the capital paid up, nor does it make loss of capital a ground for winding up. If a company is formed to acquire or work property of a wasting nature, *e.g.* a mine, quarry or patent, the capital expended in acquiring the property may be regarded as sunk and gone, and if the company retains assets sufficient to pay its debts any excess of money obtained by working the property over the cost of working it, may be divided among the shareholders; and this is true, although some portion of the property itself be sold, and in one sense the capital is thereby diminished. If it is said that such a course involves payment of dividends out of capital the answer is that the Acts nowhere prohibit such a payment as is here supposed. The proposition that it is *ultra vires* to pay dividends out of capital is very apt to mislead, and must not be understood in such a way as to prohibit honest tradings. It is not true as an abstract proposition that no dividends can be properly declared out of moneys arising from the sale of property bought by capital. But it is true that if the working expenses exceed the current gains, profits cannot be divided." There being no obligation in the articles for the creation of a sinking fund to meet depreciation, "capital lost need not be replaced" and the company has the power to divide the surplus of income over expenditure if it elects to do so.

Lord Justice LOPES said, that the contention that a company should not be entitled to pay a dividend unless its assets were of a value equivalent to its share capital was untenable. The diminution in this case, being due to the inherent nature of the company's business, and not to "improper dealing," need not be made good. If it were the case that a diminution in the value of the assets as compared with the share capital should be recouped, then a surplus owing to an advantageous sale of assets might be distributed as a dividend. Looking to the fact that the articles expressly provided that no depreciation need be written off, the Lord Justice held that unless such a provision were *ultra vires* there was no ground for question, and he said "I know of no obligation imposed by law or statute to create a reserve fund out of revenue to recoup the wasting nature of capital."

It is important to notice that in this case the articles directly provided that there need be no depreciation allowed for before striking the profits.

The abstract I have given is necessarily very incomplete, but it will at least serve to show the main principles upon which judgment was given in this case, and that these principles formed the basis of the decision of all three judges. At the first glance, it does seem as if the grounds upon which each judge based his decision were not identical, and the appellant, in a letter to the well-known professional journal, *The Accountant*, said: "the way in which the different judges have treated the same question is so different, and so conflicting, that one can hardly understand how they should have deduced the same decision from such different lines of argument." On careful consideration it will be seen, I think, that there was no conflict of opinion whatever on the main principles—certainly Lord Justice COTTON stated, that in his opinion he considered that no depreciation had taken place, but rather the reverse, but it was not on that ground solely or even mainly, that he dismissed the appeal, and, the decision did not turn on the company's articles, but on the ground that there was no obligation "by law or statute" to write off depreciation, or to make up the assets to a value equivalent to the share capital, which were the very principles upon which the other judges based their decision. It may be presumptuous in an outsider to say so, but I do not think there is any room for difference of opinion upon this decision on the point of law. I go further than this, however, and say that had the judges laid down opposite principles as those upon which the law would decide such cases, the result would have been most injurious to companies and the public. With your permission I will give my reasons for these opinions.

It is evident that at the root of the matter is the interpretation put upon capital and profits by the Companies Acts and the provisions regarding them.

Capital in its ordinary meaning, as we all know, simply refers to the surplus of assets over liabilities, and in the Companies Acts, although the term used refers to share capital, it is understood to represent such surplus—nominal if not actual. In, I should think, 40 per cent of the companies registered under the Acts carrying on a fairly profitable business, while a nominal surplus exists I fancy there is no actual or realisable surplus. The share capital is represented by patents, gold mines, &c., and it would be imposing upon them a more than Quixotic task if the Statute put upon the directors the responsibility of seeing that before declaring a dividend the actual value of the company's assets were equivalent to meet the share capital. The important fact to notice here is that the capital be represented by nominal assets, and that is sufficient unless there is fraud. The Companies Act of 1877 enacts "The word "capital as used in the Companies Acts, 1867, shall include "paid up capital and the power to reduce capital conferred by "that Act shall include a power to cancel any lost capital or "any capital unrepresented by available assets, and to pay "off any capital which may be in excess of the wants of the "company." There is nothing in the Companies Acts stating definitely that lost capital must be made up before a dividend can be paid, and it is only by a process of deduction that we infer that such may have been intended. The section I have just quoted gives power to cancel lost capital. If it were possible to pay a dividend without cancelling or making up such lost capital, then this section is not required. That is the argument, not a very strong one we must admit, and I can find no decision directly bearing upon the point. Two of the judges in the case we are considering gave it as their opinion that lost capital need not be replaced before paying a dividend, and the law decisions appear to bear this out so far as they go. But we must distinguish between direct losses of capital and losses by trading. If a company possesses buildings and there is a loss owing to, say a fire, the buildings being uninsured, as a matter of practice, Profit and Loss Account would be charged with this loss, and no dividend would very likely be declared for that year. As a matter of law it would probably be sufficient to debit this loss to an account called, say Lost Capital Account, and go on paying a dividend just as if no such loss had occurred. Of course this is a very extreme case, and no sane board of directors would act in that way, but there is nothing to prevent such being done. But a loss on trading would require to be made good before any dividend could be paid. Mr. Palmer in "Company Precedents" holds an opinion contrary to this and bases his opinion; 1st. On the Companies Acts of 1877 already referred to; 2nd. the case of *Robinson* v. *Ashton* where the judge said "that the rise or fall in the value of fixed plant or real estate belonging to a partnership was as much profit or loss of the partnership as anything else." Of course this case referred to a private firm, but Mr. Palmer thinks that the principle should, and does, apply to Joint Stock Companies, also; 3rd. In the *Ebbw Vale Company* again in 1878, where an application was made to the court for power to cancel lost capital, and the judge said, "the power was extremely beneficial inasmuch as it enabled companies to declare dividends in cases where, but for the power, no dividends would be possible." The loss here however, was a loss on trading which, as I have said, is different from a direct loss of capital. If the surplus or deficiency in any one year in the value of the assets as compared with the capital were to be carried to Profit and Loss Account the shareholders would, to say the least of it, have most perplexing dividends. Except *Dent* v. *London Tramway Company* to be referred to later, there is no decision to the effect that lost capital need not be replaced, so far as I know—at the same time there is nothing to the contrary, and the Acts are silent.

Profits.—M'CULLOCH in his "Political Economy" defines profits as the balance remaining after payment of all charges including depreciation, and Lord BLACKBURN in the *Coltness Iron Company*, v. *Black*, practically admitted the sufficiency of this definition. But the 79th and 80th clauses of Table A. show that it is intended that the profit or loss shall be ascertained by taking the gross income and expenditure and "all expenses fairly chargeable against the year's income," but nothing is said as to a valuation of assets or a provision for depreciation. The Companies Act of 1880 as Mr. Buckley points out, can only be understood on the supposition that the Capital Account and the Profit and Loss Account are kept quite separate and distinct, and that in estimating the profit or the loss you take no account of the assets and liabilities, but deal simply with revenue and expenditure. But is depreciation one of the "expenses fairly chargeable against the year's income?" In *Knowles* v. *McAdam* it was held that depreciation in respect of coal taken out of the mine must be debited to Profit and Loss Account, and in *Davison* v. *Gillies* a tramway company was held bound to make provision for depreciation of rails &c., but in these and other cases the decision turned upon the company's articles. A very strong case as exemplifying the principle upon which the court proceeds is *Dent* v. *London Tramway Company*. For some years no profits had been made, and no depreciation written off. In the particular year when a dividend was declared to preference shareholders, the court held that only the depreciation for that year required to be debited to Profit and Loss Account, and that because provided for by the articles, which read that depreciation was to be provided for, and that the dividend to the preference shareholders was "dependent upon the profits of the particular year only." This was clearly paying dividend out of capital, but in the light that capital and profits are separate the decision is quite intelligible, and the dividend was not a return of capital in the sense struck at by the Act. Mr. Palmer holds that this decision is inconsistent with *Macdougall* v. *Jersey Imperial Hotel Company* where the court prevented a direct return out of capital by way of interest at five per cent. though agreed to by the shareholders, but I think it will be seen that the cases are not alike. The 74th section of Table A. gives power to directors to set aside a sum for depreciation, and the inference from that is that apart from that sanction they would be expected to divide the entire surplus of receipts over expenditure, and the expenses properly chargeable against these receipts, of which depreciation is not one.

The principles then that rule all such questions are:—1. That capital and revenue are quite distinct; and 2. That matters of accounting such as provision for depreciation, &c., are matters of internal government and are best left in the hands of the company itself. 3. That the articles will receive the first consideration of the Court.

Now let us consider briefly what may be urged against the principles thus laid down. The decision simply leaves matters as before, except that the position is more clearly defined.

1. It is conceivable that a Mining Company might, by providing no depreciation for an exhaustion of minerals, on a liquidation taking place, have nothing to satisfy its creditors, though the shareholders, up to the last, got good dividends. That is not a likely thing to happen. The shareholders in such a case might also complain, but with much less reason.

2. It has been said, accountants would require to docquet a balance sheet as correct, while knowing the assets not to be of the value stated. The auditor's report would set that right.

3. The practice of all prudent business men is contrary to the principles of this decision. That is quite true, but you cannot compel a man or a company to be prudent.

4. Such a balance sheet would be misleading; so it would be, and so would many balance sheets be, even if depreciation were compulsory.

I know of no other objections of consequence.

Now if it were provided that directors must not pay a dividend unless their assets are of equal value to their liabilities, including share capital, wholesale resignations from Boards would at once follow. No companies of a speculative nature, though thoroughly good in themselves, would be formed, and the loss to trade can be more easily imagined than described. The effect of such a provision would only be less hurtful to trade if share capital were excluded. Besides, the assets one year, owing to high values, might allow of a 50 per cent dividend, and the company never pay another. Depreciation, therefore, if provided for by law, would require to be written off at a fixed percentage on the assets. It would be easy enough to calculate this for such wasting assets as leases, but it would be an impossible thing to apply rates to suit every business, especially looking to the very diverse views accountants hold of the rate of depreciation in the same businesses. I do not think that their is anything calling for special legislation in the present position of the questions referred to. Shareholders ought to be left free to do as they please in the matter of depreciation, and as they must trust the directors there is little doubt but that prudent directors will provide for depreciation where necessary.

If the shareholders are dissatisfied, as one set of them are in the company we have been considering, their remedy is to alter the articles, and if they are unable to carry such a proposal, they have themselves to blame for making a bad bargain. Mr. CAIRNEY ended by moving:—

"That in the opinion of this meeting it is not expedient to amend the "Companies Acts so as to make it compulsory in all companies "possessing 'Wasting Assets,' to provide for any depreciation that "may arise."

Mr. JOSEPH PATRICK, C.A., moved as an amendment:—

"That in the opinion of this meeting every company ought to provide "for the depreciation of wasting assets before declaring dividends, "and should be obliged by law to do so."

He said he would not go into the details of this particular case, nor of the legal points involved: he preferred to treat it as a question of general principles and of sound finance, and if the law was found to be at varience with these it should be altered. Even on the point of law, however, he thought this decision open to criticism. It was just a case of the payment of dividend out of capital. No doubt this was not expressly forbidden in the Companies Acts, but on general principles it might be held *ultra vires*. It had recently been held *ultra vires* for a company to purchase its own shares, though permitted by its articles to do so, on the ground that this was a way of reducing capital not contemplated by the Acts, the issuing of shares at a discount and even paying brokerage on the issue was forbidden for the same reason; and surely there could be no more certain way of reducing capital than eating it up in the form of dividends.

There appeared to be a legal superstition that there were capital assets distinct from revenue assets, but there was no real ground for any such distinction. One judge spoke of a thing being very well from an accountant's point of view, but he thought it might sometimes be of advantage to lawyers to look at financial questions from an accountant's point of view. The whole assets of a company were available for the payment, first of its liabilities, second, of its capital, and lastly, if any remained, of dividends.

The question, therefore, came to be one of a true balance-sheet, and a proper valuation of assets; and would they say that was a true balance sheet, in which, for example, a lease on the point of expiring was valued at what it originally cost? Yet that was what the decision of the Court of Appeal permitted companies to do. They could pay away their capital under the name of dividend until there was nothing left, and they would arrive at the absurd result of having their capital apparently intact, but no asset to represent that capital. The assets would profess to be there, but would be of no value, and capital without assets was an absurdity.

There was one argument of apparent weight, that if the shareholders knew they were getting back their capital along with their dividends, no harm was done. But all the time the company's balance sheet would be untrue and misleading; and creditors who were entitled to suppose that the assets in the balance sheet had a real existence, would be deceived. He concluded by moving the resolution already quoted.

Mr. T. C. YOUNG, writer, said:—This is a very practical question for Scottish Accountants. The question is whether a Scottish Accountant asked to prepare a balance sheet and Profit and Loss Account for a Limited Liability Company, having a mineral property or other wasting assets and, not incorporated with special articles, but working under table A, and especially under sec. 73 which has already been quoted by Mr. Patrick—is to go on in the old-fashioned style of writing off depreciation before bringing out the profits of the company to be divided amongst the shareholders, or whether he is to disregard that rule altogether and simply to take the receipts on the one side for coal or other material sold during the year, and on the other side the charges for working it and to treat the balance as profits available for division among the shareholders.

In this case *Lee v. Neuchâtel Asphalte Co.*, it appears to me that the *dicta* of the judges go much further than is necessary for the decision of the case. The articles provided that the Directors should not be bound to allow any sum whatever to meet wasting assets. To my mind, that fact was quite sufficient to decide the case, and therefore I do not think it is necessary to follow Lord Justice Lindley when he argues, that in no case is it necessary to lay aside anything for depreciation of wasting assets. I think we should treat his opinion to this effect, as merely *obiter*, and not having the force and strength of a decision, especially as we have various *dicta* proceeding from Scottish Judges to exactly the opposite effect.

The case of the *Coltness Iron Company* has been referred to; and although that case was decided under the Income-tax Acts, and does not raise the point purely, still there are *dicta* in the opinions of the judges which controvert the view of Lord Justice Lindley.

There is no greater authority on Company law than that learned judge, but as Scottish Accountants and Scottish Lawyers we are not to run away with the idea that we should at all times implicitly accept an English decision as settling our law. There are many occasions on which the judges of the two countries have differed in construing an Imperial statute, and then the point can only be settled by the House of Lords.

Now in the case of the *Coltness Iron Company* v. *Black*, 1881, 8 Rettie, p. 351, we find the Lord President saying: "In ascertaining the amount of net profits for the purpose of division, the state of the capital account necessarily affects the balance sheet. If any part of the capital is lost, or if, from the nature of the business, the capital employed can never be recovered or restored, that is an element of primary importance in fixing the financial condition of the Company, and the true amount of its net earnings." When the case went on appeal to the House of Lords, Lord Penzance thus lays down the law (8 Rettie, H. L., p. 69): "The cost of the mineral strata themselves, whether they have been hired or bought, should be included in any calculation which had for its object the ascertainment of the actual profit obtained by the Company out of the entire adventure—so much for the prime cost of the mineral bed, so much for approaches to it in the shape of pits, so much for working it and getting the mineral to the surface, so much for getting the mineral to the market, and against all these the price obtained for the mineral sold—these would be the elements of a profit and loss account of an entire adventure of this nature." In closing, Mr. Young said that in view of these opinions, and others which might be quoted, he would be inclined to pause before advising our Scottish Accountants to forsake the use and want of the profession in dealing with wasting assets."

Mr. Robert Carswell, C.A.—I have only to say that I concur entirely in the argument put forward by Mr. Patrick. I think the question is not one of law but of accounting, and I do not see how it is possible if the capital is being eaten up to make up a proper balance sheet. I think the case has been involved in a great amount of legal mist. I think it is entirely a matter of sound accounting, and I agree with the view Mr. Patrick has taken.

Mr. James Andrew, writer, said, from the full way in which Mr. Cairney submitted his views it is unnecessary that I should refer to the facts of this case. I should say that I join issue with my friend Mr. Young, and support very strongly the opinion of Mr. Cairney, that the decision in this case on the abstract question is right, and should be followed in all cases where you have a company possessed of wasting assets. I mean a company which is temporary in its character as distinguished from a company of a permanent kind, such as a company which would be in a position to earn dividends for ever.

It is very important in getting at this view to consider the way in which Mr. Rigby, the appellants's counsel submitted his case, for it brings out the grounds on which he asked the Court to come to a different opinion. When it came up before Mr. Justice Stirling the case was tested more upon the point which Mr. Young referred to, and it was when the case came before the Appeal Court that Mr. Rigby raised the questions in this way. "The preference shareholders are only entitled to dividends out of the net profits. There can be no profits unless the capital is kept up to the original amount . . . It is said that the 100th article permits the directors to declare a dividend without providing such a fund, but if so the article is *ultra vires* and void."

"It is in effect a permission to the Company to reduce its capital, which cannot be done except in the method provided by Act of Parliament."

He took up the position, that if you did not replace the wasting assets you are practically reducing your Capital, and in that way paying a dividend out of capital which the law did not sanction.

In a sense, that argument would be quite sound if you were dealing with a company that was permanent in its character; but where you have a company with wasting assets the shareholders will not expect that every year the portion of the capital exhausted should be set apart as a reserve fund. It would necessitate a valuation of the assets every year, and you would require to take out of profits a sum equal to the amount of the depreciation, and this would involve actuarial calculations which would give a great deal of trouble. Then as regards creditors, they know where you have say a Mining Company the assets of the Company are bound to disappear because as Lord Justice Lopes says, "The capital in an undertaking like this is in its inherent nature wasting. The scheme of this undertaking is that there should be a gradual exhaustion of material; the wasting is the business of the Company, and without such gradual exhaustion there would be no revenue. I am unable to see in this case, that either capital or the produce of capital has been dealt with in a way which is not authorised."

You can quite easily see that you can draw a distinction between a wasting asset and the machinery necessary to bring about a profit. If the Directors were interfering with the machinery which would deprive a Company from making profits, then I would say it was *ultra vires* of the Directors to do such a thing, and that the Court should step in and stop such a proceeding. Mr. Young referred to the opinions given on the question before us as mere *obiter*, and referred to the opinions of the Judges of the Court of Session in the case of the *Coltness Iron Company* v. *Black* as supporting his contention; but I venture to say that the opinions which were given in that case were merely *obiter*. That case decided that in fixing income-tax no deduction was to be made for the expense of sinking shafts.

In a question with the government, everything that was brought out of the pit was to be treated as profit. The Court did not go the length of saying, that in a question with the shareholders it fell to be treated in that way. They were not called upon to do so.

It is all very well to say that we should hesitate before differing from the opinions of the Judges of the Court of Session. We must remember however that the Companies' Acts are applicable to both England and Scotland, and that the decision of the House of Lords in the *Coltness* case must be applied here. They affirmed the Court of Session judgment, and there is nothing in the opinions of Lord Cairns nor of Lord Blackburn which would justify our holding that the House of Lords would give effect to the negative view of the case. Sir Horace Davey relied on the case of *Lambert* v. *The Neuchatel Co.* in support of his view. It brought up the very point in this case. The question was whether or not the Directors were bound to form a reserve fund. It was there held that the Court had no power to interfere, as the Directors were not bound under their articles to create a reserve fund. That I think is a decision in favour of the affirmative view of the question before us, and we thus have, in addition to the opinions of all the judges in *Lee's* case, the opinion of Vice-Chancellor Bacon that the affirmative view is sound. In considering the question we should keep distinctly before us the distinction between depreciation proper and renewals. I would urge you are bound to keep the machinery in perfect order, but in regard to providing for the renewal of the lease, or wasting asset, that is a thing which is not in the contemplation of parties, and should not be given effect to.

There would be no false balance sheet issued to the shareholders if you were to state the Capital as "nominal capital." You would show your receipts and your expenditure, and bring out the result. The profits, after writing off depreciation for machinery, would be the sum available for distribution. I would conclude by saying that I consider the decision in this case both to be law, and fair and reasonable.

Mr. D. S. CARSON, C.A.—I came here to night as an auditor in the strictly non-professional sense of the word, with no intention of speaking; but as your chairman has kindly invited me to make a few remarks on the subject under discussion, I have pleasure in doing so.

I shall not deal with the legal aspects of the case before us, leaving these to be taken up by our legal friends here.

In the minds of the learned judges there exists apparently a distinction between revenue assets and capital assets; but they have, prudently I think, not attempted to go very deeply into the question. Mr. Patrick has remarked that assets do not exist separately as representing capital and revenue account, and I quite endorse that view of it. It is impossible to split up the assets of any concern or company and say this belongs to capital, and that to revenue. To illustrate my meaning, let us suppose a company owning real estate to have sold a portion of it at a profit, and to have re-invested the whole sum so received in the purchase of, say, another piece of real estate. A balance sheet would not indicate that a portion of the cost of the recent purchase represented capital, and a portion revenue—the cost would appear as one sum. The profit which had been made on the sale would appear in the profit and loss account, and nothing further would be necessary.

Another question before us to-night is the depreciation of wasting assets. It has been suggested by one of our legal friends that in a balance sheet capital should be entered as "nominal capital," and a wasting asset, such as a coal pit, should not be written down, but be kept at its original cost, to be expressed as "nominal value." I have no objection to this, provided a Reserve Fund representing the depreciation appears as an item in the balance sheet. But if it is meant that no depreciation or wasting be allowed for, then I disagree with my friend. To my mind a balance sheet should set forth as clearly and as accurately as is possible the true financial position of the company at the date thereof. If it does not do this it is misleading and of no practical use to the common run of shareholders, to its creditors, and to those of the public who may be contemplating an investment in the shares of the company. If shareholders object to the creation of a Depreciation or Reserve Fund, and desire to have the whole income of the year divided, and if a portion only of the income can be regarded as profit, then the portion representing realised capital should be repaid to them as such, and the asset from which it has come be written down correspondingly If the Companies Acts do not permit of this being done except in a very cumbersome way, then the sooner they are amended the better.

Mr. H. ROXBURGH, writer.—The points raised are of great importance and well worthy being discussed among accountants and lawyers. There are really two points round which the discussion has revolved. (1) Whether the decision under consideration is correct or not, and (2) whether, as a question of sound finance, accountants ought, or ought not, to make a deduction for depreciation in the balance sheets of public companies having "wasting assets," or in what way they ought to deal with the question of depreciation in such cases. As regards the first question, I don't know that we can have much doubt because, as pointed out by the judges, the question came to be whether under the articles of association the directors had power to do as they did, and if they had such power, if they ought to be allowed to exercise it. Now, what was decided in the case was a negative proposition; that so far as the Companies Acts go there is nothing to make the articles of the company under which the directors acted illegal or *ultra vires*, and for the decision of the case *that* was sufficient. The court said that the directors were entitled to do as they had done. But perhaps the plaintiff (who complains of the decision), or rather his counsel, have invited the remarks of the judges upon the more general question, the soundness of which has been questioned, for Lord Justice LINDLEY says "The actual "point to be decided appears to me to be comparatively easy. "The difficulty in the case arises from *the invitation made* "*to us by Mr. Rigby* (the plaintiff's counsel) to lay down "certain principles, the adoption of which would in my "judgment paralyse the trade of the country." This is not the first time that the ideas aired by Lord Justice LINDLEY have been mooted in legal literature. In "Buckley's Treatise on the Companies Acts" there are passages proceeding on the same lines, although the author says that the questions he deals with had not up to the date of his writing been the subject of legal decision. I would suggest that the question is really one of sound finance, and the decision of it in particular cases depends on the kind of company you are dealing with. The phrase "wasting assets" covers a number of subjects varying in degree. At the one extreme it includes a lease of a coal mine where you have a substantial property which diminishes gradually in value, and at the other extreme such assets as a patent or a concession which may never have represented anything but a legal right. Now, taking the extreme case of the legal right what is to be done in the matter of depreciation? Suppose you write off a certain amount year by year, what are you to do with the money thus retained? Is it to be placed in investments, and interest only paid to the shareholders? In such cases shareholders complain at not getting the money itself. On the other hand, if the shareholders have treated the receipts as revenue, they have received back their capital in the form of dividends, which is perfectly satisfactory to them. The only other people to be considered are the creditors, but they have no right to look to the capital, as they must know from the nature of the Company in what the capital is invested. Looked at from this point of view, there does not seem any legal principle upon which we are called on to write off any depreciation, so as to keep in hand assets representing the value of the paid up capital. The same remarks would apply in a greater or less degree to other "wasting assets." The difficulty, however, in the way of allowing balance sheets to be issued in such a form, is the opportunity they afford for the issue of misleading balance sheets, and the consequent danger as to the public. Is it not possible to frame a balance sheet so at once to give effect to Lord Justice LINDLEY's ideas, and avoid this danger. I know of a case where gentlemen proposing to start a limited company for the purchase of ships are dealing with the question. In such a case the question might be dealt with in a number of ways. Might it not be a solution of the difficulty to write off depreciation from the ships in the balance sheet showing the depreciation, but, on the other side, to return that depreciation in a bonus along with dividends to the shareholders. A balance sheet in that form would shew the depreciation to the creditors and the public, while at the same time returning the shareholders their money, as, except for a small amount required to form a reserve fund for the repair of boilers, &c., the shareholders (being insured) do not require to provide, and it is better to return the whole profits to the shareholders than to keep money lying in the hands of the managers at interest. It is worth consideration whether a balance sheet in this form might not be adjusted. With regard to the law as Lord Justice Lindley puts it, he is, I think, correct in the difference between Capital and Revenue. There is a marked difference between them; and Loss may be loss of capital, or it may be loss of revenue. If the loss is of capital, then to that extent capital is not represented by assets. This not to affect the payment of dividends, but if the loss is against revenue, then it must be made up before the company can pay a dividend. In Buckley on the Companies Acts (page 4, 5, 9—4th Edit.), the case is put of a ship-owning company in illustration of this point. The company owns 10 ships. If, in the course of a year it loses one ship, that is a loss on capital, but if (without losing any ship) at the end of a year, taking its gross receipts, less its expenses, there is a loss, that is a loss of revenue, and the company cannot declare a dividend without making it up. In the first case the loss is of an asset, and would not affect the question of dividend. In the second, no dividend can be paid till the loss is repaired.

Mr. JOHN MANN, Junr., C.A., said that the Court had gone into principles not required for the discussion of the case before them; and had made statements that were rather startling from an ordinary "common sense" view of this question of depreciation.

The question before the Court really was,—Is the article of association giving the directors an option of writing off depreciation, legal or illegal? Was the discretion given by the company to the directors *ultra vires* of the company? or, were the directors bound to write off depreciation? The Court decided that the article was not *ultra vires*, that they could not interfere with the discretionary power vested in the directors, and accordingly they dismissed the appeal. Now there is no doubt that the existence of this article has a very material influence upon this decision, and as to this I cannot agree with Mr. Cairney. Indeed, I think it within range of possibility that, had that article not existed, the decision might have been different and the payment of the dividend restrained—and that more especially as the preference shares were *not* preferable as to capital. Each of the judges made careful reference to the terms of that article as partly the grounds for his decision.

Passing from that point, however, it is possible to infer as a practical result of the decision, that (in the absence of any obligation upon directors in the articles of a company to write off depreciation), it is not incumbent upon them to do so; but that they may go on living upon their capital, realizing assets of transitory nature and paying the proceeds away to the shareholders as dividends,—and all under shelter of this decision. We all recognize this to be purely a question of accounting, to be dealt with in a common-sense, business-like way, where one would expect the law would follow commercial practice. But it does not, and it therefore behoves us to have the question thoroughly ventilated. Perhaps it is our national pride that makes us say so, but there is no doubt that in the Scotch appeal of the *Coltness Company*, referred to by Mr. Young, the principle of charging depreciation before applying profits was distinctly laid down. In that case Lord PENZANCE said that the exhaustion of a mineral seam must be taken into account before any profit emerged; but *there* it was *not* a case of the administration of a Limited Company under its articles. Profit is only profit when depreciation has been charged; if anything more is paid away, it is not profit. What is it? It must be capital. Then if it is not yet *ultra vires* to pay away capital recovered in realising a wasting asset, it should be so. It should be illegal to return capital in the form of dividend—at least without saying it is capital. The practical lessons for accountants from this decision are to see that fitting provisions are made in the articles of new companies for compelling depreciation to be written off; more especially where conflict of interest is apt to arise between classes of shareholders, as here. Further, that it is the duty of accountants, as professional men and as individuals, to see that accounts and balance sheets are properly stated, that assets, wasting assets especially, are inserted, as nearly as may be, at their true value; and that no balance sheet is certified as correct unless depreciation has been duly allowed for. The fact is that, under cover of this decision, unscrupulous auditors, or interested directors and shareholders, might publish accounts and declare dividends, all calculated to mislead, deceive, if not actually defraud, creditors, present shareholders, and, above all, intending shareholders. Yet, if challenged such officials can plead, the *obiter dicta* in this decision as their justification. They might not succeed in their plea, of course, but it might be then too late to repair the mischief done. I therefore support Mr. Patrick's contention, that it should be obligatory upon a company to write off depreciation in the case of wasting assets; and that if this is not at present legally obligatory, it should be made so.

Mr. T. A. CRAIG, C.A.—Mr. Roxburgh has asked explanations on some points, and more particularly as to the mode of dealing with the sums set aside by a company out of profits to replace wasting assets. Now I am quite of opinion that there can be no profit in any case, unless the original value of the assets is kept up. With regard to the sums set aside out of profits to replace a wasting asset—say in the case of a coal company for the strata worked out—the proper course is to repay such sums to the shareholders on reduction of their capital. To pay such sums to the shareholders, either as dividend or bonus, would be quite misleading both to shareholders and creditors, or to intending shareholders. The company may hold the sums so set aside as a Reserve Fund, if so desired; but as there might be a difficulty in investing the accumulated fund securely at a remunerative rate of interest, the proper course would be, I think, to repay the amount to the shareholders in reduction of their capital.

I beg to concur in Mr. Patrick's motion.

Mr. W. WEIR, C.A.—I agree with Mr. Patrick's motion in the sense that a company should be obliged to make allowance for depreciation of wasting assets, if not for depreciation from other causes. The sum paid for the concession was virtually an addition to the royalty paid. And this is a stronger case than that of a railway company where only repairs are required to maintain the utility of earning power of the concern. If this decision represents the state of the law, it is a question whether the legislature should not be asked to impose some restraint on the paying of dividends, unless these are paid out of the net profits. Most accountants would say that in this case the dividends were being paid partly out of capital, for the whole capital would finally disappear. An exception might be made in the case of temporary companies, but only on condition that the Articles of Association set forth the fact of there being a limit to their existence.

Mr. F. N. SLOANE, C.A.—Sir, two questions arise here: a legal point, and one of pure accounting. I hesitate to speak on the first, but think that if §126 of the company's articles were read along with §100, the only logical conclusion would be, that the promoters simply did not wish a *new* lease to be provided for (anticipating, probably, that they might exhaust their mine during their current lease, and, therefore, not considering the concern as likely to be permanent), and also that while they split the shares into ordinary and preferred, they clearly intended to fix, and did fix, the interest of the two classes in the property of the company as equal—giving, of course, an advantage as regards profits to the preferred shareholders. The only error was in not having an article to indicate the manner in which the capital, which would naturally be released annually, was to be repaid to the shareholders. There can be no doubt that the learned judges have sanctioned a repayment of capital to the preference shareholders at the expense of the ordinary shareholders, as in ordinary course about £400,000 should have been written off the principal asset. I would point out that while payment of dividends out of capital is not expressly forbidden by the Act, it is actually forbidden by those clauses forbidding the reduction of capital, unless specially sanctioned by the Court. The model Articles in Table A expressly forbid it, and the whole legislation on the subject is based on the assumption that it is not allowable. The learned Lords appear to have been rather confused as to the terms "capital," "shares," "assets" and "profit." Putting these book-keeping terms aside, and taking as an example the case of a man who begins business with property valued at £200, and liabilities £100, we say that he is *worth* £100. If at the end of a year's trading the man is worth more than £100, he has made a profit; if he is worth less, he has incurred a loss. Thus the criterion by which we ascertain profit or loss is the amount a man (or a company) is worth at the beginning of his business as compared with what he is worth at its close. Book-keepers call the difference between the value of a man's property and the amount of his liabilities, his "capital" or "net assets." The capital of the Neuchâtel Company in 1867 was £1,150,000; that is, after deducting its liabilities from the value of its assets, there was a surplus, or a capital, or net assets, to that amount. Had the Court instructed a valuation of the assets (which cannot be judged by the market value of the shares), the question of whether a profit had, or had not, been made would have been at once decided. Such valuations do not require the employment of actuaries. The company's servants, or a civil engineer, are quite capable of doing this. All classes of traders and companies value their assets at balancing dates, and there is no good reason why the Neuchâtel Company should not do so. Mr. Roxburgh considers concessions cannot be reckoned as tangible assets, but I do not see that they demand exceptional treatment. They only differ from other assets by having a rather uncertain and very fluctuating market value.

The Chairman.—It seems to me that every case must be considered and dealt with on its own merits. One thing I am quite satisfied about is that it may sometimes be quite legitimate and proper for a company to pay dividends, although its assets, after providing for liabilities to third parties, may be much below the capital expenditure. In considering provisions for redemption of capital, deterioration and such like, a distinction has to be made between what is permanent capital expenditure, and what is circulating capital expenditure. For instance, and speaking very generally, in the case of a railway the costs of forming the company and making and equipping the railway is permanent capital expenditure, if the railway company is not limited in respect of the time for which it is to carry on, but the stores for working and such like are circulating capital expenditure. These stores must at every balance appear at their then value, and not at the sum expended on stores, and the difference is charged against revenue, on stores used. The permanent capital expenditure stands at cost, but revenue must bear the expense of keeping the undertaking in effective working order before any dividend can be declared. Where there is no limit to the time during which the undertaking may carry on business, there is no motive for writing off for redemption of capital permanently invested. We are not called on to value every year what is to remain for an unknown number of years, and particularly as the subject may any year increase or decrease in consequence of circumstances which the company could not forsee, and could not control. The company may, so far as any one knows, carry on its business till the end of time, and what is the good of having a reserve for redemption of capital, which may only be available in the next world.

I do not consider that Capital invested in a wasting subject is permanently invested, and, but for the decision in this case, would have thought it should be redeemed, before a dividend could be paid, because there must be an end to a wasting subject. Take, for instance, the case of a Company working a concession limited to a certain number of years. Let us suppose the terms of the concession were a stump sum for the whole time, or a fixed rent payable annually over the period. As I read the opinions of some of the Judges, then if the Company pays the stump sum for the concession, it can pay dividends without providing for redemption of the Capital involved. But, supposing it pays the annual rent, will any one say that capital is to be applied in paying the annual rent, and that such rent need not come out of revenue before a dividend is declared. Yet both payments are made for exactly the same thing only in one case the payment is made in stump before hand, while in the other, the payment is made at certain agreed on terms If one needs to be provided for out of revenue so does the other, and I think therefore, that capital invested in a wasting subject should properly be replaced before dividends are declared, if these are to be declared from profits only. I do not for a moment say that the redemption money should not be divided among the shareholders, but it should not be divided as profits. There is a section in the Company's Act of 1880, which, I think, provides for such a division, but then it increases the uncalled capital *pari passu*. I do not see why this should be in such a case as I have imagined, because, supposing the affair had been conducted at a loss, and no dividends had been made, creditors could not have asked the shareholders to make up the waste, as they could if the uncalled capital were increased in terms of the section referred to.

The amendment moved by Mr. Patrick was almost unanimously carried, only three supporting Mr. Cairney's motion.

THE CALCULATION OF DEPRECIATION

O. G. Ladelle

THE CHARTERED ACCOUNTANTS STUDENTS' SOCIETY OF LONDON.

THE CALCULATION OF DEPRECIATION.

BY MR. O. G. LADELLE, A,C.A.

The following Paper was written by MR. O. G. LADELLE, A.C.A. (First Prizeman at the Final Examination in June, 1890), and circulated among the Members with a view to its di-cussion at a Meeting held on the 22nd October.

In consequence of Mr. LADELLE's sudden indisposition the discussion was posponed; and his illness terminating fatally on the 31st October, the consideration of the paper was adjourned *sine die.*

PREFACE.

DEPRECIATION is a subject on which we have of late heard much. Much has been written, and said, upon the necessity of taking account of it, and also upon the different ways in which this may be done.

We have heard, that to obtain the true measure of Depreciation of an asset we should take various courses, as *e.g.*:—

(1).—Take the actual decrease in its market value.
(2).—Divide the cost (less residue) by the number of years that it is expected to last, and write off each year the quotient thus obtained.
(3).—Write off each year a constant proportion of the balance then standing.
(4).—Set aside each year such a constant sum, as, with its interest, will accumulate during the life of the asset to an amount sufficient to replace it.
(5).—And yet sundry other ideas are adopted.

but there is, I think, a field still untouched, for these rules are all defective, either from inaccuracy or from being applicable to special cases only; and though theoretical discussions are sometimes apt to be dry, yet I venture to submit, that to us accountants, having to take account of almost every sort and kind of asset, rules for special cases, however practical and useful, are insufficient; and that to be ready in every variety of cases that may come before us, not merely to propose a scheme of our own, but to review the particular system that has been already adopted, to see exactly how far it is true and how far fallacious, and to point out its particular defects and their consequences, it is important to have distinctly formulated in our minds, the abstract theory upon which calculations of depreciation in general should rest, and this in a form so general, as to be universally applicable.

It is therefore, to a discussion of this general theory that I now venture to ask this society to honour me with its attention. It is, of course, seldom convenient to work out this theory in its full detail, but my meaning in saying at the close of my paper that we must revert to the general principle, is, that it is this theory which should form the base of our considerations, and guide our general ideas, in propounding or assenting to, the scheme of depreciation for use in any case that may come before us.

I shall, for simplicity, assume the rate of interest to be constant, and this, I think, will generally suffice; but if it should be desired to deal with varying rates we may do so, by adopting symbols yet more general (a)

(a) for writing i_n for the interest of 1 for n

f_n for $(1+i_n)$

and $|f_n$ for $(f_1 . f_2 . f_3 \, .. f_n)$

our expression in notes (d) and (g) becomes $b_n - i_n \; (P - \Sigma v_n) |f_{n-1}$

O. G. LADELLE

London, 15*th Oct.*, 1890.

PAPER.

Allow me, in opening this discussion, to assume, for convenience of illustration, that a large number of persons, numbered from 1 upwards, purchase as a joint venture, an asset, which they do not propose to use simultaneously, but agree to use for a year apiece, in turn, and that we are asked to determine the method of apportioning the cost between them (*b*).

(*b*) for, if we can do this, it is quite clear that the union of all these persons into one firm can make no difference to our calculations, and that the same figures, will give the amounts which that firm ought to charge to each year in its accounts.

Now here it is clear that we must not re-value the asset each year, but must entirely disregard market fluctuations, for each speculator is as much entitled to the benefit of any rise, and liable to the loss of any fall, in the market value of their joint asset, as is any of his fellows; and even though after No. 1 has used it for his year, the market should be so risen that the asset is fairly worth its original cost, yet No. 1 cannot call upon the remaining joint speculators to share that value and that cost amongst them, but must pay his just proportion with the others.

To ascertain what this proportion is, it may be stated that as the purchase price is the present value of the total future enjoyment of the asset, so, it is equivalent to the sum of the present values of its enjoyment during each successive year of its duration—so that if we write

b_n for the value of the enjoyment of the asset during its nth year, and

v_n for the present value of this b_n

then if No. 1 pay v_1-, No. 2, v_2 and so on, in each case No. n paying v_n the vendor will receive in the aggregate the exact purchase price, and each speculator will pay exactly his fair share for the use of the asset during his year—and if then we can determine the values of v_n our apportionment is complete. (*c*)

(*c*) Let P=Purchase price.

. $P = \Sigma v \infty$ where the symbol Σ is used to denote that we are to sum the series stated, giving to the variable (∞) every integral value from unity to the limit indicated (infinity.)

But it may be that those speculators who are to enjoy the asset in future years, will not care to pay for it now, and they may, therefore, agree that No. 1 shall pay at once the whole cost, and that the others shall recoup him at the end of his year the proportions thus paid on their accounts, together with interest thereon for the interval—these payments to be actually made, however, by No. 2, who will in turn recover from No. 3 the shares of his posterity; and so on until the asset is exhausted, simultaneously with which v_n will vanish.

In this case the cost to each speculator will be, the difference between the amounts paid by and to him (d) *i.e.*,

(*d*) Writing i for the interest of 1 for one year, and f for $(1 + i)$
so that f^n = the amount of 1 accumulated during n years –
No. 1 will pay P but recover $(P - v_1)f$. That is to say, he will have expended v_1 but having also invested throughout his year,
$(P - v_1)$ will have earned
$(P - v_1)\,i$ interest on that capital.

Similarly No. 2 will pay $(P - v_1)f$ but recover $(P - v_1 - v_2)f$ and so for the general expression No. n will pay........$(P - \Sigma v_{n-1})f^{n-1}$ ......

but recover $(P - \Sigma v_n)f^n \equiv \left\{ (P - \Sigma v_{n-1} - v_n) f^{n-1} (1+i) \right\}$

so that his cost will be $v_n f^{n-1} - i\,(P - \Sigma v_n) f^{n-1}$ ......

each year the tenant for the year will expend during his year, the original present value of his year's enjoyment, with interest thereon to date of payment, but will earn from his posterity one year's interest upon the amount that he pays for them (e).

(*e*) Viz. upon the original present value of their shares accumulated to the commencement of his year.

Obviously the rates of interest and of discount here employed must be equal, but how are they to be determined?

I submit that since, in such a case, every prudent speculator must, and does, either consciously or otherwise, at the time of making his purchase, carefully estimate the value of the interest upon his money, over the period for which he is about to invest it, and include this estimate as a factor in determining the price he is willing to pay—it is this same estimate which supplies the answer to our present question—*i.e.* The speculators must at the time of purchase jointly agree upon an estimate of the fair rate of interest to represent the value of their money during the life of the asset, and then base their calculations of discount and interest upon this rate, and adhere to it. It may be that this rate will prove to differ from those actually prevalent in future years, but if so the differences caused, will be, *not* profit or loss *of the years in which they occur*, but an original error of the speculators at the date of purchase, and must be dealt with in their accounts, not as normal depreciation, but as an unexpected variation in the market value of their property.

Concluded from our last issue.

Similar remarks will apply to fixing the values of b_n. It may be uncertain what the real value of the enjoyment of the asset during future years will be, and it may be very difficult to estimate these values, but undoubtedly, it is upon his estimate of this value and of the interest on his money, that, consciously or otherwise. (f)

(f) And either for the one year, or for several, in which he may be interested,

each prudent speculator fixes the price he is willing to pay, and makes his purchase.

A list, then, of these estimated values of the enjoyment of the asset during each year of its life, is obtainable; and given this, with the actual price paid for the asset, and the rate of interest, the values of b_n can be found by calculation (g)

(g) For representing this series of estimated values by the compound symbol ab_n where a is an arbitrary constant, and taking y as the life of the asset, we have:—

$$P = \Sigma v_y \equiv \Sigma \frac{b_y}{f^{y-1}}. \qquad b_n \equiv ab_n \times \frac{1}{a}$$

$$a P = \Sigma \frac{ab_y}{f^{y-1}}$$

$$\text{,,} \equiv ab_n P \Sigma \frac{f^{y-1}}{a_y}$$

$$a = \Sigma \frac{ab_y}{Pf^{y-1}}$$

whence, returning to the formula in note (d) for

$$v_n f^{n-1} - i(P - \Sigma v_n) f^{n-1}$$

we may now write $b_n - i(P - \Sigma v_n) f^{n-1}$.

and the general expression for the cost to each speculator, becomes a known quantity, payable during his year, and equivalent to the agreed value of his year's enjoyment of the asset, less his year's interest upon the amount paid by him for his posterity.

Here, then, we have the cost which each successive joint speculator should bear, and since it can make no difference whether these speculators be separate traders or be co-partners in one firm (h)

(h) For in any case the amounts chargeable to the respective years will be unchanged.

it is clear that this s also, the true principle upon which we should distribute the cost of, *i.e.*, write off Depreciation from, any asset, of any individual, firm or company (i).

(i) In the case of a company we may carry the analogy even closer, by regarding the shareholders as changing from year to year, and the directors as acquiring assets as agents of, and in trust for, the various sets of shareholders whom they will represent n he respective years.

and now, putting this into bookkeeping form, we have the theory for each year working thus:—

Bring forward the amount from the previous year (or in first year charge cost).

Deduct the agreed value of the current year's enjoyment (*i.e.*, b_n).

Add a years interest at the agreed rate upon the balance, and carry forward the sum thus shown.

Let us now compare this theory with the rules cited in my preface.

Suppose the asset to be part of the plant of a gasworks, costing £120, and having an estimated life of 20 years, when it will be worth £20 for old material; and that, after 10 years use, the electric light is adopted generally in the neighbourhood, so that the plant is now far too large for the company's use, and the market value of it greatly reduced.

By the first method cited, upon the re-valuation at the end of year 11 there would have to be a great reduction.

Is our 11th speculator to bear the whole of this loss? The idea is clearly preposterous. There is a reduction in the capital value of the joint venture, and the loss must be shared by all.

By the second method, each year would bear £5. But we may well conceive that this plant might be nearly as useful, and productive of revenue in the 10th year as in the first. Yet whilst each of our speculators would pay off £5, No. 1 would in addition, have to keep £115 of capital lying out through his year, and No. 10 £70 only, which is arbitrary and often unfair.

Trying the third method, we should find that approximately No. 1 would pay off £11·3 and invest £109, whilst No. 10 would pay off £4·6 only, and invest £49, thus increasing yet further the arbitrary advantage of No. 10.

If we turn to the fourth method, so often put forth as the true and scientific one, we find no improvement. For though our plant may be *nearly* as useful through the 10th year as the first, it clearly will not be *quite* so—there will be more flaws discovered, and more repairs needed to keep it up to its work. Surely, then, it is not fair that with these increasing expenses to pay, *i.e.*, with less net benefit to each successive speculator, the amounts to be contributed to the cost should be uniform. But if we apply the theory expanded above we shall find none of these objections.

Our estimates may be made on various bases--we may agree to estimate the benefit of each year under normal circumstances only; or we may agree that all chances shall be taken into account, and the values of b_n be reckoned accordingly.(k)

(k) And similarly any number of special circumstances may be dealt with, each having its appropriate bearing upon the original estimates of b_n.

In the first case we should, in the the 11th year write off capital (l)

(l) Or our speculators would all subscribe to a fund, for the use of Nos. 11 to 20.

an amount equivalent to the extraordinary loss that had occurred — not as depreciation, but as a special loss of capital to be dealt with by itself. In the second case Nos. 11 to 20 could not complain. They have agreed to take their chance, and have already had a fair allowance for so doing. In fact when this second method is adopted we may generally consider the charge born by each year as consisting of two parts, which may be stated either in one sum, or separately, one part being for the enjoyment of the asset under normal circumstances, and the other part, an insurance premium against casualties.

Here Nos. 11 to 20 have received this premium, to cover the risk which has now ripened into loss, and must stand to their bargain. Still not throwing it entirely on to No. 11, but sharing it between them (m) and in practice we may

(m) Either by adhering to their original estimates, or by paying at once to No. 11, such a proportion of the present values of their respective shares, as shall together, amount to the loss sustained. Or in our books—by writing off from the asset as a special item, the amount of the loss; and reducing the charge to each present and future year accordingly.

often prefer to adopt this plan; remembering, that it is safer for future years, to have these premiums in hand, than to have a right to contribution from years which are past and gone. But to proceed, the objections to the second, third, and fourth methods, are entirely met—as to the varying capital employed, by the fair interest allowed upon it; as to their arbitrary character, by our whole system being based upon *reasonable* estimates; and as to the decreasing revenue, by the yearly benefits having been fairly estimated in view of that circumstance.

Having now concluded our discussion of this theory—if it be desired to glance also at the practical application of it in detail we shall see that the main points of it, are, the fixing the rate of interest and the values of the series of b_n.

For the interest—we have simply to settle the rates which may fairly be expected from investments such as we are dealing with, during the life of our asset—being careful, generally, for the sake of safety, to keep the rate low enough. (n)

(n) For since a part of the charge to later years consists of interest earned from them by earlier years; if the rate of this interest be higher than the real value of money, the effect will be, to unduly tax these later years, in favour of the earlier ones. By increasing the rate of interest, the total charge is increased, but the vendor gets the same, and the difference, is profit to the early years, at the expense of the later ones.

Coming however to the values of b_n our task is sometimes much more intricate, for to arrive at a fair estimate of the net value of the future enjoyment of our asset we must consider alike, the chance of ever getting that enjoyment, the income to be derived from it when got, and the outgo to be spent in making that income.

And here we may require the advice of other experts intimately acquainted with the business concerned.(o)

(o) As for example, when our chance depends upon the survival of a life, the life of plant, machinery, or buildings; or the stability of various works, &c.; or where our income and outgo are not constant, but require time for development, have their prime and their decay, are likely to increase or decrease, to be depressed, or augmented, by new inventions; or depend upon the many other special circumstances which affect the revenues from different classes of property—we may have to seek the assistance of actuaries, engineers, architects, merchants, &c.—and frequently those concerned in managing our particular business.

We may frequently too find it desirable to deal with these points separately, and for the purposes alike of convenience in working, and of supplying useful information in our account, to state, as one item, the depreciation based on calculations as to the normal income alone; as another item, an amount based on calculations as to the normal outgo alone; and as a third, a reserve to meet contingencies. (p)

(p) as *e.g.* with our gas works, we may write off depreciation on the assumption that the plant is kept in constant repair free of expense to us, and then state separately the amount payable to a repairs fund, from which to pay this expense, and those carried to a reserve to provide for casualties.

And when this is done we may conveniently arrange the book-keeping thus:—

In a ledger ruled with two money columns on each side, open an account from the particular class of asset—say gasometers—a second for depreciation of gasometers, a third for repairs of gasometers, and a fourth for reserve on gasometers. To gasometers' account debit in the inner column the cost of gasometers, extend yearly the total (or balance) of the year's expenditure, and cast the outer column after each extension. To the depreciation account credit each year (by P. & L.) the agreed amount of depreciation, irrespective of repairs.

To the repairs account debit the cost of repairs, extending yearly as before, and credit each year (by P. & L.) the agreed charge for that year's repairs.

To the reserve account credit each year (by P. & L.) the agreed amount of reserve for that year.

In drawing the accounts it may be well to show the balance remaining on gasometers, after adding or deducting the balance of these other accounts, but in the books themselves I prefer to keep them distinct, showing upon the gasometers account the total cost to date, on the depreciation and reserve accounts, the total sums charged or reserved to date, and on repairs account the yearly balance, for I find that this gives a ready view of the position, and is very convenient in working.

If gasometers be realized (or thrown aside) we should credit to gasometers account, the original cost, debit to depreciation account the depreciation that has been charged in respect of them, and then carry to the reserve account the difference between the balance of these two items and the price realized (or value of residue). And in books thus kept this is easily done, for, having each part of the account by itself, we can readily ascertain the cost, and the depreciation charged against it to any given date, and so cease charging at the proper time, whereas when the depreciation is credited yearly to the plant account, and the balance only carried forward, these are not so readily seen, and it is easy to charge depreciation of assets, either in excess of their original cost, or after they have ceased to exist.

The repairs account should balance, or nearly so, at intervals, and if it fail to do so, it may be necessary to assist it by a transfer to the reserve account.

The reserve account will, of course, be a continually increasing credit, subject to such debits as may be occasioned by the casual losses charged against it, but it clearly cannot survive the particular assets to which it is related, so that when they disappear this account too should be carried to a general reserve, or dealt with in other suitable way.

In doing thus, however, we must bear in mind that we are really dealing with different parts only of one subject, and that though we may state them separately, we should consider them together—(q).

(q) In determining our quantities the same arguments and the same formulæ will apply. Our symbols may be sometimes positive, and sometimes negative, but we shall be using the same principle, and subject to the same considerations.

and we should be careful, too, to keep our yearly estimates as regular as circumstances will allow. (r)

(r) As *e.g.* Find some regular progression, applicable to our particular case and then deviate from it as little as possible, for this generally adds greatly, not only to our convenience in making our calculations, but also to the readiness with which others can grasp their business import when made, whilst accounts in which such items fluctuate from year to year are generally open to suspicion.

We may frequently find results thus obtained agree with those given by the methods cited in my preface, and particularly with the second of them, and some might thereby be led to think that all these investigations were useless, as we might have adopted at once the simpler method.

But this is fallacious—The results will agree, not invariably, but under certain conditions only. (s)

(s) Where the yearly profit happens, as it so often does, to decrease throughout by constant sums, our results will agree with those of this second method. Where it decreases in a constant ratio, we shall agree with the third method: and where it is stationary, through a given time, and then lapses entirely, we shall agree with the fourth, and sometimes, too, correct results may be obtained from a combination of these rules, for in these particular cases, our formulæ happen to be identical with those giving these rules.

We may often see what the conditions are, and apply at once a suitable rule, but except where these particular conditions occur, these particular rules, which are attached to them, are useless, and we must revert to the general principle.

ON THE PROFIT OF COMPANIES AVAILABLE FOR DISTRIBUTION

T. A. Welton

CHARTERED ACCOUNTANTS STUDENTS' SOCIETY OF LONDON.

ON THE PROFIT OF COMPANIES AVAILABLE FOR DISTRIBUTION.

By Mr. T. A. Welton, F.C.A.

At a meeting of the above Society—open to all members of the Institute—held at Winchester House, E.C., on Wednesday, Dec. 3rd, Mr. F. Whinney, F.C.A. in the chair, Mr. Welton read the following paper:—

I have undertaken to revive the subject treated by Mr. Ernest Cooper with great care and ability in the year 1888.* In doing this I intend to dwell rather fully upon the two important cases of *Lee v. Neuchatel Asphalte Company*, and the *Leeds Estate Building, &c., Society* which must have an enduring interest for members of our profession.

In taking this course I have been actuated by the view that the method adopted by Mr. Cooper was not the best fitted for eliciting the true principles which should govern our profession, and not our profession only, but the highest legal authorities, in coming to decisions upon a very difficult class of questions. I recognise that when called upon to construe the laws, the Judges do not always agree, and that their disagreements are not more often founded upon different views concerning precedents and the grammatical construction of the Statutes, than upon divergent opinions as to what is reasonable, fair, and workable, and therefore consonant with public policy. I feel assured that no judge on the bench would willingly create or confirm a precedent, inconvenient or prejudicial to honest interprise, or if obliged to do so, would omit to express at the same time his sense of the matter. On the other hand it is undoubtedly better that any endurable inconvenience should be borne patiently than that unsound principles should be allowed to be introduced into the management of public companies.

My method of treating this question as to divisible profit, with which is inextricably bound up the further question as to capital being intact, will be first to weigh it as a mere question of public policy, and next to consider how far, if at all, the legal decisions conflict with the conclusions at which I arrive, and what principles were in the minds of the judges when arriving at such decisions. I hope that I may be able to seize their ideas and harmonise them with my notions of what is best for the nation, or at least to minimise and distinguish the points of difference.

*Reported in *The Accountant*, November 10, 1888.

Like Mr. Cooper, I will confine myself to the divisible profit of a Limited Company registered under the Companies Acts, 1862 to 1886, though I may refer to other classes of companies by way of illustration and example.

The definitions of capital quoted by Mr. Cooper refer to two distinct things,

(*a*) The capital of the proprietors, and

(*b*) The capital laid out by the proprietors in the creation and extension and working of the undertaking.

The definition of the capital of the proprietors of a company is perhaps imperfectly expressed in the words "The aggregate of the sums contributed by its members for the purpose of commencing, or carrying on, business, and intended to be risked by them in the business," because capital not called up or called up and not yet paid can hardly be said to be contributed, and yet is really risked in the business. But on this definition there is little need to comment.

The capital of the proprietors may not be the sum by which the assets exceed the liabilities. There may be a balance either of profit or loss which has to be taken into account. For instance, supposing the facts were

Assets	1,000,000
Liabilities	250,000
Paid up Capital	700,000
Undivided Profit	50,000

I certainly should not assert that the capital was £750,000, and if there were a Reserve Fund formed out of profits I should equally exclude that fund from the computation of capital.

I think it is expedient in considering the capital laid out by the proprietors to have regard to the elements of which it is composed, which in the main may be ranked in three categories, viz:—

1. Cost of the permanent portion of the undertaking, such as the way and works of a railroad.
2. Cost of any less permanent portion of the undertaking, such as leasehold property, minerals, patent rights, and even the factory or the ship in the case of a manufacturing or shipowning company; which cost may properly be reduced by an allowance for depreciation to cover the effect of the lapse of time.
3. Cost of such floating assets as are necessary for carrying on the business.

Any assets not necessary for carrying on the business ought in my opinion to be regarded as investments and not as capital. I consider the whole of the three elements above stated to constitute capital outlay, and if such capital outlay is greater in amount than the paid up capital of the proprietors, I regard the difference as being borrowed capital, or capitalised profit, as the case may be.

Here, it will be observed, I join issue with Mr. Cooper, who says, "it is as well to bear in mind that the real capital is the surplus of assets," and adds, "every increment to capital is profit and every diminution a loss." I simply say that such a use of the word "capital" as he claims to be correct, is not a convenient one, nor one which assists us in dealing with the problems which have to be faced.

If every accretion of value ought to be regarded as profit, the companies, whether under limited liability or not, whose stocks are justly valued above par, ought to introduce into their Balance Sheets figures representing the true values of assets and of goodwill, and per contra would be obliged to create a credit balance or reserve representing such accretion, which would in Mr. Cooper's opinion be profit. In like manner Companies whose stocks are justly valued below par would have to exhibit in their Balance Sheets, such values of assets as would leave a deficit more or less nearly equal to the discount at which the stock could be sold, and such deficit would be loss.

Now I for one am of opinion that there is danger of confusion if we apply the word "profit" to that which no practical man could think of dividing as profit, for instance to the improved value of London and North Western Railway Stock, in the case of a Parliamentary company, or to that of Messrs. Guinness and Co's shares, in the case of a limited company;—or if we apply the word "loss" to that which for similar reasons ought not to be set off against income, for example the discount on the London, Chatham, and Dover Railway Company's ordinary stock.

The public interest is not served by a continual revaluation of the permanent assets of a company, classed in the 1st category above. Nor is it expedient that items in the 2nd category should be revalued, though they all require to be "written down." Let us consider these two propositions.

First, as regards permanent assets. Since the object of a railway company is to employ almost the whole of its capital in a permanent form, a comparatively small amount being needed for working the undertaking, such a company affords an excellent type for our consideration. The sound practical course is to charge against the capital account all that must necessarily be spent in order that the undertaking may be brought into existence, including the expenses of Parliamentary contests, and law charges attendant on the acquisition of land, as well as all taxes and expenses incident to the formation of such a Company down to the time of its undertaking being opened for traffic, and to charge against Revenue only those expenses which arise in consequence of the undertaking being worked and requiring to be maintained. The cost of any unprofitable extension is as justly charged to capital as that of the most productive section of the line. If a great success is attained, the line itself could doubtless (with Parliamentary sanction) be sold at a vastly enhanced figure beyond its cost. But this fact affords no justification for valuing the line at a sum exceeding its cost. No purpose is to be served by such revaluation, for it could not on any sound principle affect the distribution of dividends, nor would it prevent the market value from fluctuating daily, just as much as it does now.

Take now the case of iron works. The appliances and buildings might be acquired from a previous owner, or might be put up by the company. When erected, if fortunately situated where ore could easily be had, where labour was plentiful, and where a great and permanent demand was found to exist, the return would probably be large and the value of the stock held by the proprietors should exceed par. But where would be the use of expressing this higher value on the face of the Balance Sheet? It would no more affect either the interest of the continuing shareholder, or that of the purchaser in the market, than in the case of a railroad.

There is, indeed, a distinction to which attention may usefully be paid, namely, that whilst a railroad is, in a sense, perpetually renewed, any kind of factory may in course of years need to be rebuilt, not only because of natural decay, but from the necessity of removing what is obsolete and introducing the latest improvements. A reserve out of profits beyond mere maintenance may therefore be recommended in order to meet the value of the superseded parts, which should be written off when the Capital Account is charged with the new outlays. But this can be provided (and ought to be provided) without any revaluation, and totally irrespective of whether the stock of the proprietors stands above or below par.

A manufactory may in some cases be a comparatively unessential part of the undertaking, for instance, in a case where the cost of a patent is the main item of outlay, and for reasons of policy a factory may first be erected or hired in one place, and then replaced by another many miles distant. Such a comparatively ephemeral factory should (if the possibility of its demolition be forseen) be the subject of an ampler reserve than if it were not intended to vary the seat of operations. On the other hand it may fairly be said that if an important new industry is being created, and a valuable goodwill raised up, the mistakes and experiments which accompany the creation of that goodwill are part of its cost—and cost, for the purpose of correctly assessing what should be charged against capital outlays, is an element of the first importance.

Passing to the second category, I think no one will have much difficulty in admitting that leaseholds should be ordinarily depreciated at a rate calcutated to extinguish their cost and provide a fair sum for dilapidations during the residue of the period they have to run. But, as in some cases, a leasehold may advance in value during the earlier years of the term, it is perhaps safest to say that when the residue of a lease is less than forty years in duration, it is expedient that provision be made for depreciation as just stated. This I think may best be done by means of a special reserve, credited with compound interest out of profits, and set off against the book value. Real value is not to be considered, but merely cost, in settling the amount of this reserve.

Brick earth, as well as coal, may be estimated as to quantity, and the value of the freehold reduced to the small price attaching to denuded land, in the period required for its exhaustion. This case is like that of buildings requiring to be replaced in an estimated period, and may equally be met by a Sinking Fund credited with compound interest in addition to a fixed annual contribution. Steam ships may be dealt with similarly, with special provision for renewal of boilers much earlier than other parts. The fact that a Sinking Fund is maintained need not imply any special provision for the investment of such fund. Where it represents depreciation of ships, or of mineral resources, the natural course is to apply the profit held in reserve in procuring new ships or additional minerals. In many other cases the amount of a Sinking Fund may be judiciously used in aid of the floating capital employed in the business, so as to keep down the amount due to creditors, and prepare the way either for the exercise of borrowing powers, or for raising new capital when the occasion arises for expending such fund. But the expediency, or otherwise, of making special investments of reserved profits can only be determined after a careful review of the circumstances in each particular case. I lay the more stress upon this matter because it has become the fashion in some quarters to urge that all reserves, including those of banking companies, should be specially invested, without any regard to the nature of the prospective requirements, to meet which they are provided.

The case of Patent Rights is one of the most difficult which can be raised, especially since the practice has arisen of paying very heavy sums for such rights. In dealing with a matter of this nature it is proper to consider the motives and expectations of those who undertake the working of new inventions. They must be presumed to know: (1) that the term of a patent is but limited; (2) that an important part of that term is usually consumed in perfecting the means of production and gaining the favour of the public; (3) that therefore the adventure is not in general worth undertaking unless there be a prospect of large profits during the latter years of the patent, and a further benefit in the shape of the goodwill of a going concern when the patent shall have expired, and (4) that any remote advantage is subject to an increased risk of its neutralisation through some new invention superseding the patented one. They expect, therefore, to receive little or no dividend on their outlay for two or three years, or even a longer term. But their motive being profit, they submit to this deprivation in the hope that when profits are reached they will allow of a liberal distribution of dividend. And, unless their hopes are disappointed, the surplus earnings beyond a handsome dividend on the capital during the latter years of the patent should suffice either to extinguish its cost or to reduce such cost to a figure not exceeding the value of the goodwill which may remain after the patent has run out.

In the case of a successful Company, the difficulty is not much felt, and resolves itself into the question, when and at what rate the cost of the Patent should be provided for out of Profits. On the whole, I am inclined to think it would be a convenient course to deal with that question in advance when founding the Company, as for instance to prescribe for that beyond a cumulative dividend at the rate of five per cent. per annum, all profit during the term of the Patent shall be carried to a Reserve Account until the cost of the Patent (or some prescribed amount) shall have been reached. Such a provision in the Articles of Association would be notice to all the world as to the intended procedure, and should alike satisfy the shareholders and the creditors of the company, and relieve the directors from a heavy responsibility.

But assume an unfortunate issue to the adventure; as matters usually stand, the question whether the shareholders are to have any dividend at all, or must devote all the profits to the sinking the cost of the patent (even assuming there are no creditors to be considered), has undoubtedly to be met. I know of no golden rule which can be applied in such circumstances. If the laws admitted of a return of capital being made out of profits, in such a way that the amount returned could not again be called up, I certainly should advocate treating distributions of profit under such doubtful circumstances as being returns of capital, and would not commence the payment of dividends so called until after the expiry of the patent, when experience had been acquired as to the ordinary earning power of the concern. At that date, in the worst event, a portion of the cost of the patent would remain unextinguished which would exceed the value of the goodwill. This balance of cost would in my opinion require to be dealt with exactly as if the goodwill had been acquired at that price.

In the absence of any governing provision in the Articles of Association by which reserves against the exhaustion of value of patent rights could be regulated, and in the absence of power to treat distributions of profit as irrevocable returns of capital, I think a well-advised board will act as nearly as possible on the assumption that some reasonable anticipatory provisions were part of the company's constitution, and will give the proprietors only moderate dividends, or none at all, until the success of the undertaking is so obvious as to render so much caution superfluous.

It is open to proprietors of such companies who find the denial of dividends too irksome to resort to a reconstruction. The cost of a merely mechanical change of this nature is by no means prohibitory. The new Articles of Association would have to contain provisions governing the valuation of goodwill and the amount of any Sinking Fund, which provisions I hope may, in future, when similar companies are being established, be inserted in anticipation of such difficulties arising.

The whole of the items in the second category have now been gone through, and in no instance do I find that the proper conduct of a company's affairs demands that they should be revalued. It follows, I think, that in a Balance Sheet none of these items ought to be regarded as more than book figures. Like the railway undertakings already adverted to, these parts of capital outlay mainly depend for such value as they possess on the concern being kept going and being productive of profit. Only when the railway is to be abandoned or the iron work to be discontinued does it become important to consider whether any and what value for other uses may attach to the land and materials remaining.

The items in the third category ought by universal consent to be of full value. The constant renewal of floating capital brings its value to a test which as to permanent assets is unattainable. There are, however, one or two qualifications which affect the treatment of floating assets, and which I will endeavour to indicate.

In the first place, stocks of manufactured goods ought to be valued upon some *uniform system*, whether at or below cost. Otherwise, the profit annually reported will not represent in reality the profit of the year, but something less or more, according to the effect of the alteration in method. And the more we are convinced of the impossibility of attaching other than book values to permanent assets, the more obligatory becomes the duty of truly representing the annual profit earned, by which above all the value of such assets must be measured.

Next, stocks of materials and of partly manufactured goods should be valued either at cost, or at some fixed per centage below cost. It may happen that on the balancing day the market value of some of the materials is much higher or lower than cost; but as I think it inexpedient to place an enhanced value on materials cheaply bought, so also I do not consider it necessary to abate the valuation of dear materials below cost. It is one of the natural incidents of the business year that materials must to some extent be procured in advance, and the profits of the year ought, I think, to be affected favourably or otherwise by the cost of those materials, which constitute the stock at its commencement.

Thirdly, book debts should be valued with due regard to discounts and risk of loss. This, in the case of a manufacturing company, can generally be done with a very close approach to correctness. But where debts constitute a great part of the Assets, as in the case of a bank, much less certainty is attainable, and the risk which in the case of a railway or a factory attaches to the values of permanent Assets, may be said in the case of a bank to attach, though in a lesser degree, to floating assets. The bank has to do business on the footing that the industries amongst which it works will remain for the most part going concerns, and any such decline of trade as would largely affect the earnings of local railways may be expected also to influence materially the cash value of the floating assets of local banks. The true policy of a Bank is therefore to gradually accumulate a private reserve large enough to meet any such decline in values as in bad years may reasonably be feared.

I think I have now said enough concerning the three categories of capital outlays required for carrying on business. As to investments not necessary for that purpose, the usual practice is to value them at cost, or at a less figure, but there is no real reason why marketable investments such as railway stocks, consols, &c,, should not be re-valued at every balancing date, provided the thing is done systematically and all investments not currently saleable are valued low:

It remains to be said that goodwill, in my opinion, must be treated as belonging to the first category, and ought neither to be valued above nor below cost. Where it is worth less than cost, the effect will be seen in the unsatisfactory income and consequent low market value of the Company's shares. Where it is worth more than cost, there is no advantage in entering an enhanced figure in the Balance Sheet. If, by reason of accumulated losses, the flow of dividends be stopped, so that a reduction of capital is expedient, I would recommend that such reduction be applied to the cost of goodwill, as well as to the extinction of the adverse balance of "Profit and Loss" account. In the absence of such adverse balance, none but sentimental considerations appear to call for a modification of the item of cost in the Balance Sheet. The cry for a gradual extinction of the cost of goodwill out of profits is founded principally on ignorant prejudice, so liable to be fostered by interested persons, but such extinction, like the formation of larger reserves than necessary, is obviously a matter for the free action of the proprietors—or that of the directors to whom their interests are entrusted, and whose acts they endorse.

Having now explained, I hope in sufficient detail, what course as to the valuation of assets and ascertainment of profits seem to be called for by the circumstances under which joint-stock enterprises are conducted, I will turn to Mr. Cooper's paper, and notice any conflicting ideas, regarding them from the point of view of the shareholder present or prospective, and the creditor, beyond which classes I think it unnecessary to look.

The first great question which arises is that as to the Double and Single Accounts respectively. The Double Account could not be more distinctly defined than in the words of Mr. Buckley, thus:—

> "If a shipowning company's capital be represented by ten ships with which it trades and one is totally lost and is uninsured, such a loss would be what is here called a loss on Capital Account. But if the same company begins the year with ten ships, value say £100,000, and ends the year with the same ten ships, and the result of the trading after allowing for depreciation of the ships is a loss of £1,000, this would be what is here called a loss on Revenue Account."

It will be remarked here, that if a merchant or private firm owned ten ships and lost one as suggested, that would undoubtedly be a loss on Capital Account, and the merchant would certainly feel at liberty to expend the income derived from the nine remaining ships without replacing lost capital. So also if the company Mr. Buckley refers to had no creditors, or only such creditors as are inevitable on working accounts, there would be no difficulty in carrying out a reduction of capital from £100,000, to £90,000 by consent of the Court, and thus the flow of profit would not be stopped. I am of opinion that no inconvenience would attend such an application to the Court, beyond the expense, which might possibly be reduced, if our legislators would consider how applications of this kind may be facilitated.

Though I see much reason for agreeing to place against revenue any *absolute loss* of capital, I do not think it necessary or desirable to revalue capital outlays so as to write off unrealised losses. The assertion of Mr. Palmer that "the Single Account view is in accordance with the "practice adopted by the commercial world in ascertaining "the profit or loss of an ordinary partnership" is only true if we add, that the commercial world no more revalues the permanent items than I should, but often leaves them untouched for a long series of years. With this qualification, it seems to me that the difference between single and double accounting practically vanishes, since I cannot suppose that Mr. Palmer would create divisible profit by adding to the value attributed to permanent assets. I certainly think it a matter of taste and convenience only, whether the Balance Sheet of a company of any sort is shown in two divisions, or as a whole. The really critical question is as to what expenses and what reserves for depreciation have to be placed against profit. I fail to realise "the necessity of keeping the capital funds distinct "from the revenue in Parliamentary companies," as being essentially greater than in the case of ordinary companies, though, as a matter of practice, the Legislature having prescribed a form of account, doubtless such form has necessarily to be used. What Mr. Cooper calls "a charge "in favour of the public on the railway," seems to me to be no such thing. And when Mr. Cooper speaks of a company evading "its legal obligation under the Companies Acts to "ascertain, before paying dividends, that it has the value "of its capital intact," it seems to me that he involuntarily begs the whole question. For, as I have endeavoured to show, there is no such obligation in fact, and if the law so decreed, it could not be obeyed. To pretend "to take into "account the value of all liabilities and assets in ascertain-"ing profits available for distribution," means, either to value the assets as I should do, or else (if value means cash value) to do the very thing I have ventured to assume that no practical man would do, namely, to revalue not only tangible assets, but goodwill, at every balancing, and thus to show on the Balance Sheet a capital (including reserves) about equal to the market price of the stock.

The opinion of Sir Geo. Jessel that "the rise or fall in "value of fixed plant or real estate belonging to a partner-"ship, was as much profit or loss of the partnership as "anything else," is correct, doubtless, but requires to have something added, namely "upon realisation." Sir Geo.

Jessel would never have accounted as profit or loss variations in valuers' estimates, in cases where realisation had not occurred. Other legal opinions, such as that quoted from Vice-Chancellor Kindersley, seem to proceed upon the assumption that some definite value in the nature of things attaches to each asset, but no judge fails to appreciate in practice the difference between breaking-up value and value in use, and the extreme difficulty of arriving at either save by means of "the higgling of the market." Mr. Justice Chitty's dictum as to valuation in the *Midland Land and Investment Company's case*, merely assumes that "all the "precautions which ordinarily prudent men of business "engaged in a similar business" would take, are attended to. But these precautions, I contend, are not greater than those which I have described, and fall far short of Mr. Cooper's standard. I agree with Mr. Cooper that capital is not represented by specified assets, but I contend that all assets are to be dealt with after their kind, and that some of them ought not to be revalued.

The remarks made by Mr. Cooper as to under-valuation of assets apply, it will be seen, to those assets which are permanently held. I agree in thinking that it may be difficult to forecast the probable action of the Courts supposing such under-valuations were brought under their consideration, but I would point out that the very reasons which render re-valuations undesirable, are of a nature to justify any under-valuations which the proprietors approve. In short, since such low valuations do not affect the income, except that of the years when the reductions were made and approved, and since market values are dependent on income almost exclusively, the proprietor is not damaged, and the intending purchaser of shares, or creditor, is not misled, unless in the direction which leads him to exercise more caution than is absolutely necessary.

I entirely controvert the allegation that large secret contingency funds so operate, that retiring shareholders in banks or similar institutions are losers. Whilst such funds are being accumulated, the declared profits are lower than those actually made, and in that way market values are prevented from rising unreasonably high, as they otherwise would do, on the tacit assumption that adequate reserves must exist. No sooner is the required fund completed, than the profits assume their full dimensions, (including the benefit of interest from such secret reserve), and no one is then without information as to the earning power of the concern, and the consequent value of the shares. The most enlightened holders of shares would be the last to desire any departure from the system of making secret reserves where thought necessary, especially in the case of joint stock banks.

When Mr. Cooper comes to the heading "works and plant" the principles he lays down are in conformity with sound common sense, and what he there writes justifies me in holding that he is but half serious in other parts of his paper with which I have ventured to disagree. I only part company with him when he says "if the depreciation is . . . considered of a permanent nature, I know no means by which the directors of a tramway or shipping company can justify showing profits until the loss in value is provided for." This doctrine is the same impracticable one as before, and notwithstanding all Mr. Cooper has said, I am convinced that its acceptance implies writing down the value of a railway to the extent that its capital is or may be estimated to be worth less than par. At the least it implies the application of such a monstrous doctrine in any case where *a limited company* constructs any work which produces a poor return.

Preliminary expenses are in my opinion justly maintainable permanently as an asset, akin to the cost of goodwill. They are customarily written off, chiefly because they are relatively of small amount.

Brokerage on Shares.—I cannot hold with Mr. Justice Kay that such brokerage ought not to be paid on the formation of a company. Nor do I understand how on ordinary business principles the public issue of shares at a discount can be impeached. The judges in these matters seem to me rather to be fighting with shadows. Any arrangement between partners (whether shareholders in a company or not) the nature of which is disclosed, and which leads to the introduction of new capital, must be innocuous as regards creditors and the public.

As respects prospecting or exploring, and also the removal of superincumbent rock in slate quarries and the like, I think there is no way of attaining a fair result save by writing off such expenses in a period of years not exceeding the time during which benefit is derived through them.

As respects "interest during construction," I am bold enough to say that the decision in *Bardwell* v. *The Sheffield Waterworks*, quoted by Mr. Cooper, was obviously right, and the reason given was the true one, viz: "That if the "company, instead of themselves constructing the works, "had employed a contractor, he would have included "interest in his estimates." The doctrine is analogous to that under which law charges are included in the capital cost of a railway, *i.e.*, that incurring such law charges, or such loss of interest, is a necessary incident in the creation of such an undertaking, and for which capital must be forthcoming in order to carry out the enterprise, that is to say either share capital or borrowed capital.

The latter decision of Mr. Justice Fry in the Alexandra Palace case was given under peculiar circumstances. In the first place, the Articles of Association contained a very unusual clause, running thus—

"The amount of all calls and moneys paid to the company "in respect of shares, and all moneys borrowed, and all "moneys raised or produced by sale, conversion, or realising "of the property or any part thereof, ... and all "moneys received under insurance of the property against "destruction or damage by fire, or wreck, or perils of the "sea, shall be deemed capital."

In the next place the interest charged to Capital Account was in that case not interest upon borrowed money, but upon preference shares, and although I must hold that in the case of borrowed money, following the decision in *Bardwell* v. *The Sheffield Waterworks*, it matters not whether interest be paid to the contractor or to a lender, such interest being in either case part of the cost of the undertaking, yet where the money is raised upon shares, it is clearly a matter of contract between partners whether such shares are to bear interest prior to the completion of the works, and whether guaranteed or preferential interest or otherwise.

Thirdly, it happened most unfortunately that the enterprise was so far unsuccessful, that there was no profit for the first year of working as a whole, though profit was made during certain months, nor was any clear profit ever shown by the accounts laid before the company down to the date of the liquidation. But by the articles it was provided, as is usual, that "all dividends and bonuses on shares shall be "declared at the ordinary general meeting, and shall be made "only out of the clear profits of the company."

Part of the money paid away in dividends upon the preference shares raised for the purpose of rebuilding the palace after its destruction by fire, was taken from the insurance money, and the residue was borrowed for the purpose from the financiers who were creditors of the company. No portion came from the excess of receipts over payments.

Mr. Justice Fry was of opinion that the terms upon which the preference shares were issued gave the holders a right to receive out of profits only a preferential dividend at the rate of 6 per cent. with a contingent addition out of surplus profits which might remain after paying 6 per cent. to the ordinary shareholders. It was declared by the Articles of Association that the insurance money was capital replaced and it therefore could furnish no fund for payment of dividend. Loans certainly could not be regarded as available profits.

The question remained whether, if the accounts had been carefully made up, on the principle of crediting receipts and debiting expenditure *after the opening*, a profit would have appeared, applicable to the payment of dividends? On the part of the directors, nothing of the sort was set up, but only a contention that *in the summer months succeeding the opening*, money was made, which was seemingly absorbed by losses prior to the regular balancing. The judge expressly says "The general meeting which was held in "December had not before it any materials, as it appears to "me, for declaring a dividend, and I do not understand that "any dividend was declared at that meeting." Again, later in his judgment, he says, "There is no balance sheet which "it can be for a moment suggested induced the directors to "come to the conclusion that there were divisible profits."

Now, if there had been a surplus of income over expenditure at the first balancing, and the back dividends on the preference shares had been paid out of that surplus (and it seems, according to the terms of the issue, the preference shareholders could not otherwise claim payment) then the directors would have been exonerated, and moreover, such back dividends, not because of the nature of things, but because of the special bargain made with the preference shareholders, would have fallen on revenue and not on capital. The true answer to Mr. Buckley's ingenious contention, which has so much reason in it, viz.: "that it is quite proper to debit to "Capital Account the interest on capital expended on works, "such as buildings, so long as they are unproductive during "the period of construction" is that under such circumstances it is not applicable.

In this, as in so many cases, the apparent discrepancies between judgments are greatly reduced when details come to be considered and distinctions duly made. The doctrine laid down in *Bardwell v. The Sheffield Waterworks* has certainly been acted upon in many important cases by existing companies, and I shall be much surprised if it is ever upset.

Before proceeding to deal with the legal cases which I referred to at the commencement of this paper, I think it may be useful if I refer to one or two variations from the simple cases we have been considering, such as the case where two classes of shares exist, or where the vendor for a term of years guarantees to make up a certain dividend. The existence of deferred shares, as in the case of the *Edison and Swan Electric Light Company*, or of a vendor's guarantee of dividend, as in the early years of the *Bodega Company*, or of founders' shares in most cases where there are such shares, renders it necessary to ascertain profits with greater strictness and to divide them more completely than would be necessary or advisable if only one class had to be considered, and I am therefore compelled to regard the existence of such deferred interests as in a measure unfortunate for the proprietors as tending to disable the management from acting with a due degree of caution. Another case where somewhat unusual conditions had to be dealt with, was that of the *English and Australian Copper Company*. Its permanent assets were some of them much overvalued, whilst one at least was largely undervalued, and although in point of fact the capital was reduced by leave of the court, and the valuations adjusted according to the latest data, I think we may conclude that supposing the undervalue of one asset of a permanent character matched the overvalue of another such asset, the two figures might have been adjusted by the mere vote of the proprietors. I by no means object on principle to the operation of writing down capital where this can be done without disturbing income, but have only desired to point out that in many cases nothing is gained by the process. I have already suggested that liberty to return capital out of profits without incurring the liability to put it back, would in some cases be very useful to proprietors, and to those who might be called upon to give the company credit, as guarding them from forming a flattering estimate of capital values. I recur to the suggestion for the purpose of indicating mining companies, especially gold and silver mining companies, as being peculiarly likely to profit by such a law. Nobody knows, as a rule, how long the productiveness of a gold mine will continue, and if large profits were customarily distributed, part as dividend and part as returned capital, the proprietors would form a juster idea of their position, the market value of their shares would not rise so high, and the directors might, when the eventful collapse came, have the satisfaction of feeling that with a capital largely reduced or even extinguished, less scope for complaint would exist.

An important company, following the advice of an eminent lawyer, has lately decided to carry straight to the credit of "profit and loss" the whole proceeds of some of its assets, on the footing that the book value of the mass as shown in their balance sheet is far below the real value, and that they may go on treating their assets in this way until the estimated value of those which remain is, whilst still above the book value, much nearer to it than it is at present. I regard this as a very dangerous precedent, and hope it will not be followed, for it amounts to nothing less than a continual revaluation of assets held for sale, for the purpose of swelling divisible profits. Had it been proposed that these assets should be revalued in detail, the book value being split up rateably into many parts, so that on sale of any one of such parts, the profit compared with the book value could be treated as available, I should have considered this to represent the utmost which could be safely done towards the augmentation of divisible profit.

Lee v. Neutchatel Asphalte Company, Limited.

In this case some of the circumstances are so peculiar that the decision come to may not apply to many other companies, and the chief value of the judgments for our guidance is rather contained in the incidental remarks made by the judges than in the final order. For instance, this is a company which has a distinctly terminable undertaking, indeed one which must inevitably come to an end for want of material after a time, yet by its articles it was expressly provided that the directors were not bound to form a fund or otherwise reserve moneys, for the renewal or replacing of any lease, or of the company's interest in any property or concession. In the absence of such a clause it is plain that in the circumstances fair dealing would demand the creation of a reserve. The plaintiff desired to override this clause, and on the other side it was contended, not so much that a reserve was unnecessary, but that by the extension of the concession, both as to area and time, the company had been placed in a better situation than at the date of its formation. A further and highly important peculiarity of the case was, that by common consent the purchase money in the form of nominally paid up capital enormously exceeded the value of the assets at the date of the formation of the company, and those assets even if fully maintained could not be expected ever to make that capital good. If a sinking fund to provide for the wasting interest of the company in the concession were proportioned to the purchase price paid in shares, it would absorb a very large annual sum and prevent the distribution of profits, thus depriving the preference shares of the benefit of their priority, but if such a fund were proportioned to the actual value of the concession, it could be borne, and yet the dividend objected to could be paid to the preferred shareholders.

Mr. Justice Stirling was the judge who decided the case in the first instance, and he held:

1. That unless it could be shewn that after payment of the dividend the assets of the Company would fall short of those acquired at its formation, it could not be said that the dividend was being paid out of capital.
2. That upon the evidence it was not established by the plaintiff that the assets so fell short.
3. It having been urged that if the company were to do in every year down to the expiration of the con-

cession as was proposed to be done in 1885, the concession would expire and no fund would exist to represent its value, he said: "It may be that in "some future year the company will have to set "apart a substantial sum to represent depreciation "in the value of the concern; but, so long as the "capital remains intact, and the current receipts "exceed the current expenditure, both according "to the general law and under the provisions of "these particular Articles of Association, it rests "entirely with the shareholders whether the excess "should be divided among them or set apart to "provide for replacing wasting assets, and the "court has no power to interfere with their decision, "however foolish or imprudent it may seem to be."

It is one of the peculiarities of the case, that whilst the interests of the preference and ordinary shareholders are antagonistic, they have to decide the question last referred to by voting together, and consequently it is of great importance that the holders of preference shares shall hold a large number of ordinary shares (there are 33,700 preferred and 80,000 ordinary shares) otherwise the interests of the preferred shareholders might be overridden. This fact does not appear to have been touched upon by Mr. Justice Stirling. His decision seems to me to contain these principles—

(*a*) That a provision like that in the Articles of the *Neuchatel Asphalte Company, Limited*, is ineffectual to absolve the company from the obligation to keep its capital intact,—a reasonable provision for replacing of wasting Assets must be made.

(*b*) That capital may be held to be intact, although there is no valuation of assets, and there can be none such as would show that the shares are worth par.

(*c*) That a company may do foolish and imprudent things without breaking the law.

The contention of Mr. W. Pearson, Q.C., and Mr. Buckley to the effect "that a company does not value its fixed "capital and ascertain whether it has available assets "representing that, before it declares a dividend. For "instance, a railway company would not make a valuation of "its line of rails for such a purpose. The floating capital "is in a different position, and that ought to be valued, "and the company ought to have assets representing that "before it pays any dividend," seems to me to have been accepted by the judge, who took the trouble to go into an alleged loss of £32,736 1s. 10d. on floating assets, and decided that "profits to a greater extent have been made "and retained in the coffers of the company."

On appeal, the judgment was confirmed. It was contended for the plaintiff that "the nominal amount of the share capital must be taken as the value of the capital when the company was formed. and the value ought to be kept up to that amount." In reply it was urged that "an acceptance of the principles contended for by the appellant would be ruinous to companies, for it would make it impossible for directors ever to recommend a dividend without going into elaborate calculations as to the value of their assets."

Lord Justice Cotton held that "there is no obligation in anyway imposed upon the company or its shareholders to make up the assets of the company so as to meet the share capital, where the shares have been taken under a duly registered contract, which binds the company to give its shares for certain property without payment in cash."

As to the question whether a sinking fund was necessary he arrived at the same conclusion as Mr. Justice Stirling, saying that though "there is nothing in the Act which says that dividends are only to be paid out of profits," yet "there is this firmly fixed, that capital assets of the company are not to be applied for any purpose not within the objects of the company, and paying dividend is not the object of the company, the carrying on of the business of the company is its object;" and he went on to say, "In this company, as in other companies, the directors and others who have the control ought to consider whether in a fair reasonable way what they are going to divide is to be considered as profits but, in considering that they may well have regard to the Articles. There is no such necessity as was contended for by Mr. Rigby, to set apart every year a sum to answer the supposed annual diminution in the value of this property from the lapse of time."

In the course of his judgment his Lordship defined capital to be "permanent assets, and assets not to be expended in providing for the profit earned by the company,' *i.e.*, I suppose to be meant, not such things as materials of manufacture, or ores, a definition evidently in harmony with the views which I have ventured to express as to the 1st category of capital outlays in the early part of this paper. Again, he says "here for the purpose of getting the profit there is necessarily a consumption year by year of part of the capital of the company," and adds that "the question whether what has been done is really a division of capital by way of dividend must be considered in a reasonable and sensible way," Here the 2nd category of outlays was obviously what he had in mind.

In the judgment of Lord Justice Lindley the language used goes beyond that of the Judges whose opinions have so far been quoted: yet I am able to accept cheerfully the dictum that when minerals are raised, "every ton of stuff which you get out of that which you have bought with your capital may, from one point of view, be considered as embodying and containing a small portion of your capital, and that if you sell it and divide the proceeds you divide some portion of that which you have spent your capital in acquiring. . . If that is a return of Capital it appears to me not to be such a return of Capital as is prohibited by law." This dictum must be correct, otherwise no mining company could divide its profits, as is commonly done, without any provision for the replacement of capital. I think it would be better perhaps if the law stood otherwise, but it is a question of extreme difficulty for the legislator, and comparatively a simple one for those who have a particular case presented to them.

His Lordship also held most liberal views as to the freedom which men of business are allowed to have, in deciding how profits are to be reckoned, what is to be put into a capital account, what into an income account. I ask for nothing in the way of latitude beyond what he was willing to grant.

On another point his Lordship grappled very vigorously with a case which I have not myself ventured to handle so boldly. He said "I may safely say that the Companies "Acts do not require the capital to be made up if lost." This seems on all fours with Mr. Buckley's illustration of the loss of one ship out of ten, but the context shows that it was hardly that class of cases which was in the mind of the learned Judge. He quotes the outlay on establishing a daily newspaper, and says, that if £250,000 were sunk in building up a property which might not be saleable for £10,000, yet, provided they pay their creditors, the company may go on earning and dividing profits, without taking any steps towards replacing the £250,000. Here his Lordship is in effect dealing with the case of goodwill, and lays down the doctrine, which I fully accept, that goodwill is to be deemed for purposes of account to be worth its cost.

It will be seen that, differing from Mr. Justice Stirling and Lord Justice Cotton, he gave it as his opinion that the wasting nature of the concession or lease did *not* necessitate a provision by way of sinking fund. He therefore saw his way to accept the stipulation contained in the Articles of Association, by which as already stated, the company may distribute profits without making a reserve for the renewal or replacing of any lease, &c., a stipulation obviously representing a bargain at the time the company was formed, and which for that reason ought not to be set aside without absolute necessity.

His Lordship applied the doctrine which, as I have already remarked, is commonly acted upon in the case of a mine, to that of a company formed to work a patent, holding that "if the company retains assets sufficient to pay its "debts, it appears to me that there is nothing whatever in "the Act to prevent any excess of money obtained by working "the property over the cost of working it, from being "divided amongst the shareholders." Here I do not question the correctness of his Lordship's exposition of law, but I feel the inconvenience of its application in practice, and have been careful in the preceding part of this paper to say what I regard as the best course.

It is unnecessary to detail the views of Lord Justice Lopes save so far as to remark that they accorded nearly with those of Lord Justice Lindley. Where investments of capital diminish in value, by reason of causes over which the company has no control, or by reason of its inherent nature, that diminution need not, in the opinion of his Lordship, be made good out of revenue. He added that "for "the purpose of determining profits, accretions to and "diminutions of the capital are to be disregarded.

The Leeds Estate Building, &c., Society v. *Shepherd*

In examining this case I propose to confine myself to two points, viz:—

1. The principles laid down as to the proper statement of accounts, the violation of which enabled the Society to pay dividends out of capital.
2. The reasons assigned for attaching liability to the auditor.

The articles provided that a dividend might be declared upon such estimates of accounts as the directors may see fit to recommend, but subject to that, no dividend should be payable except out of the profits arising from the business of the company. Under Article 88 it was provided that the statement to be submitted to the General Meeting should "show arranged under the most convenient heads "the amount of gross income, distinguishing the several "sources from which it has been derived, and the amount "of gross expenditure distinguishing the expenses of the "establishment, salaries, and other like matters. Every "item of expenditure fairly chargeable against the year's "income shall be brought into account so that a just "balance of profit and loss may be laid before the meeting, "and in cases where any item of expenditure which may "in fairness be distributed over several years has been "incurred in any one year the whole amount of such item "shall be stated, with the addition of the reasons why only "a portion of such expenditure is charged against the "income of the year."

The Judge (Mr. Justice Stirling) gave full effect to the provisions in the Articles, including that which authorised dividends not out of "realised profits" but out of estimated profits. If the accounts had been drawn up on some definite principle not contrary to common sense, he would apparently have been satisfied with the action of the directors. But no evidence was offered in explanation of the accounts as rendered, save that the defendant Crabtree, the secretary and manager, gave an explanation as follows; "The principle on which we ascertain the sum of "£4,855 18s. 10d. as margin was, that we first ascertained the amount required for dividend and then left the balance of 'deferred interest' as a margin." In other words, the accounts were deliberately "cooked."

Supposing the outstanding payments had been rebated at a rate of interest nearly approximating to the rate of interest used in constructing the Society's tables, or if it had simply been estimated that the Society's profit must equal the amount of interest at such rate upon the moneys from time to time invested, the balance of interest charged being carried forward, I think these would have been amongst the several modes of estimation which the judge deemed to be available.

Another point on which the judge was very liberal in his construction of the law, was as to the re-valuation of freeholds. Had there been a real valuation showing the Albion Street property to be worth £5,180, his lordship was not prepared to say that the directors might not, in proposing or recommending dividends, act upon such a valuation.

Although I am reluctant to narrow the freedom of action of the managers of commercial undertakings, I feel bound to regard this doctrine with extreme jealousy.

The answer to the first question therefore is that the accounts were not even apparently in the form prescribed by the articles: the unearned interest was not dull estimated, and in the matter of revaluation of freeholds mere hearsay was acted upon.

The second question may be answered thus: The auditor Mr. Locking, was not a professional accountant; but he knew enough of business matters to see that the accounts were not in the proscribed form, and to be aware that something more than the mere assertion of the secretary as to the sum of interest which should be carried forward as not having been earned, or as to the value of the freeholds, ought to have been required by him. Moreover, the accounts which he signed were not really based on the Society's books. His Lordship says, "In each of those "years (1878-9 and 1879-80) Locking certified that the "accounts was a true copy of those shown in the books of the "company. That certificate would naturally be understood "to mean that the books of the company showed (for example) that on the 30th of April, 1879, the Company were "entitled to moneys lent to the amount of £29,515 15s. "This was not in accordance with fact."

In another part of the judgment his Lordship said, speaking of Mr. Locking's certificates, "They are not in any sense "such reports as are prescribed by Article 101. It is true in "one sense as stated in them, that the Accounts to which "the certificates are appended are copies of those shown in "the books of the company, for in each year there was inserted in the ledger of the company a Share Account, a "Cash Account, a Stock Account, and a Profit and Loss "Account, exactly as shown in the printed Balance Sheet, "but except in this most literal sense the certificates are not in "accordance with fact. No such items as 'Monies Lent, "'£21,289 9s. 8d.,' or 'Deferred Interest Account,' £3,030,' "which occurs in the Stock Account for 1874 are to be found "in the books of the company, and similar remarks apply "to similar items to be found in the subsequent Balance "Sheets."

His Lordship seemed to think it doubtful whether the Statute of Limitations applied to Locking's case, but as the plaintiffs, without arguing the question, had admitted the validity of the plea, he did not go into that matter

It follows then that where an auditor has manifestly failed in his duty, and the improper payment of dividends appears to be the natural and immediate consequence of such breach of duty. he may be held liable to damages to the amount of the dividends so paid. No caution in the wording of the actual certificate will protect him. The judgment being without prejudice to the rights of the directors to recover the dividends, this fact, together with the joint responsibility of the directors, would in practice relieve the auditor to a certain extent, but apparently he might be called upon at once for the full sum, and left to reimburse himself by taking some steps against his co-obligants, the nature of which does not appear. The judgment was without prejudice to any question of the liability of the defendants *inter se*, upon which the judge refused to say anything

It may be thought hard that a man who received but a very small remuneration, and who gained nothing by the wrongful acts which he failed to point out, should be required equally with the evil-doer himself to make good the money paid away. But it was part of his duty, which he had voluntarily accepted, that he should see that the accounts were at least on the surface correct. Had he failed to fathom some dark mystery, the failure would not have been visited on him as severely as this manifest neglect of a simple duty has been.

Mr. Ernest Cooper, F.C.A., then read some notes upon the paper, he having been furnished with a copy prior to the meeting, expressing dissent with the views of Mr. Welton, his notes, he said, were all put forward in his paper read in 1888.

The Chairman then said that the matter dealt with in Mr. Welton's paper and Mr. Cooper's reply contained very valuable material for reflection, and he suggested that they should meet and have a discussion that day fortnight. This being duly carried, the meeting terminated.

NOTES ON MR. T. A. WELTON'S PAPER

"ON THE PROFIT OF COMPANIES AVAILABLE FOR DISTRIBUTION"

Ernest Cooper

The Chartered Accountants Students' Society of London.

NOTES

ON MR. T. A. WELTON'S PAPER

"ON THE PROFIT OF COMPANIES AVAILABLE FOR DISTRIBUTION."

BY Mr. ERNEST COOPER, F.C A.

At a meeting of this Society held on the 3rd ult., a paper was read by Mr. T. A. WELTON, F.C.A. (16 *Accountant*, *p.* 677), a sort of outcome of the paper by Mr. ERNEST COOPER, F.C.A. (14 *Accountant*, *p.* 740), read before the members in 1888. At the conclusion of Mr. WELTON'S paper Mr. COOPER read the following notes, which he has since been induced to publish with the prefatory paragraph which appears below.

IN spite of the suggestion I made when asked at the meeting to print these remarks, that doing so may tend to draw attention from the subject, Mr. HANSON has urged that members desire to have them printed. In assenting I venture to ask students who desire to acquaint themselves with the points upon which discussion has arisen, to first read my paper in the "Transactions" of 1888, and I would impress upon them the importance—as a necessary preliminary—of clearly understanding the essential difference between a Limited Company under the Companies Acts and a Parliamentary Company for Public Works. This will make intelligible what is described as Double and Single Account and the consequences that result from the law not requiring the share capital of Companies' Act Companies to have a restricted destination or be represented by specified assets. These points, I think, form the basis of the difference of opinion among lawyers as to "What is Profit of a Company."

E.C.

15th December, 1890.

I am indebted to Mr. WELTON'S kindness for an early copy of his paper.

It should first be pointed out that although Mr. WELTON begins by saying he revives the subject treated in my paper of November 1888, entitled "What is Profit of a Company," he raises by his title a somewhat different subject, viz., "available and distributable profit." His paper shows that this distinction is not unimportant, for he deals with the subject from a different standpoint to mine. Whereas I sought to ascertain by what principles we are bound in ascertaining profit, whether by Statutes and judicial interpretation of them, or by custom and usage, Mr. WELTON has taken far higher ground. To quote his words (p. 1), he weighs the question as one of "public policy," (p. 2), he seeks "what is best for the nation," and he points out "where (p. 4) the public interest is not served," he guides us to (p. 4) "the sound practical course," or (p. 7) "a convenient course"; he tells us (p. 5) what it "is safest to say," and what he "would certainly advocate," and (p. 8) how a "well-advised Board" will act and what is the "true policy of a Board" and (p. 10) what he would recommend, and (p. 11) he treats the vital matter of single or double account as a matter of "taste and convenience."

Now some of these things may, or may not, have to do with what is available or distributable or divisible profit, but they have nothing whatever to do with the question, "What is Profit?"

But it is right to point out that Mr. WELTON, at starting, claims to seek for "true principles," and he considers what principles were in the minds of the Judges, and—to take his words—he hopes to be able to seize their ideas and harmonise them with his notions of what is best.

Mr. WELTON treats separately of the cases of *Lee* v. *The Neuchâtel Asphalte Co.* (41 Ch. Div. 1), and the *Leeds Estate, Building and Investment Co.* v. *Shepherd* (36 Ch. Div. 787). I do not propose to refer to his remarks upon these cases further than this, that I was at first surprised he did not employ *Lee* v. *Neuchâtel Co.* to scourge my paper, as he might well have done, but he has evidently discovered that the case would recoil upon himself, for throughout his general paper he ignores the judgments in this case, and (p. 22), in referring to it separately at the end, he says, "I "do not question the correctness of his Lordship's (L. J. "LINDLEY'S) exposition of the law, but I feel the inconvenience "of its application in practice." I think we shall all agree with Mr. WELTON as to the inconvenience of this decision, and for the present, we shall do well to wait for more light upon it from lawyers, which cannot, it may be hoped, be long withheld.

I must thank Mr. WELTON for the courtesy with which he has treated my paper, more especially as it is evident my views have severely strained his patience. He is even complimentary, crediting me with much care, and, in one instance, with sound common sense. When he has to be severe, he is politely so. He finds I beg the whole question, but I do so involuntarily, and when he detects levity, he only finds me half serious; nothing short of the repetition of "the same impracticable doctrine" will induce him to part company with me, and when finally he is obliged to describe my doctrine as monstrous, he only charges me with implying it. I shall follow Mr. WELTON's lead in speaking plainly and perhaps severely of his views, but not, I hope, failing in the high respect due to himself.

Now, I assure Mr. WELTON I am quite serious. I regard this question of the difference of opinion among lawyers as to what is profit as very far from a joking matter for us Accountants, and if this difference, or rather confusion, of ideas is to extend to Accountants, it becomes still more serious. Whether it does exist to any great extent among us, I hope this discussion may show and may lead to at least a narrowing of the divergence.

After reading Mr. WELTON's paper carefully, I venture to recommend Students not to accept his conclusions, with none of which, where they conflict with my paper, can I, although sincerely desirous of doing so, bring myself to agree.

Coming now to the matter of Mr. WELTON's paper; on page 2 he refers twice inaccurately to my paper. First he says, "like Mr. COOPER I will confine myself to *divisible* profit," &c., which I did not by any means do, and then he says, my quoted definitions of Capital "refer to two distinct things." If this means that I said, or implied, they were distinct things, I say I did not do so, and I say, so far from being distinct they are the same. The capital brought in by the proprietors, and that laid out by them are one and not two.

Mr. WELTON says the Capital of the proprietors may not be the surplus of assets, because there may be a balance of Profit and Loss. I said (page 8) the surplus of assets whether called Capital, Reserve Fund, or Profit and Loss, is the real Capital in a business and this I repeat; but I will quote from the very next page of Mr. WELTON's paper, "I regard the balance . . . as Capitalised Profit," and I say by this he contradicts and refutes himself, for if the balance of Profit and Loss is capitalised then it is Capital.

I refer him to the judgment of Lord HERSCHELL in *Bouch* v. *Sproule* (12 App. Ca. 393-4).

Mr. WELTON divides assets into four elements or categories, and finds that three are capital or capital outlay. These three categories are permanent, less permanent, and floating. He says, "any assets not necessary for carrying on the business "ought to be regarded as investments and not as capital. The "three elements . . . constitute capital outlay, and if such "capital outlay is greater in amount than the proprietors' "capital, the difference is borrowed capital or capitalised "profit."

All this is original and startling, coming from an Accountant of experience, but it is not more startling than it is manifestly unsound. I cannot occupy the time of the meeting in refuting it in detail. I say it means that book debts are capital and consols not, and stock-in-trade bought and not paid for is money borrowed. To ascertain the capital in the business of a company on Mr. WELTON's principle, you must ascertain the precise sum necessary for carrying on the business, and then the surplus, whether cash in hand, bank balance, or any other asset not wanted for carrying on the business, becomes an investment, and ceases to be capital at all.

Then as to the three elements of capital outlay. They amount, say to a million, and the company has no other property, so you deduct the proprietors' capital, £500,000, (you do not notice the liabilities), and the remainder is what? According to Mr. WELTON, it is borrowed capital, or capitalized profit. But has Mr. WELTON considered where he is if the three elements he calls capital outlay are less than the capital of the proprietors. Then there must be a deficiency of capital according to his system, although there may be a surplus in fact. Is it possible to pursue the subject?

I will return presently to the three categories, but before leaving page 3, there is some more astonishing matter to refer to.

I said that every accretion to capital is profit. Mr. WELTON argues that if this be so, we ought to introduce into Balance Sheets figures representing the value of the goodwill. He passes by my quotation from Lord Justice LINDLEY, that goodwill is an asset only so far as it has saleable value, but surely I need not say goodwill is such a peculiar species of asset that it is seldom, or hardly ever, inserted in a Balanc Sheet unless it happens to have been bought, and then only at or under cost; so of course it would not constitute what is called an accretion to capital at all. If we may assume a case in which goodwill could properly be included in the Balance Sheet above cost, the surplus over cost, I contend, would be profit.

But Mr. WELTON goes very much farther than this. Not only goodwill, but the premium or discount, at which shares in the company are sold in the market is to be taken into account.

But upon what are these extraordinary suggestions based? Merely upon this—whereas some lawyers say the accretion is Capital and others that it is profit, and I agree with the view that it is profit—upon this foundation Mr. WELTON bases the astounding suggestion that what I have said implied that the improved market value of Guinness's Shares is profit of that Company, and so he goes on to warn us of the danger of applying the word profit to "what no practical man could think of dividing." I am afraid profit must be called profit, what ever the practical man may think of doing.

On pages 4, 6 and 9, Mr. WELTON gives his views as to revaluation of the three categories of assets. In these views there is much that I agree with, but I find difficulty in separating his views of what is, or is not, prudent from what can, or cannot be legally justified.

What is clear is that he wholly disagrees with my conclusion as to the fundamental difference between a parliamentary company and a limited company. Until we reach page 10, I can find no indication of his having read what I say on double and single account. He instances a railway to support his argument in favour of keeping assets permanently at cost in the Balance Sheet of a limited company, whereas no one pretending to a fragment of knowledge of the subject would suggest a railway under the Clauses Acts need be re-valued.

He cites Mr. BUCKLEY's ship case apparently with approval, and remarks that if a merchant or private firm lost one out of ten ships, that would undoubtedly be a loss on Capital Account, and the merchant would feel at liberty to go on spending the income of the nine ships without replacing the capital. Why, this is carrying the double account system into private accounts. Surely there Mr. WELTON will find himself alone; Mr. BUCKLEY even will not, I presume, follow him. But why "undoubtedly"? I should say he will find no one who understands the matter will agree with him for a moment.

I am driven to the conclusion that Mr. WELTON had not at all in his mind what is the meaning of double and single account, and I think I am abundantly confirmed in this by what he says on page 11, where, by merely inserting a qualification, he finds the distinction between double and single account vanishes, and he clearly implies the opinion that the distinction between double account and single account is merely the stating a Balance Sheet in two divisions or as a whole.

Now let us examine the new theory of the three elements of capital laid out. There seem to be four elements, but No. 4 is, we are told, "Investments" and not capital. The three elements are No. 1, "Permanent," like a railway; No. 2, "Less Permanent," like leases, patents, and ships: and No. 3, "Floating Assets," necessary for carrying on the business.

From these elements Mr. WELTON develops his ideas as to re-valuing assets.

As to the first element, I will not follow him into his remarks about a railway for the reason I have given. But he takes the case of Ironworks, and he asks "where would be the use of expressing" enhanced value on the Balance Sheet. Now this seems to me to be begging the question, but involuntarily, I am sure. The question is not "what is the use of it," which the Board may be left to decide, but is the company legally entitled, and I ask for anything in the law to prevent this being done.

Take the case of a brewery built on inexpensive land in London fifty or a hundred years ago. The value has multiplied ten or twenty times. I say there is no legal objection, and certainly no objection on the ground of prudence to the Directors showing the enhanced value of the brewery in their accounts, and as to the use of it, as Mr. WELTON asks, I will answer. The proprietors' interests will become of greater marketable value, the credit of the concern will become greater from showing enhanced value, and debentures would be more readily issued upon the security of the property. But what have we to do with the use or uselessness? Does Mr. WELTON doubt that companies that have increased capital against increased value of so-called permanent assets, going to the trouble to reconstruct the company for the purpose, have not been able to judge whether it was useful for them? But on this subject, again, Mr WELTON refutes himself on the next page, for he owns that his "ephemeral factory" must be the subject of reserve. So although we may not value up, we must value down. Now I invite him to produce his authorities against valuing up, and I remind him that *Lee* v. *The Neuchâtel* is an authority against the necessity of writing down.

Then the second element. The less permanent. Here is what Mr. WELTON tells us:—

> He has gone through the whole of the items, and in no instance does he "find the proper conduct of a company's "affairs demands that they should be re-valued." So, "it follows," they are no "more than book figures," and their value depends, like a railway, mainly on the concern being kept "going."

Now I dispute every word of this, and I ask for no other witness against Mr. WELTON than his own paper. As to not re-valuing these mere "book figures," why, he re-values them all himself. Leaseholds, he says, must be lowered in value every year to meet the exhaustion of the cost by lapse of time, and advance in value, he tells us, is to be taken into account in doing this. He says, real value is not to be considered, and in the same breath he considers real value. "Brick-earth as well as Coal,"—in face mind of the three judgments in *Lee* v. *The Neuchâtel*—is to be estimated as to quantity; steam-boilers are to be provided for, and so the value of the ship will be raised when the new boilers are put in. You are to raise a fund against the depreciation of your mineral resources, and apply it to the purchase of new minerals, and even a prospecting or exploring company is to write down its outlay out of profits. My doctrine, which never surely went so far as this, is described as monstrous and impracticable.

Then I will simply, to save time, say that of the items of assets he refers to, few can properly be described as "no more than a book figure." They are mostly real, tangible, and saleable assets, and not necessarily or probably dependent mainly for their value on keeping the business going.

To Mr. WELTON's ideas about a patent, I see little reason for taking exception, but he strangely ignores the judgment in *Lee* v. *The Neuchâtel* in telling us that the shareholders must meet the question of devoting all the profits to writing down the patent.

Turning to the last of the three elements, Mr. WELTON properly points out that the constant renewal of what he calls floating assets, tests the value in a manner impossible with permanent assets. But this does not surely argue in favou of not applying such tests to the value of permanent assets as are practicable.

Mr. WELTON tells us that stocks of manufactured goods "ought to be valued upon some *uniform system* whether at or "below cost." Here, again, I hold that Mr. WELTON is wrong. Why does he deal only with manufactured goods, and does he mean only those manufactured by the company? A uniform system is impossible in regard to stocks. The test of the proper valuation of stocks in their convertibility "at or below cost," is a safe rule in many, perhaps most cases; but if an article is saleable in open market in Mincing Lane at any moment without trouble or expense, it can fairly be taken nearly at selling price; but if it is an article which involves expense and uncertainty in finding a customer, it should be taken at a price which leaves provision for the expense and uncertainty and all risks, and also the full proportion of profit properly attributable to the completion of the sale. But a proportion of profit may fairly be attributed to the expenses and trouble attendant upon purchasing and on partially completed manufacture. Then as to materials, I disagree again. Mr. WELTON says whether the goods have been bought cheaply or dearly, cost is to be the test. As he considers it inexpedient to value up, so he finds it unnecessary to value down. Thus, if the stock of a coppersmith fall in value fifty per cent. below cost, Mr. WELTON would take it at cost, and presumably he would leave an incoming shareholder or partner to bear the loss in the succeeding year. But would not the incomer be entitled to say he had been deceived?

Next, leaving the "capital outlay" (mind it is Mr. WELTON, not I, who so calls it) we come to "investments." But here he seems to lose sight, for the moment, of his remarkable idea of making everything not required for carrying on the business an "investment." Still, I am unable to agree with him when he says "the usual practice is to value investments at cost or at a less figure."

On page 7 we find another very original proposition. It sounds strangely like the third section of the Companies Act, 1880, which Mr. Buckley "found so much difficulty in "struggling to understand" (5th ed. p. 562), so perhaps I ought not to describe the proposition as original.

Here is Mr. WELTON's suggestion enforced by repetition.

P. 7. "If the laws admitted of a return of "capital being made out of profits in such a way "that the amount returned could not be called up" and

P. 17. "I have already suggested that liberty "to return capital out of profits without the liability to "put it back would in some cases be very useful."

The Act of 1880 attempted the impossible feat of returning capital by dividing profits. But that Act presumably was not drawn by an Accountant, or he should have known that by dividing profits you do not and cannot return capital.

Then Mr. WELTON does not agree at all with my remarks about undervaluation of assets, but here, again, he inadvertently misquotes me. He says my remarks apply to permanent assets, whereas I expressly included investments. Mr. WELTON deals with undervaluation as a matter which the proprietors approve, whereas the whole question turns on concealment from the proprietors. But strangely, on the next page he returns to the subject of secret reserves.

I cannot, again, from necessity of putting some limit to my remarks, discuss every point in which I disagree with Mr. WELTON. I wholly and entirely disagree with his remark that market values of shares are "dependent on income "almost exclusively," and I assert, in spite of Mr. WELTON's emphatic contradiction that secret reserves do operate to the prejudice of a seller of shares.

Mr. WELTON will, I think, carry few with him in his imputation of "ignorant prejudice" against those who favour the extinction of the cost of goodwill out of profits. Goodwill is not a desirable item in a Balance Sheet, and using profits to write it off is, in most circumstances, a sound and commendable practice. But here, again, I cite Mr. WELTON against himself, for he recommends that if a company finds it expedient to reduce capita , such reduction should be applied to goodwill. I must point out that on page 11 Mr. WELTON quotes me again inaccurately; I did not say the public had a charge on a railway, but by insuring the application of the whole of the capital to the work, and the retention of the capital in it "something in the nature of a charge" was created.

One very strange circumstance is that whilst Mr. WELTON on page 11 tells us he has shown me there is no obligation on the part of a company to keep capital intact, on page 19 he quotes three times in almost the same words without disapproval from Mr. Justice STIRLING's judgment, references to this obligation, and there is no question that that learned Judge held that such an obligation existed.

I think Mr. WELTON should give his authority for saying the words "upon realisation" must be added to my quotation from Sir GEORGE JESSEL's judgment in *Robinson* v. *Ashton* (20 Eq., 28) as to the rise or fall of the value of fixed plant. I have read the judgment again and find no ground for the suggestion, so I prefer to take this great Judge's law as he gave it to us.

I feel that I have laid myself open to the charge of speaking at too great length, but I have been impressed with the necessity of answering Mr. WELTON's paper, and in doing so I think the length of my answer must be attributed to the very numerous points on which I have been compelled to disagree. I have employed few words upon those parts of Mr. WELTON's paper which do not conflict with the views I expressed two years ago. Those views are not, I submit with all humility, shown in one single point to be unsound by Mr. WELTON's paper. [*The Discussion will appear in our next.*]

THE PRINCIPLES UPON WHICH THE ASSETS OF A JOINT STOCK COMPANY SHOULD BE VALUED FOR BALANCE SHEETS

Alex W. Payne

The Chartered Accountants Students' Society of London.

THE PRINCIPLES UPON WHICH THE ASSETS OF A JOINT STOCK COMPANY SHOULD BE VALUED FOR BALANCE SHEETS.

By Mr. Alex. W. Payne, A.C.A.

The following Prize Essay was read on the evening of the 2nd December, 1891, Mr. G. van de Linde presiding, in the absence of Mr. Waterhouse:—

The Committee is, I think, to be congratulated upon its choice of a subject for this Essay. From an accountant's point of view it would be almost impossible to over-estimate its importance, for without principles of some kind to guide us in such a matter a proper Audit of Accounts is impossible. The worth of an audit to those whose interests we are appointed to protect must always largely depend upon our ability as experts to deal with the question of the value of the assets at the time of audit, and to ascertain therefrom the balance between assets and liabilities. The responsibilities and duties of an auditor are year by year becoming more clearly defined, and whilst Chartered Accountants are showing themselves prepared to accept all the enhanced weight of obligation which recent legal decisions and the demands of a keen and critical commercial community has cast upon them as auditors, there is an important and imperative duty resting upon us as younger members of the profession to render ourselves qualified not only to vouch the clerical accuracy of the accounts put before us, but, what is far more, to agree or disagree with the *principles* upon which such accounts are based, the principles, in other words, upon which the assets have been valued.

It is often urged that accounts are unreliable, and that figures can be made to prove anything. It should be impossible to bring such a taunt against us as auditors, and we ought to be able to gain for our profession the confidence of the public by proving that our management of figures is not "an application of the art of legerdemain," but that statements audited by Chartered Accountants may be relied upon as showing in a clear, impartial and complete manner the position of the company's affairs. As auditors we should always bear in mind the nature of our appointment, and how an imperfect discharge of our duties may prejudice those on behalf of whom we are at law supposed to act. Our position is undoubtedly a judicial one, and its duties call for the exercise of the greatest impartiality and thoroughness. But such services can obviously only be rendered with credit to ourselves and advantage to the community by our becoming masters of those guiding principles in regard to accounts which experience and equity dictate.

I have stated that the duties of an auditor are judicial. As an expert to whom the accounts of a company are referred, he is bound, I submit, to consider such accounts in their relation to *all* the parties who are or may be interested in them. In the case of the accounts of a Joint Stock Company, such interests are many and often conflicting. The claims shareholders and creditors, present and future, upon the auditor's attention, often render the task of adjustment no easy or enviable one. Then, too, as the representative of the shareholders, the auditor's duty may lead him into disagreement with the directors, and call for the exercise of those sterling qualities of tact and judgment that are of such inestimable value in our profession. But these considerations all point to the necessity for an auditor having sound principles at the back of his opinions, so that in case his judgment upon the value of particular assets at the time of audit is called in question, he may be able, if necessary, to give a reason for his decision.

It is clearly impossible in the time at my disposal to deal exhaustively with this subject, or to state the principles upon which every conceivable kind of asset should be valued. But it should be borne in mind that the provisions contained in Table A. of the Companies Act, 1862 (arts. 92-94), undoubtedly cast upon the Auditor important duties in regard to the assets of a company. The intention of the Legislature was clearly at least this, to make the auditor share in the responsibility for all statements appearing in the accounts he professes to have investigated. The Act of 1862 only contemplated apparently the employment of professional accountants to assist the auditors in the discharge of their duties, but I think it may safely be inferred both from the regulations contained in Table A., as well as from the present attitude of the Courts in regard to the responsibilities of an auditor, that where Chartered Accountants are appointed auditors of the accounts of a company, their reputation as professional men will increase their obligation to make the audit a real and reliable matter, and where necessary to employ other persons, such as professional valuers, to assist them in examining the Balance Sheet, and arriving at a judgment as to the value put upon the assets of the company by the directors and others in the accounts rendered to the shareholders. The standard of fitness for the important duties of an auditor is very rightly being raised, for experience has demonstrated that in order to make an audit the real protection to the shareholders or public interests that it should be, auditors must be suitably qualified for the discharge of their duties.

There has been a good deal of discussion of late as to the form in which we should certify our approval of the accounts submitted to us for audit; but I cannot but think that in future it will be more difficult, and I hope ultimately impossible, for an auditor to shelter himself behind the terms of a formal certificate. Accounts are referred to us for examination, and we are bound to make such examination as thorough and exhaustive as possible. No doubt, to a certain extent, in the case of the accounts of a private firm, we may be protected by the terms of our instructions, but I submit that in the case of a Joint Stock Company where our clients are many, and as a rule unknown to us, and the interests we have to consult are so important and often conflicting, we cannot and ought not to so limit our responsibility. Confidence is placed in our ability as professional accountants, and not in the extent of our investigation as defined in a certificate, however comprehensive; and as the public can scarcely be required to judge of the relative importance of what we do or leave undone, I think we may very properly be held liable for any damage to such parties arising from a neglect to fulfil all the reasonable obligations of our office.

Having obtained a clear idea of our relation as Chartered Accountants to the subject before us, let us now consider seriatim the principles that should, I think, be applied in the valuation of particular kinds of assets. And our duty to maintain an attitude of the strictest impartiality becomes at once obvious. Either an *under*-valuation or an *over*-valuation of the assets may prejudice those interested in the accounts, and we must therefore see that we obtain a reasonable ground for believing not only that such assets exist, but, that in the interests of all concerned, the accounts disclose such assets at a proper and fair valuation at the time of audit.

(1). *Freehold Land and Buildings.*—It is clear that an auditor should exercise considerable caution as to the value appearing in the balance sheet in respect of such assets as these. Assuming that he has had produced to him the deeds, and has satisfied himself as to the existence of the property, there still remains the important question as to its value. To determine this it may be necessary in some cases to have a valuation made, and especially so if the auditor has reason to believe that the actual value of the property is *below* its ledger value. Because unless the proper depreciation is written off, the auditor may become responsible for the payment of dividends which have never been earned, and for giving an undue preference to the existing shareholders at the cost of future ones. On the other hand if the property has *increased* in value he should be careful to see that such increment is not distributed as profit, until there is every reasonable ground for believing it to be practically a realised profit. As a rule, the safer course in *all* cases must be to postpone the distribution of such an increase in value, until actually realised by the sale of the property; but in any case the real value should, I think, be stated on the face of the accounts, so that present shareholders may have their share in such enhanced value, through the increased price that such disclosure would give to the shares.

This suggests the practice of banks and other similar concerns of making *secret reserves* by under-valuing their assets. No doubt it is most politic and necessary for a bank to have strong reserves, upon which to rely in case of need to cover contingent liabilities. Mr. T. A. Welton in his paper on the "Profit of Companies Available for Distribution," (Transactions 1890, page 141), approves of such risks as these being covered by *secret reserves*, his words being, "The "true policy of a bank is to gradually accumulate a *private* "*reserve*, large enough to meet any such decline in values as "in bad years may reasonably be feared." It seems to me, however, that the mere phrase *secret reserves* is opposed to the idea of an impartial audit, one of the essential aims of which ought to be the detection and prevention of such a policy, and the protection of the interests of all parties by placing a full and fair Balance Sheet before the shareholders. Such risks as are referred to, are those which must necessarily attach to the business of banking, and the proprietors must be aware of the necessity for accumulating a Reserve Fund large enough to protect their interests. There does not seem to me therefore to be any reason, whatever, why as Chartered Accountants, presuming to act in the interests of all parties, we should become connected in any way with a policy having for its object, an accumulation of reserve funds without the direct knowledge and consent of the shareholders, and the effects of which can only be to further the interests of future, at the expense of present, shareholders, and to increase the risk of directors and managers undertaking business of a too speculative character. The question of the proper valuation of assets of this kind may, therefore, often become a matter of the greatest importance, especially where there are differing classes of shareholders, and it can hardly be contended that every proper charge upon the year's income has been brought into account until such important assets as freehold property and buildings are fairly valued. In the case of a building society or similar institution, the gravest mis-statement of the accounts may be made unless, for instance, the properties on hand are properly valued, and it is therefore the duty of an auditor to see that there is a fair and correct value put upon all such assets, so as to prevent a distribution as profit among the present shareholders of what is in reality capital. There can be no doubt, I presume, as to the actual depreciation in the value of buildings, and this should, of course, be provided for out of profits at a fair rate.

(2.) *Leaseholds.*—As this class of property is by its very nature subject to depreciation in value, an auditor should satisfy himself that a sufficient sum has been written off each lease and charged against the profits to enable the original cost to be liquidated on the expiry of the term for which the lease is held. The amount properly chargeable to Profit and Loss may be roughly ascertained by dividing the cost of the lease by the term of years for which it is granted or which remain unexpired; but the preferable method is that by which a fixed annuity, actuarially determined, is charged to Profit and Loss and accumulated at an agreed rate of interest (5 or 6 per cent.) until at the end of the lease it amounts to the original outlay.

(3.) *Mining and Colliery Properties.*—Assets of this nature should also be mentioned where the value is diminished year by year by the gradual exhaustion of the mine. In such cases a charge must be made against Revenue for depreciation, and the amount of this should be ascertained by calculating the approximate cost per ton, assuming the mine to be of such an area and to contain so many tons of mineral, and then charging Revenue Account at that rate per ton on the output for the estimated exhaustion of the mine. Of course, provision should be made for the value of the plant, &c., at the end of the lease. As you are aware, the decision in the case of the *Neuchâtel Asphalte Co.* has made it somewhat doubtful whether directors are bound to make such provision for the gradual wasting of assets of this character. But the ruling is so utterly at variance with the views of all practical accountants and prudent men of business, that I think it is more than ever the duty of auditors to see that the shareholders are fully informed as to the actual value of their property from time to time.

(4.) *Purchase Leases.*—These are contracts under which railway wagons, pianos and furniture, &c., are hired, the lessor agreeing to let the goods for a certain rent or charge during a fixed period, at the end of which the property belongs to the lessee, or he has a right to purchase it at a nominal price. In the event of the lessee failing to keep up the payments, the lessor can take possession of the goods. The object of the parties to such an agreement is to spread the cost over a term of years, and to afford, meanwhile, security to the vendor for the price of the goods sold and interest thereon to date of payment. The auditor should here also satisfy himself that the proper charge has been made to Profit and Loss. The instalments payable are usually based upon the annuity system, so that care should be taken in the case of each payment to separate the amount representing interest on the balance of purchase money unpaid from the amount paid on account of such purchase money.

(5.) *Steamers and Shares in Ships.*—In cases where a company owns these assets an auditor should at least see that the amount appearing in the Balance Sheet is fully explained. In the case of Single Ship Companies it is not thought advisable to accumulate a reserve for the depreciation in value of the vessel, and the earnings are usually paid away to the shareholders in dividends, leaving them to provide for the gradual depreciation of their property. It is clearly the auditor's duty in cases where shares in ships form part of the assets of a company to see that the cost of the shares is properly written down, and that the whole of the dividends received is not included in the accounts as revenue. Where vessels are entirely owned by the company, the auditor must see that an adequate Reserve Fund is raised sufficient to liquidate the original cost within the life of the ships.

Of course, in regard to all these assets the value must be assessed upon them as the property of a going concern, and it seems to me impossible for us as auditors to certify the amount available for distribution as profit until such assets are fairly valued and any depreciation provided for. I do not say that as auditors we should always insist upon a revaluation of all assets of a permanent nature, but our duty certainly is to report whether the Balance Sheet is drawn up "so as to exhibit a true and correct view of the state of the company's affairs," and for this purpose we are bound to consider whether such assets as I have already mentioned are fairly stated in the Balance Sheet. Care should, however, be taken in every case to distinguish clearly between contingent and realised profits.

(6.) *Stock-in-Trade.*—In regard to this asset an auditor has an important duty. Upon its value and character the prosperity of any business must largely depend, and care should be taken that all loss upon goods in hand arising from change of fashion or other causes, is properly met. Of course, an auditor cannot be directly responsible for the value of the stock-in-trade, but he must take every reasonable means of ascertaining whether the stock has been properly taken on some uniform system at or below cost price by the manager or some other responsible person. As a sound principle accountants should not, I think, permit profits to be anticipated by allowing the stock, or any part thereof, to be valued at more than cost price, as profit arising from temporary fluctuations in the market price would otherwise be taken credit for, and so lead to confusion and error in the accounts. Although it would in most cases be impossible for an auditor to check the quantities and value of stock, yet he should invariably examine very carefully the stock sheets, so as to detect any clerical error, and see if the values generally correspond with the invoice or market prices of the articles at the date of stock-taking. The principles upon which the stock is valued should, I think, be stated in the accounts, and the responsibility for the correctness of the quantities should be acknowledged and certified by the manager or some other responsible servant of the company.

(7.) *Plant and Machinery.*—The auditor should examine carefully the valuation put upon these assets. The period of service of machinery is limited, and its depreciation from ordinary wear and tear, or from its pattern being improved upon by newer inventions, is so certain that a reserve should be made so as to reduce the amount standing to the debit of these accounts to its real value at the date of the Balance Sheet. The percentage of depreciation will vary with different articles; but, as a rule, the ordinary life of a machine can be ascertained, as well as any residual value it may thereafter possess, and from these data the charge to revenue can be easily arrived at. In addition to this charge for gradual deterioration, the cost of any repairs and renewals should I think be debited to Profit and Loss; but in any case the auditor should, before certifying the correctness of a Balance Sheet have reasonable grounds for believing that the value put upon the plant and machinery is a real one, and that a fair deduction for depreciation has been made.

(8.) *Mortgages and Loans on Bill or other securities.*—In regard to these assets there is not much need for valuation. The original advances or loans, less any part repaid, would appear in the books to the debit of the mortgagees or others, but the auditor should be satisfied that the balances are actually due as stated in the books of the company, and also that the securities held are real and sufficient. He should, of course, have the securities, in the shape of mortgage and other deeds, and bills of exchange, &c., produced to him, and he should protect the shareholders, as far as possible, from relying upon an insufficient or depreciated security for advances, by calling attention to the fact, and advising that a proper reserve be made to cover contingent loss. It would be well to have confirmatory evidence, by the production of Pass Books, &c., as to the balances due, so as to prevent the misappropriation of repayments, and the auditor should also see that the stipulated interest has been properly charged. In the case of building societies, &c., the repayments are usually made by fixed instalments including interest, and care should be taken to see that such repayments are properly dealt with in the accounts. In the accounts of a Joint Stock Company, subject to Table A. of the Act of 1862, an auditor is bound to see also that the balance due in respect of loans on mortgage of property out of the United Kingdom is separately stated in the Balance Sheet.

(9.) *Book Debts.*—These should receive the auditor's special attention, and be valued subject to discounts and risk of loss; and care should be taken to see that an adequate reserve is made for bad or doubtful accounts. It is manifestly difficult for an auditor to go outside the books, but he ought, strictly speaking, to have some further evidence that the debts are actually outstanding. Unfortunately, it is only possible in a few cases at present to secure such confirmation from the debtors themselves, but until the method of circularising each debtor is adopted, accountants must use such care and experience as they possess in valuing such assets. In the accounts of a bank it may often be exceedingly difficult for the auditor to estimate the risk of loss from bad debts, but he must obtain all the evidence he can, and this, supplemented by the experience of the managers, etc., will in most instances enable him to deal fairly and reasonably with such matters. In the case of a Joint Stock Company, subject to Table A. of the Act of 1862, he is bound to see that any debts due from a director or other officer of the company are separately stated in the Balance Sheet.

(10.) *Stocks and Shares.*—With regard to the valuation of the investments held by a company, an auditor should be extremely careful. In the case of Insurance Companies, Banks, and other financial concerns, such assets may represent the bulk of the property held, and it is, therefore, of the greatest importance that the securities should be fairly valued. As you are aware, in Insurance offices a periodical re-valuation of the assets is required, but even then a prudential policy should be adopted, so as to prevent a temporary rise in value, the advantage of which may never be secured by the company, being taken credit for. In the case of other companies, including Banks, etc., I am very strongly inclined to agree with the principles advocated by Mr. F. Whinney during the discussion on "The Profit of Companies," held on 17th December, 1890 (*Transactions, 1890*, page 171), that stocks and shares should in all cases be valued at or below cost, unless, I presume, such fall in price is believed to be only temporary. It seems reasonable and safer, in view of the serious liability to which we, as auditors, are exposed, that we should absolutely decline to admit as profit what at best is contingent upon an immediate sale. Such profit is not actually made, and there can scarcely be said to be reason to believe at the time of the balancing that such profit would ever be realised if there was no intention of converting such investments into cash. Investments held as reserve funds should, I think, be separately stated in the Balance Sheet. An auditor should always, of course, where possible, have the securities produced to him for examination, and, in the case of Inscribed Stocks, should ascertain that the proper trustees are duly entered as holders. In the event of any dealings in the securities since the last audit, the brokers' Contract Notes should be examined, so that any profit or loss may be properly dealt with, and the auditor should satisfy himself that all income due in respect of the investments up to the date of the accounts is accounted for.

(11.) *Patent Rights and Goodwill.*—The valuation of such assets as these must clearly receive the most careful attention of an auditor. There has of late been much discussion among the leaders in our profession as to the duty of accountants in regard to assets of this kind. And, I think, it may be safely taken for granted, as a result of such discussion, that Accountants agree in the *desirability* of writing off such assets as soon as possible. The controversy has chiefly turned upon the point whether the gradual liquidation of the cost of Goodwill ought to be effected by a charge against capital or income. Mr. Welton in the paper I have already referred to (*Transactions, 1890*, page 141), appears to prefer the retention of the cost of Goodwill as an asset in the Balance Sheet, except where, "by reason of " accumulated losses, the flow of dividends" has "stopped, so " that a reduction of capital is expedient," when he " would " recommend that such reduction be applied to the cost of " Goodwill, as well as to the extinction of the adverse balance " of Profit and Loss." In other cases, apparently, where the "flow of dividends" into the shareholder's pocket has continued, whatever the actual source from which they have come, Mr. Welton considers the "gradual extinction " of the cost of Goodwill out of profits" unnecessary and unreasonable. On the other hand, Mr. F. Whinney (*Transactions, 1890*, page 167), sees a necessity for writing down Goodwill, because it is not an actual realisable asset upon which the shareholders can rely. " Whether it is a vanish- " ing quantity or not, whether the Goodwill remains the same " after ten years as it was when you bought it is," he thinks, "somewhat beside the question. It is not an asset you can " depend upon to make the company stable, and just at the " time when the company wants to borrow money you will " find that your Goodwill is going and the asset itself is dis- " appearing." "Some day or other the case will arise where " directors for several years back have paid dividends which, " on the face of the accounts, appear to be earned, but they " made no provision whatever for writing anything off Good- " will. The company winds up, the Goodwill has vanished, " and then comes the question whether the directors were " justified in paying those dividends without writing off Good- " will. I think," he says, " that it is very likely that a Court " of Law would hold the directors so liable." "They ought " to have made provision for the depreciation of Goodwill just " in the same way as for other items."

I think such a statement as this shows clearly what our duty as accountants is in this matter. Mr. Welton contends (*Transactions, 1890*, page 141), that this is a question " for " the free action of the proprietors—or that of the directors to " whom their interests are entrusted, and whose acts they " endorse." But while this is, no doubt, technically correct, yet as auditors, representing the shareholders in examining the transactions and accounts of the directors, we are bound, I think, to place the matter unmistakeably before the shareholders. We have no right, it seems to me, to pass without comment an asset, often of the largest possible Ledger value, as if it were in the same category as the other realisable assets of the company. And we should, therefore, urge with all the weight of our authority the advisability and even the necessity in the real interests of the company of writing off such an asset as soon as circumstances will permit.

Let us consider for a moment, then, if some sound and practical principles cannot be found to guide us in the matter. The cost of Patent Rights is a form of Goodwill that can easily be dealt with. The patentee pays for a monopoly of the article patented for a number of years, at the end of which the patent becomes common property. Here, an auditor should see that the ledger value or cost of the patent is gradually written off, on the same principle as the cost of a lease, so as to liquidate the original outlay by the time the patent right or monopoly has ceased to be of value.

The treatment of the cost of Goodwill, as we are accustomed to meet with it in the accounts of Joint Stock Companies, is a more difficult matter, and the issues involved are far more important. I should like therefore to refer to an illustration given by Mr. Francis More, in the admirable and suggestive paper on this subject, read before the Chartered Accountants Students' Society of Edinburgh, and reported in *The Accountant* of April 11th 1891 :—

"Take for example," he says, "a trading concern with

"tangible assets, the full going value of which is ascertained "to be £100,000, and suppose it is earning and is likely to "earn 8% or £8,000 a year. I would say that the total price "should not exceed the value of the tangible assets, viz:— "£100 000, because no more than an ordinary return is "being got. But suppose the concern is earning and is "likely to earn 13%, or £13,000 a year, then I think a fair "price might be seven annual payments of the extra £5,000, "or a present payment of £26,030, less 8% discount. In "this case the price would be the above £100,000 plus "£26,030, or together £126,030. Suppose, again, it is "earning 18%, or £18,000 a year; then I think a fair price "might be the above £126,030 plus five annual payments "of £5,000, or a present payment of £19,963; in this case the "price would be £145,993," and so on.

"It appears to me," he says further on, "that the period "within which the price paid for Goodwill should be re- "placed out of Revenue ought - to a large extent, at least— "to be regulated by the number of years' purchase of the "profits which the price represents. For instance, in the "case which I have assumed in order to illustrate my views "as to how the price should be ascertained," (quoted above), "I assume that £26,030 would be a suitable present pay- "ment to make for a Goodwill which produced £5,000 a year "in excess of the ordinary return. This present payment of "£26,030 represents seven yearly payments of £5,000 (less "discount at 8 per cent.), and I am disposed to think that in "such a case one-seventh of the present payment of "£26,030 should be set aside yearly out of Revenue until a "reserve of £26,030 was reared up. If this plan were "adopted, the result would be, so far as the payment of divi- "dends is concerned, that the ordinary shareholders would "only get during the first seven years 8 per cent. on their "money plus any increase on the profits beyond the amount "dealt with in fixing the price, and plus also any saving "which might be effected by raising money either on deben- "ture or on preference stock at a lower rate than 8 per "cent. Of course, the profits might fall below the amount "reckoned on when the purchase is made, and in that case "the shareholders would have to judge whether they would "continue to set aside yearly the amount I have indicated, "and be satisfied with smaller dividends. The shrinkage of "the profits would, however, only emphasise the risk which "had been run in purchasing the Goodwill."

I think the above affords a sound and practical method of dealing with Goodwill. There may be no *legal* obligation on directors or shareholders to make that reserve which prudent men of business would certainly make to replace capital sunk in Goodwill. But, as I have already urged, our duty as auditors includes the protection of interests other than those of the present proprietors. There should be some recognised principles as to the purchase of Goodwill, but whether these can be agreed upon or not, the necessity remains, I think, that Chartered Accountants should hold some sound and workable principle in regard to the liquidation of such an intangible asset as Goodwill, "for," as Mr. Francis More rightly contends "it must be apparent to all that every "penny that is paid away in the shape of dividends to ordinary "shareholders which ought in prudence to have been applied "either in replacing capital, or in securing capital, lessens the "security which by right belongs to the holders of debentures "and preference stocks."

The foregoing Essay cannot pretend to be a complete statement of the principles upon which the assets of a Joint Stock Company should be valued. Its length has necessarily and advisedly been curtailed, but I hope that in spite of its imperfections and errors, it may prove a useful contribution to the consideration of a most important subject.

A discussion followed the reading of the Essay, and the meeting terminated with the customary votes of thanks.

THE CAPITAL OF A COMPANY WITH SPECIAL REFERENCE TO ITS REDUCTION

P. O. Laurence

Liverpool Chartered Accountants Students' Association.

THE CAPITAL OF A COMPANY, WITH SPECIAL REFERENCE TO ITS REDUCTION.

By Mr. P. O. Laurence, Barrister-at-Law.

At a meeting of this society held last month, Mr. Lawrence read the following paper :—

One of the main principles of the Companies Act 1862, designed for the purpose of protecting persons dealing with companies, is the unalterable character of the Memorandum of Association. Every company formed under that Act is required to state certain fundamental particulars relating to its constitution in a document which is called the Company's Memorandum of Association, which is registered and is accessible to all the world. Except in two particulars not calculated to affect persons dealing with the company, the Act of 1862 provides that the Memorandum is to be unalterable.

With regard to matters of constitution and regulations for internal management which are not required to be contained in the Memorandum of Association, these may be contained in documents called the Articles of Association of the Company. Unlike the Memorandum, the Articles of Association can, under the Act of 1862, be altered at the wish of the members of the company, though not by a bare majority, for the Act requires a special resolution to be passed—that is, a resolution passed by a majority of three-fourths at one meeting, and confirmed within fourteen days at another meeting by a simple majority.

The principle that the constitution of a company so far as contained in the Memorandum is unalterable has, since the passing of the Companies Act 1862, been gradually encroached upon by successive Acts of Parliament, the last of which is the Companies (Memorandum of Association) Act 1890. These Acts have almost done away with the principle, and now the Memorandum of Association can be altered in every particular except one, but the sanction of the Court is in most cases necessary.

There are two kinds of companies which may be formed under the Companies Act 1862, namely, companies with unlimited liability and companies with limited liability; the latter kind is further sub-divided into two classes, namely, companies limited by shares and companies limited by guarantee.

With regard to all three kinds of companies, the Act of 1862 provides that the Memorandum of Association shall contain three particulars, namely:

(1) The name of the company; this is one of the particulars which the Act of 1862 allows to be altered; requiring, however, the sanction of the Board of Trade.

(2) Whether the registered office of the company is in England, Scotland, or Ireland—that is, the domicile of the company. This is the only particular which is left unalterable by subsequent legislation. And

(3) The objects for which the company is formed.

No further matters are required to be stated in the memorandum of association of a company with unlimited liability, but with regard to companies whose liability is limited, certain particulars, from which the limit of the liability of the members of the company can be determined, are, as we might expect, required to be contained in the memorandum.

In the case of companies limited by shares, the limit of the liability of a member depends upon the amount unpaid upon the shares held by him. Sec. 38 (4) providing that, in the case of a company limited by shares, no contributions shall be required from any member exceeding the amount, if any, unpaid on the shares in respect of which he is liable as a member, past or present. The amount of the share capital, therefore, affords the requisite data for determining the limit of the liability of the members of the company, and accordingly the Memorandum of Association is required to contain a statement of the amount of the capital with which the company proposes to be registered, divided into shares of a certain fixed amount. The Act of 1862 permits the capital to be increased by special resolution, this being not calculated to injure but to benefit the outside world, and being, therefore, one of the exceptions to the rule permitting no alteration in the Memorandum. But no reduction of capital was allowed, this having the effect of reducing the liability of the members.

In the case of companies limited by guarantee the method of defining the limit of the liability of the members is by requiring the Memorandum to contain a declaration (binding on all the members) that each member undertakes to contribute to the assets of the company in the event of the same being wound up during the time that he is a member, or within one year afterwards, for payment of the debts and liabilities contracted before the time at which he ceases to be a member, and of costs of winding-up, &c., such amount as may be required, not exceeding a certain amount.

It will be seen, therefore, that the amount of capital of a company limited by shares is an important part of the machinery by which the liability of the members of the company is determined, and is to be contained in the memorandum of association. But with unlimited companies, and companies limited by guarantee, the amount of capital plays no such important part in the constitution of the company, and is a matter which may be relegated to the articles of association, and can, therefore, be altered by a special resolution, and no difficulties of a legal character arise as to reduction of capital.

I will, therefore, confine this lecture to the capital of companies limited by shares. When used with regard to this kind of company, the word acquires no less than three artificial meanings in addition to its ordinary meaning. And the question in which of these meanings it is used, even when occurring in Acts of Parliament, is not always easy to answer.

I will now proceed to examine these various meanings of the word capital; and first I will explain what I have called the three artificial meanings; and I think I shall best do this by means of an illustration. We will suppose that a company limited by shares is registered with a capital, as stated in its memorandum of association, of £300,000, divided into 30,000 shares of £10 each. Of the 30,000 shares we will suppose that only 20,000 are subscribed for. We will suppose for simplicity that all the shares are paid for in cash, and that £5 per share is paid up, leaving the balance of £5 per share liable to be called up, either for the benefit of the company, or, if it is wound up, for the benefit of the company's creditors. Now, in speaking of the company's capital, we may mean one of three things, namely:—

(1) Its nominal capital, that is, the amount stated in the memorandum, viz., £300,000, divided into 30,000 shares of £10 each.

(2) Its issued capital, that is, that part of the nominal capital which has been taken up, viz., £200,000, or 20,000 shares.

(3) Its paid-up capital, that is, that part of the issued capital which is represented by actual payments, viz., £100,000, or £5 per share.

With regard to the paid-up capital, I have assumed in my illustration that this is all represented by cash paid by the members on the allotment to them of their shares, but it was held [a] not necessary that the members should contribute cash only, but they can contribute property in specie, or money's worth upon which a value is set, and the amount of such value is credited to them as if it had been paid in cash. The usual method of effecting this is by means of an agreement for sale to the company in consideration of shares credited with an amount paid up upon them equal to the value set on the property sold. The amount credited on these shares is generally their full nominal amount, so that no liability attaches to them.

It is evident that this method of selling property to the company in consideration of fully or partly paid-up shares is liable to abuse. The vendors are often in a position to obtain a far greater nominal price in shares than the true value of property sold, and therefore both the shareholders who pay in cash and the creditors of the company who rely on the amount of the company's capital are liable to be deceived. To remedy this the Com anies Act 1867 was passed, which provides [b] that every share in any company shall be deemed and taken to have been issued, and to be held subject to the payment of the whole amount thereof in cash, unless the same shall have been otherwise determined by a contract in writing and filed with the Registrar of Joint Stock Companies at or before the issue of such shares.

The Act then clearly recognises, though it does not expressly affirm, the validity of a contract involving the crediting of the amount of value of property or labour sold or supplied to the company as actually paid, but imposes upon it the condition of being filed with the Registrar of Joint Stock Companies before the issue of the shares.

The paid-up capital of a company may, therefore, be defined as that part of the nominal capital which is represented, in the first instance, by payments of the same amount in cash, or contribution of money's worth.

It was thought, at one time, that this was not necessarily so, and that paid-up capital might be represented by payments of a less amount than the nominal amount of the paid-up capital; in other words, that the company might issue its shares at a discount, subject, of course, to the filing of a contract. Mr. Justice Chitty decided this to be legal in two cases which came before him in the year 1883 [a], relying on the analogy of statutes governing railway companies [b] which permit this. The decisions were, however, overruled by the Court of Appeal [c], and more recently by the House of Lords [d]. The judgment of Lord Herschell in this case is well worth reading, and shows how very slight the reasons for the decisions are, so far as regards the provisions of the Companies Acts.

Closely allied with this question is the question whether, where the shares of a company are admittedly at a discount, the company can evade the effect of these decisions as to not issuing shares at a discount, by purchasing goods or remunerating labour by giving shares instead of money, on the footing that these are treated as of less than their nominal value. This question has yet to be decided [e], though, under ordinary circumstances, and especially before the companies' shares have been put upon the market, there is some expression of judicial opinion that the Court will not go into the question whether the property contributed is worth the amount credited on the shares given in exchange for it, unless a case of fraud is made out, any more than it would interfere with an improvident contract by the company to buy property at a greater price in cash than the true value of the property [f].

These meanings of the word capital, which I have distinguished by the names, nominal capital, issued capital, and paid-up capital, arise from the peculiar constitution of companies whose liability is limited by the amount unpaid

[a] See cases cited by *Buckley*, 6th Ed., p. 553.

[b] Section 25.

[a] *Plaskynaston Tube Co.*, 23 Ch.D. 542, and *In re Hall Co., ibedem* 545 *n.*

[b] See Companies Clauses Act, 1863, as amended by sec. 27 of the Railway Companies Act, 1867, and Companies Clauses Act, 1869, sec. 5 and 6.

[c] *Almada & Tirito Co.*, 38 Ch.D. 415.

[d] *Ooregum Gold Mining Company*, 1892, A.C. 125.

[e] See *Almada & Tirito Co.*, 38 Ch.D., per Cotton L.J., at p. 415.

[f] See, for instance, *Lee v. Neuchâtel Asphalte Co.*, 41 Ch.D. 1, per Stirling, J., at p. 9, per Cotton, L.J., at p. 15.

on their shares. The word capital has, however, another, and more general meaning, which is not confined to this class of companies; but is equally applicable to the case of unlimited companies and companies limited by guarantee, and also to private partnerships, that is, capital in the sense of all the property of the company which is not distributable among its members as income or dividends. This meaning of the word capital I shall call for distinction "capital as distinguished from income."

What part of the property of a company limited by shares is income, and what is capital depends on the system of accounts adopted by the company, and is a matter which no doubt is more familiar to accountants than to lawyers, which perhaps accounts for the considerable difference of opinion there exists among lawyers as to which is the right system of accounts.

There are two rival systems of accounts, namely, the Single Account system and the Double Account system.

According to the Single Account system, what is income and what is capital is determined by a Balance Sheet prepared at stated intervals. In this Balance Sheet, on the debit side, are written the debts and liabilities of the company and the amount of its paid-up capital. That is, the amount of the paid-up capital is treated as a debt due to the members. On the credit side of the account is placed the value of the various items constituting the property of the company. Then, if there is any excess on the credit side, this appears in the shape of the "balance" on the debit side. This balance, which is the excess of the value of the company's assets over its liabilities (including paid-up capital) is the measure of the income of the company.

This system is well adapted for a company whose principal business consists in buying and selling, and, in a recent case ([a]), Mr. Justice Chitty laid down that it was the proper principle to be adopted for the purpose of ascertaining the profit of a trading company.

But where the principal property of the company is of a more or less permanent character, such as ships, or a tramway, or a mine, opinions of lawyers have differed a great deal as to whether the Single Account system or the Double is the right one.([b]) It is objected to the Single Account system that this involves, in cases of this sort, the periodical revaluation of assets of a permanent character, which may be difficult and perhaps impracticable, and, moreover, turn out to be false after the imagined surplus of assets over liabilities has been realised and distributed. Those who advocate the Single Account system reply to these objections that these revaluations are not necessary so long as there is no known reason to suppose that the assets have become depreciated and that temporary fluctuations may be disregarded. Moreover, as regards any increase in value, there is no necessity to realise and distribute the amount of this increase at once, but it can be kept as a reserve fund till it is established beyond doubt that the increase in value is permanent.

([a]) *Lubbock v. British Bank of South America* [1892] (2 Ch. 198). This case seems, however, to carry the principle too far, see *Solicitors' Journal*.

([b]) See the note in *Palmer*, 5th Ed., p. 345, where the Single Account system is advocated; and *Buckley*, 6th Ed., p. 513, where the Double Account system is advocated.

The Double Account system, on the other hand, is this, namely, that Capital Account and Revenue Account should be distinct accounts, and that, for the purpose of determining profits, you must disregard accretions to, or diminutions of, capital. According to this system the capital of a company is its permanent property, and the income is the excess of receipts over expenditure.

It will be seen that, so long as the permanent property of a company has not been known to have permanently depreciated or increased, in practice there is not much difference which system is adopted; but we will consider two instances in which a great deal depends upon this.

First take the case of a ship company owning ten ships, none of which are insured: one of these is lost. Now, if the Double Account system is adopted, the profits arising from the remaining nine ships can be distributed; but, if the Single Account system is adopted, no profits can be divided until the value of the lost ship is replaced.

Another instance is the case of a company owning a mine held on a lease: the permanent property of this company is of less value every year, as the unexpired term the lease has to run becomes shorter, and the minerals are worked out. If the Double Account system is adopted, the company may go on distributing profits till the expiration of the lease, when its capital would be nil. If, however, the Single Account system were adopted, the company would be obliged every year to set aside part of the earnings of the mine to form a fund out of which other property could be acquired, or a renewal of the existing lease obtained.

The Single Account system claims this advantage in cases of companies with permanent capital, that it affords a criterion for the amount to be expended out of the earnings upon repairs and improvements, that is, the amount required to keep the capital up to its original value.

In the recent case of *Lee v. Neuchatel Co.* (41 Ch.D. 1) ([a]) however, the Court of Appeal decided that a mining company working wasting property is under no obligation to adopt the Single Account system; but that it can divide the excess of the earnings of the mine over the working expenses as dividend; and this case points to the conclusion that the Double Account system is the right one in all cases where the assets of the company are of a permanent character.

Armed with these definitions of the different meanings of the word capital, we are now in a position to attack the main subject of this lecture, namely, the reduction of capital.

([a]) See also *Bolton v. Natal Land & Colonisation Co.* [1892] (2 Ch.D. 125), following this decision.

We have seen that, under the Act of 1862, no reduction of capital was allowed, as that was altering the memorandum of association to the prejudice of persons who might rely upon it; and this remained the state of the law till the Companies Act, *1867*, was passed. This Act enabled a company limited by shares *to reduce* its capital upon obtaining the sanction of the Court and the consent of all the creditors of the company whose debts were not paid off or fully secured.

The machinery for the reduction of capital, which we find in the Act of 1867, is as follows: The 9th section provides that any company limited by shares may so far modify its memorandum of association if authorised so to do by its articles as originally framed, or as altered by special resolution, as to reduce its capital; but no such resolution shall come into operation until an order of the Court is registered with the Registrar of Joint Stock Companies. Section 10 provides that the company shall, after the passing of the special resolution, add to its name, until such date as the Court may fix, the words "and reduced," as the last words of its name. Section 11 provides that the Court may, on petition—if satisfied that, with respec to every creditor entitled to object, either his consent has been obtained or his debt discharged, or secured as provided by the Act—make an order confirming the reduction upon such terms and conditions as it deems fit. Section 13 defines the creditors entitled to object as those who, at the date fixed by the Court, are entitled to any debt or claim which if that date were the commencement of the winding up of the company, would be admissible in proof against the company, and the Court is to settle a list of creditors. Section 14 defines the nature of the security required to be given to a creditor in order to dispense with his consent. Section 15 provides that the order of the Court and minute (approved by the Court) shewing the amount of the capital of the company and the number and amount of shares in which it is to be divided as allowed by the order, is to be registered; and Section 16 provides that this minute is to form part of the memorandum, and that, subject to the saving clause contained in the Act, no member of the company, past or present, shall be liable in respect of any call or contribution exceeding in amount the difference (if any) between the amount paid on such share and the amount of such share as fixed by the minute. Section 17, which is the last section we need notice, contains a saving of the rig_ts of creditors ignorant of the proceedings for reduction.

It will be seen that the Act empowers the company "to reduce its capital." There is no definition given either of the whole phrase or of the word "capital," and the question naturally arises as to what operations are included in the phrase.

One of the operations which is evidently authorised by the Act is the reduction of the nominal amount of each share by cancelling the whole or part of the amount unpaid on each share, the effect of which is to reduce each member's liability to the amount of the difference (if any) between the amount which has been paid on his shares and the amount of the share as fixed by the minute embodying the order sanctioning the reduction, as is provided by Section 16 of the Act of 1867. For instance, a company with the capital of £100,000 divided into 10,000 shares of £10 each, on which £5 has been paid up, obtains the sanction of the Court to reduce its capital from that amount to £75,000, divided into 10,000 shares of £7 10s. The effect of this is to reduce the liability of the members from £5 per share to £2 10s. per share.

That this operation was included under the phrase reduction of capital in the Act of 1867 is clear from the provisions as to the consent of, or giving security to, the creditors, and from the provision contained in Section 16 as to the reduction of capital; but there are certain other operations which might be also included in this phrase. One of these is the reduction of the company's paid-up capital—that is, reducing the nominal amount of each share by cancelling part of the nominal amount paid up, without reducing the nominal amount unpaid, and therefore without reducing the liability of the members. This is done so as to make the nominal amount of the paid-up capital accord with the true value of the assets of the company, when the latter have been reduced in value by sudden loss or gradual depreciation, as in our previous example of the loss of one of ten ships and the case of the company working a mine held on lease. The object of such a reduction is obvious if the Single Account system is used—that is, to enable a dividend to be declared before the loss of the company's assets is made good out of capital. If the Double Account system is used the object is not quite so obvious, but is explained, by those who defend that system, in this way: Income or dividend is defined as excess of gross receipts or earnings over gross expenditure. If there had been an excess of expenditure over earnings in any year this must be made good out of the earnings of the next year before any dividend can be distributed. If, however, the capital is reduced, part of assets appearing in the capital account can be applied in reduction of the loss without being liable to be replaced out of income; in other words, it enables part of the capital to be transferred from the capital to the Income Account and to be treated as income. [a]

It seems that reduction of capital by cancelling lost capital was generally understood to have been included in the power given by the Act of 1867, [b] but in the year 1877 Jessel, M.R., decided that this was not included, [c] on the ground that the whole frame of the Act showed that it applied to the case of reduction of liability only.

The learned Master of the Rolls, in his judgment, expressed a hope that, if the Legislature were to amend the Act of Parliament, some provision would be made for enabling the Court to do that which it could not do then; which

---

[a] See *Palmer*, 5th Ed., p. 352, citing *Buckley's* 4th and 5th Ed.

[b] See *Buckley*, 6th Ed., and the unreported cases there cited.

[c] *Re Ebbw Vale Co.*, 4 Ch.D. 833.

hope was destined to be speedily fulfilled, for in less than seven months the Companies Act 1877 was passed, enabling such a reduction to be made.

The Act of 1877 recites in its preamble that doubts had been entertained whether the power given by the Companies Act 1867 to a company of reducing its capital, extends to paid-up capital, and that it is expedient to remove such doubts, therefore not recognising the decision of the Master of the Rolls as necessarily good law. The Act then declares that "capital," as used in the Companies Act 1867, shall include paid-up capital; and that the power to reduce capital, conferred by that Act, should include a power to cancel any lost capital or any capital unrepresented by available assets or to pay off any capital which may be in excess of the wants of the company, and that paid-up capital would be reduced either with or without extinguishing or reducing the liability (if any) remaining on the shares.

This section therefore permits two operations, namely, the cancellation of lost capital, which I have described, and the paying off of capital, that is returning it to the shareholders, which does not involve, but can be combined with, the reduction of the nominal amount of the shares, and may thus leave the amount returned liable to be recalled ([a])

The 4th Section of the Act provides that, where the reduction of the capital of a company does not involve either the diminution of any liability in respect of unpaid capital, or the payment to any shareholder of any paid-up capital, thus (1) the creditors of the company shall not, unless the Court otherwise direct, be entitled to object or require to consent to the reduction; (2) it shall not be necessary, before the presentation of the petition for confirming the reduction to add, and the Court may, if it thinks expedient, so to do, dispense with the addition of the words "and reduced."

The 5th Section gives power to any company limited by shares to reduce its capital by cancelling unissued shares by special resolution merely, and without the sanction of the Court.

It will be seen, therefore, that there are four different methods of reducing capital authorised by the Acts of 1867 and 1877, which are as follows:--

(1) Reduction by cancelling uncalled capital, and so reducing the liability of the members.

(2) Reduction of paid-up capital by returning part of the paid-up capital to the members with or without being liable to be recalled.

(3) Reduction of paid-up capital by cancelling lost capital; and

(4) Reduction of the nominal capital by cancelling unpaid shares.

The Acts of 1867 and 1877 contain all the provisions now in force relative to the reduction of the capital of a company limited in force, unless we include in that expression the operation authorised by the Companies Act 1880. That Act authorises a company, by special resolution, to apply accumulated profits, which may be distributed as dividend or bonus in reduction of the paid-up capital of the company, the unpaid capital being increased by a similar amount. This operation is, indeed, a reduction of the nominal amount of the paid-up capital, but it is evident that, except on paper, the only effect of it is to increase the liability of the members, nothing having been paid to the members which was not payable to them before, and the capital—in the sense of capital as distinguished from income—of the company is not reduced.

([a]) See *Palmer*, 5th Ed., p. 373, citing *Northmore Co.* (unreported), confirmed by Kay, J., 9 Feb., 1883, since frequently followed.

I have said that the only effect of an exercise of the power given by the Act of 1880 is to increase the liability of the members, and this is so if the Double Account system is used, as is evidently intended.([a]) But if the Single Account system were used the result would be very startling, and would defeat the provisions of the Acts of 1867 and 1877. Suppose, for example, a company with a paid-up capital of £20,000 has £5,000 in hand, representing accumulated profits. This would appear in the balance sheet by the assets being £5,000 more than the liabilities and paid-up capital. Now, suppose the £5,000 is paid to the members in reduction of the paid-up capital, which would be reduced to £15,000, and if a balance sheet were then made out it would still show a balance of £5,000, (for the nominal amount of the paid-up capital and the assets have been each decreased by the same amount), and this £5,000 might be again distributed so as to reduce the paid-up capital to £10,000, and again showing a balance of £5,000. And so this process might be repeated till £20,000, in addition to the original £5,000, had been distributed. This can hardly have been intended by the Act; indeed, it is hard to say what was intended, for if the only object was to enable the company to increase its liability no new Act was needed for this, as the Companies Act 1862 permits the increase of capital, and all that would be necessary to increase the liability of the members would be to pass a special resolution to increase the nominal amount of the shares. The only difference that this method has would be that in future the dividends would be at a less rate per cent. than if the operation sanctioned by the Act of 1880 were adopted, so that the company would look more prosperous on paper.

We have now completed our survey of the provisions of the Companies Acts relating to the reduction of capital of a company limited by shares. I shall conclude this lecture by noticing two ways of reducing capital which, though not expressly prohibited by the Companies Acts, have been held to be impliedly prohibited, and consequently illegal. They are: (1) paying dividends out of capital; (2) the company acquiring its own shares; (3) or improperly cancelling or accepting a surrender of its own shares.

With regard to the payment of dividends out of capital, there is no express prohibition of this in the Companies Acts. Table A. in the schedule of the Companies Act, 1862,

([a]) See *Buckley*, 6th Ed., 595.

which is a model set of articles of association, and which apply to any company limited by shares unless excluded by its own articles, contains a clause (73) providing that no dividend shall be payable except out of profits, and most articles of association contain a similar provision. The matter does not, however, depend upon the provisions of the articles, as seems to have been assumed by the earlier cases [a]; but it rests upon the general law. The reasons for holding payment of dividend out of capital illegal are two, namely: (1) It involves the reduction of paid-up capital, for which the Acts of 1867 and 1877 prescribe a particular procedure, and, therefore, they impliedly prohibit any other mode of reducing paid-up capital, which is the effect of payment of dividends; (2) It involves the application of the capital of the company to objects not specified in the memorandum of association.

These two grounds for supporting the principle seem to have been first recognised by Jessel, M.R. [b]. Both grounds are equally conclusive, so that the principle, which is now established beyond doubt [c], cannot be evaded by an apt provision in the memorandum of association giving the company power to apply its capital in payment of dividend [d], though some of the cases appear to go only on the ground that the memorandum gives no power to so apply the capital [e].

Closely analogous to this principle is the principle that the company cannot purchase its own shares, and the same reasons are given, namely, that it is in effect a reduction of the company's capital without going through the procedure prescribed by the Companies Acts, and that it is an application of the company's capital for purpose not authorised; and the House of Lords have affirmed the principle, which is now beyond doubt on these grounds [f].

---

[a] *Dent v. London Tramways Co.* (16 Ch.D. 344); *Davies v. Gillies* (16 Ch.D. 347); *National Funds Co.* (10 Ch.D. 118, 127); *Wills v. Northern Railway of Buenos Ayres Co.* (5 Ch.D. 621). The decision in the case of *MacDougal v. Jersey Hotel Co.* (2 H. & M. 528, 1864), was irrespective of the articles.

[b] *Flitcroft's case* (21 Ch.D. 519, 533).

[c] *Guinness v. Land Corporation* (22 Ch.D. 375) approved; *Trevor v. Whitworth* (12 App.Ca. 409); *Denham & Co.* (25 Ch.D., 752); *Oxford Building Society* (35 Ch.D., 509); *Leeds Estate Co. v. Shepherd* (36 Ch.D. 787).

[d] In *Trevor v Whitworth* (12 App.Ca. 409); *Raines' case* (1 L.R. 203); *Messina & Adana Co.* (5 T.L.R. 680), &c.

[e] See *Guinness v. Land Corporation of Ireland* (22 Ch.D.).

[f] *Trevor v. Whitworth* (12 App.Ca. 409).

The third operation, which I have described as a prohibited method of reducing capital, is by the company improperly cancelling or accepting a surrender of its shares. A company can no doubt in a proper case cancel and accept surrender of its shares, but this becomes illegal precisely where it amounts to a reduction of its capital. The law on the subject is well summed up by Lord Herschell [a]. He says "The forfeiture of shares is distinctly recognised by "the Companies Act, and by the articles contained in the "Schedule [b], which, in the absence of other provisions, "regulate the management of a limited liability company. "It does not involve any payment by the company, and it "presumably exonerates from liability those who have "shown themselves unable to contribute what is due from "them to the capital of the company. Surrender, no doubt, "stands on a different footing. But it also does not involve "any payment out of the funds of the company. If the "surrender were made in consideration of any such pay-"ment, it would be neither more nor less than a sale, and "open to the same objections. If it were accepted in a "case when the company were in a position to forfeit the "shares, the transaction would seem to me perfectly valid. "There may be other cases in which a surrender would be "legitimate [c]. As to these I would repeat what was said "by the late Master of the Rolls, in *re Donfield &c. Co.* [d]. "It is not for me to say what the limits of surrender are "which are allowable under the Act, because each case as "it arises must be decided upon its own merits."

We have now touched on all the more important topics connected with the capital of a company and its reduction, and we have seen what an important part it plays in the constitution of a company limited by shares, and I hope that this lecture will serve to impress firmly on your minds the fundamental principles on the subject which are to be found in the Companies Act, and the body of law built up upon their foundation by the decisions of our Courts.

---

[a] 12 App. Ca., 417.

[b] Table A., cl. 19.

[c] Lord Herschell was no doubt alluding to such a case as *Teasdale's Case*, (9 Ch.D. 54), where the surrender was in consideration of fresh shares with greater liability. The case is, however, of doubtful authority.

[d] 17 Ch.D. 76.

VERNER *Versus* THE GENERAL AND COMMERCIAL INVESTMENT TRUST (LIMITED)

[IN THE CHANCERY DIVISION AND IN THE COURT OF APPEAL.]

STIRLING, J.
1893.
Nov. 23, 24.
1894.
March 2, 6.
LINDLEY, L.J.
KAY, L.J.
SMITH, L.J.
March 14, 15, 16, 20.
April 7.

VERNER *v.* THE GENERAL AND COMMERCIAL INVESTMENT TRUST (LIMITED).

Company—Payment of Dividends out of Capital—Loss of Capital by Depreciation—Obligation of Company to keep up Capital—Reduction of Capital — Companies Act, 1877 (40 & 41 *Vict. c.* 26), *s.* 3.

Where a limited company has sunk its capital in any trade or business authorised by its memorandum of association, and part of such capital is lost, the company is not bound, in the absence of any special provisions in the memorandum or articles, to make good the loss before declaring a dividend.

Decision of STIRLING, J., *affirmed.*

This was an action by W. H. Verner, on behalf of himself and all stockholders of the General and Commercial Investment Trust (Limited) other than the defendants, against the company and four of its directors, for an injunction to restrain the defendants from declaring or distributing any dividend for the financial year ending the 28th of February, 1894.

The company was incorporated on the 26th of January, 1888, with a memorandum and articles of association. The objects of the company, as defined by section 3 of the memorandum, were (*a*) "to raise money by share capital and invest the amount thereof in or otherwise acquire and hold" a variety of investments enumerated in the memorandum; (*b*) "to borrow or raise money by the issue of . . . . debentures or debenture stock of the company, or in any other manner, . . . and to invest the money so obtained in any such investments as aforesaid," (*c*) to acquire any such investments as aforesaid by original subscription or otherwise in manner therein mentioned; "to vary any such investments, and generally to sell, exchange, or otherwise dispose of, deal with, or turn to account any of the assets of the company"; (*i*) "to receive the dividends, income, profits, bonuses, and advantages of every description from time to time payable or receivable in respect of the company's investments, and to apply the same respectively according to the provisions of the articles of association in force for the time being."

The articles provided as follows:

"80. The share and debenture capital moneys of the company, including any moneys received from the payment off of investments or securities, shall, after paying thereout all expenses of a capital nature, be invested in investments and securities of the kinds mentioned in the memorandum of association."

"81. The trustees shall on making any change of investment or other financial transaction of the company maintain as nearly as possible the relative rights of and separation between capital moneys and income, and shall deal with the same accordingly."

"84. Subject to the rights of members holding share capital issued upon special conditions, the receipts of the company from the dividends, income, profits, bonuses, and advantages payable or receivable in respect of the company's investments shall be applicable as follows:

"1st. To the payment of a dividend for the particular year at the rate of five per cent. per annum on the preferred stock.

"2nd. To the payment of such a dividend on the deferred stock as the same shall suffice to pay.

"And the trustees may, with the sanction of the company in general meeting, declare a dividend to be paid to the members accordingly."

"85. The trustees may, before recommending any dividend, set aside out of the profits of the company such sum as they think proper, as a reserve fund to meet contingencies or for equalising dividends, or for any other purposes of the company; and may from time to time apply the whole or any part of such fund for any purposes of the company."

"86. When in the opinion of the trustees the profits of the company permit, interim dividends not exceeding five per cent. per annum may be declared and paid by the board on account of the dividend for the then current year on both preferred and deferred stocks, and if the profits for the whole year shall in such case prove insufficient to pay the full dividend of five per cent. for such year on the preferred stock, the holders of such stock shall not be entitled to have the deficiency made up."

"110. The surplus assets of the company upon the winding-up thereof shall be applied, first, in repaying the holders of the preferred stock the amount paid up in respect thereof; then in repaying to the holders of the deferred stock the amount paid up in respect thereof; and the residue, if any, shall be divided among the members in proportion to the nominal amount of the capital held by them respectively."

The capital of the company consisted of 600,000*l.*, divided into 60,000 shares, all of which had been issued and fully paid up. They were subsequently converted into stock of two classes—preferred and deferred.

In addition to these funds the company borrowed 300,000*l.* on security of debenture stock of a like nominal amount, bearing interest at four per cent.

The 900,000*l.* thus obtained was invested in stocks of various kinds. The present market value of the investments stood at 654,000*l.*, shewing a depreciation of 246,000*l.*; and of this depreciation 75,000*l.* represented the amount which there was no prospect of recovering within a reasonable time. The receipts of the company in respect of income derived from these investments, after deducting the current expenditure—such as the expenses of management and interest on the debenture stock—amounted for the past financial year to 23,000*l.* This action was brought to determine the question whether this 23,000*l.* could be applied in dividends without first making good the loss of 75,000*l.* in respect of capital. The plaintiff now moved for an injunction in the terms of the writ.

Graham Hastings, Q.C., and *Kirby*, for the plaintiff.

Buckley, Q.C., and *Eve*, for the defendants.

Cur. adv. vult.

STIRLING, J. (on March 6), stated the facts, and continued: The first enquiry is, What is the law upon the subject? Up to a certain point that is clear. The general propositions I may take from a case of the highest authority—namely, *Trevor* v. *Whitworth* (1), in the House of Lords. [His Lordship read a passage from the judgment of the Lord Chancellor (Lord Herschell), commencing with the words "The Companies Act, 1862, requires," and concluding with the words "was considered to be."] It has been held, and is well-settled law, that where the annual receipts do not exceed the expenditure, or there happen to be, from any cause, no annual receipts at all, the capital cannot be applied in payment of dividends upon shares. That has been determined in many cases, and I may mention, among others, *Flitcroft's Case* (2) and *Guinness* v. *The Land Corporation of Ireland* (3). In the present case it is not proposed to resort to capital for the payment of dividends. What is in dispute is the question whether the excess of receipts over expenditure can be applied for the payment of a dividend while there remains a deficit on the capital.

A point of a very similar nature came before the late Master of the Rolls in the case of *In re The Ebbw Vale Steel, Iron, and Coal Company* (4), where a petition was presented to obtain the sanction of the Court to a reduction of capital. [His Lordship referred to the facts in that case, and continued:] The Master of the Rolls says this: "I am very sorry I cannot accede to this application, which is a most reasonable one; and I have no doubt that if the Legislature amends the Act of Parliament some provision will be made for enabling the Court to do that which I think it cannot do at present. When a joint-stock

(1) 57 Law J. Rep. Chanc. 28, 31; Law Rep. 12 App. Cas. 409, 415.

(2) 51 Law J. Rep. Chanc. 525; Law Rep. 21 Ch. D. 519.

(3) 52 Law J. Rep. Chanc. 177; Law Rep. 22 Ch. D. 349.

(4) 46 Law J. Rep. Chanc. 241; Law Rep. 4 Ch. D. 827.

company has lost a portion of its capital, nothing can be more beneficial to the company than to admit that loss—to write it off; and, if it chooses to go on trading, to trade with the diminished capital which remains, the dividend being declared on the capital actually remaining. The object of the present application is to authorise this to be done—that is, a portion of the share capital having been lost, it is desired that something should be written off each share so as to make the share of less nominal value, and to enable the company, still going on trading, to pay a dividend on the amount of the capital actually remaining; but, as I understand the Companies Act, 1867, such was not the object of the Act." That decision having been given in January of the year 1877, in the July following the Legislature passed the Companies Act of 1877. It recites that "doubts have been entertained whether the power given by the Companies Act, 1867, to a company of reducing its capital extends to paid-up capital, and it is expedient to remove such doubts." Then it enacts in section 3 (after providing in section 2 that the Act is to be incorporated and construed as one with the preceding Acts) "that the word 'capital' as used in the Companies Act, 1867, shall include paid-up capital; and the power to reduce capital conferred by that Act shall include a power to cancel any lost capital, or any capital unrepresented by available assets, or to pay off any capital which may be in excess of the wants of the company." I believe that after the passing of that Act an order was made by the late Master of the Rolls, on a petition presented by the same company, authorising the reduction of the capital in question to be made.

Now, speaking for myself, I confess that I have always read the passage which I have just cited from the judgment of Sir George Jessel as indicating his opinion to be that when a loss of capital had occurred in a company governed by the Act of 1862, dividends could not be paid unless the loss was made good. It seemed to me that the view taken by the late Master of the Rolls was this—that for the purpose of ascertaining whether a dividend should be paid or no, a balance-sheet must be made out in the same way as a balance-sheet of an ordinary trading partnership. On one side would be set down the assets of the company; on the other side would be set down, firstly, the liabilities to the outside world—namely, the creditors—and, secondly, the liabilities of the company to its own shareholders in respect of capital; and if on one side—on the side of the assets—you found an excess over the liabilities of the two classes I have mentioned, then what remained was profits, and a dividend might be declared of a proportionate amount. The application of that rule in practice, as we all know, is not without difficulty. Questions may arise on valuation of the assets, on valuation of the liabilities, and on the ascertainment of what was the capital of the shareholders; but that appears to me to be the view of the Master of the Rolls as indicated in that passage, and, I believe, in other cases which came before him.

It was suggested in argument before me that that was putting too extensive an interpretation upon the language of Sir George Jessel, and that the object of the petition was not really to enable dividends to be paid, but to reduce the amount of the shares so as to increase the apparent amount of dividend. It is said, and I believe truly, that shares would be thus rendered more marketable. For example, shares in a company with a capital of 50,000*l*., paying dividends of six per cent., would, it is said, be more valuable and sell at a higher price than shares in a company with a capital of 100,000*l*., and paying a dividend of three per cent. I can only say that if this was all that was intended I can scarcely suppose that the Legislature would have been so ready to interfere. But, however this may be, in point of fact, the Companies Act of 1877 does provide a means by which a company which has lost capital, or whose capital is to any appreciable extent not represented by available assets, may reduce that capital and so be enabled properly to pay a dividend on the reduced capital; and we all know that to this process of reduction of capital for the purpose of enabling dividends to be paid, recourse has been largely had in practice. This, I am bound to say, seems to me to be a consideration to which great weight ought to be given, and so much so that, but that I have the guidance of the judgment of the members of the Court of Appeal in the case of *Lee* v. *The Neuchatel Asphalte Company* (5), I should probably come to the conclusion that the only proper course which could be taken by a company constituted as the present company is would be to present a petition, and obtain the sanction of the Court to a reduction of capital before a dividend was declared; but, in my judgment, such a view is inconsistent with the judgment delivered by the Court of Appeal in the case to which I have referred—*Lee* v. *The Neuchatel Asphalte Company* (5). That case came before me in the first instance, and, so far as the facts go, the decision in that case does not govern the present. It was found by me that the receipts there exceeded the expenditure, and that the capital, as I understood it, remained intact; and these conclusions of fact were expressly assented to by Lord Justice Cotton, and were not dissented from by either of the other members of the Court of Appeal; but I think that, when their judgments are read, I am bound to come to the conclusion that their decision was rested on other grounds than those which appeared to justify my decision, which was affirmed. [His Lordship referred in great detail to the judgments of the Lords Justices, and continued:] It seems to me, therefore, that I must have regard to the constitution of the company and the articles of association. I must examine them and see what provisions they contain, and observe whether they authorise, not a mere division of profits, but a division of capital, meaning, in the language of Lord Justice Cotton, "permanent assets and assets not to be expended in providing for the profit earned by the company." [His Lordship then read the memorandum of association of the company, and proceeded:] Now, on that memorandum, speaking broadly, the object of the company is to raise money and to invest it. There is a power of sale of the investments, and it might be contended that that authorised the carrying on of a business in the nature of that of a stock or share broker.

(5) 58 Law J. Rep. Chanc. 408; Law Rep. 41 Ch. D. 1.

I do not think that is the true meaning. I think that what was intended was an investment company, not the business of stock or share broking at all; and in point of fact, as I understand, no such trafficking in shares has taken place, although the investments have, in accordance with the power, been from time to time varied.

The articles of association which are material are articles 80, 81, 84, 85, 86, and 110. [His Lordship read them, and continued:] The result, therefore, of not declaring a dividend, and of putting the excess of receipts over expenditure to the credit of the reserve fund, would be to preserve the capital of the company really for the ultimate benefit of the deferred shareholders, a similar result to that which would have followed in *Lee* v. *The Neuchatel Asphalte Company* (5) if the decision had been other than it was; and therefore in that respect the present company and the Neuchatel Company stand on a similar footing.

Having regard to articles 80 and 81, I read the words "profits, bonuses, and advantages" in clause (i.) of the 3rd section of the memorandum of association and in the 86th article of the articles of association as meaning profits, bonuses, and advantages in the nature of income, and not applying to any increment of capital. The scheme of the company appears to me to be to put the shareholders for the time being in the same position as regards dividends as are tenants for life under an ordinary settlement of personal property, while the persons amongst whom the capital would be divided in the event of a winding-up are intended to stand in the position of the remaindermen entitled to the *corpus* of the settled property. Tenants for life under such a settlement would take the whole income of all duly authorised investments, notwithstanding any shrinkage or decrease in their value, and would not be entitled to share in any augmentation in the value of the *corpus*, however great that might be, or however insignificant in comparison might be the increase of the income. The word "profit" in articles 85 and 86 I read as meaning "excess of income over expenses of management," and, so reading the word, I think such excess was intended to be applicable for the payment of dividend, notwithstanding shrinkage in the value of the investments or loss of capital occasioned thereby. The investments seem to me to constitute permanent assets within the meaning of Lord Justice Cotton in the passage which I have read from his judgment. Those assets remain intact save by causes over which the company has no control. Any diminution in their value has arisen not from any dealing with them by the company itself, but from their own inherent nature, and it is not sought to expend any portion of them in providing for profit or dividend.

Lastly, it appears to me that the creditors stand amply provided for, and that there is no apprehension of their being cheated, to use the expression of Lord Justice Lindley. The interest on the debenture stock, which constitutes the main liability of the company, is provided for out of the income arising from the investments, and the capital of those investments at the present time appears amply sufficient for payment of the principal.

Under these circumstances, I think it is not made out that the payment of a dividend is beyond the power of the company. Whether it is right or prudent that under these circumstances a dividend should be paid is not for me to decide, but for the men of business of whom the company is constituted. I base my decision on the peculiar nature of the constitution of this particular company, and it is not to be assumed that I should have arrived at the same conclusion if I had been dealing with an ordinary trading company—if, for example, the object of the company had been to carry on the business of a stockbroker, and the investments had been the ordinary stock-in-trade of that business.

It follows from my view of the nature of the company that the shareholders would not be entitled to divide for the purpose of dividend any increase in the value of the investments, however great. It is urged that, if this be so, my decision conflicts with the decision of Mr. Justice Chitty in *Lubbock* v. *The British Bank of South America* (6). The answer appears to me to be this—that the nature of the two companies is quite different. The British Bank of South America was evidently constituted as an ordinary trading company, and the mode which the learned Judge thinks is the proper one for making out the account of that company in respect of dividends, as stated in his judgment, shews me that that was his meaning, and he expressly distinguishes the case before him from that of *Lee* v. *The Neuchatel Asphalte Company* (5). On the contrary, in this present case I distinctly do not hold the defendant company to be an ordinary trading company.

Lord Justice Lindley, in concluding his judgment in the case of *Lee* v. *The Neuchatel Asphalte Company* (5), says this: "I hope I am not inadvertently—certainly I am not intentionally—laying down any rule which would lead people to do anything dishonest either to shareholders or creditors." I take leave, on my own behalf, to express a similar hope, and to add this—that I trust I have not misinterpreted the views of the Court of Appeal in a matter of so much importance; and, further, that, if I have, any misconceptions of mine may be speedily removed by the decision of a higher tribunal.

The plaintiff appealed.

Graham Hastings, Q.C. (*Kirby* with him), for the plaintiff.—This company is bound to make good a loss arising from the depreciation of its investments before declaring a dividend. Where the paid-up share capital has been lost, the company must obtain the sanction of the Court to a reduction of capital under the Companies Act, 1877, before a dividend can be declared—*In re The Ebbw Vale Steel, Iron, and Coal Company* (4).

Lee v. *The Neuchatel Asphalte Company* (5) is distinguishable, because in that case the Court held that, at the date of the proposed dividend, the value of the concession was greater than it was originally.

If the value of all the investments is increased, such increase is profit which may be divided—*Lubbock* v. *The British Bank of South America* (6); and conversely, if there is a decrease in the

(6) 61 Law J. Rep. Chanc. 498; Law Rep. [1892] 2 Ch. 198.

value, nothing can be divided until such decrease is made good.

Buckley, Q.C., and *Eve*, for the defendants.—In determining this question the capital account and the revenue account must be kept distinct. The profit available for dividends is the balance of receipts over expenditure. Apart from special contract, there is no obligation to make good depreciation of capital. If the capital of a company is used for the objects specified in its memorandum of association, and is lost, that is a risk which persons investing their money in the company must be prepared to take—*Trevor* v. *Whitworth* (1), *Lee* v. *The Neuchatel Asphalte Company* (5), *Dent* v. *The London Tramways Company* (7), and *Bolton* v. *The Natal Land and Colonisation Company* (8). Here the object of the company is to invest its share capital in securities and divide the income of the investments, and if the capital has been diminished while so employed, the company is not bound to make it good to the shareholders.

Kirby, in reply.—The result of the year's dealings shews an actual loss on the capital account more than sufficient to counterbalance the profit on the revenue account. The profit of the year is the result of the year's dealings looked at as a whole. The assets of the company must be either profit or capital, and if the capital is lost there can be no profit till it is made good, although part of the capital may be derived from the revenue account. If a dividend is declared under such circumstances, it will be a return of capital to the members of the company, because there is nothing to resort to but capital. Putting aside a fund for contingencies is a matter of internal management, and is within the discretion of the directors; but here there is an absolute loss of capital, which the directors are not at liberty to disregard.

Cur. adv. vult.

LINDLEY, L.J., delivered the judgment of himself and SMITH, L.J., as follows:

(7) 50 Law J. Rep. Chanc. 190; Law Rep. 16 Ch. D. 344.

(8) 61 Law J. Rep. Chanc. 281; Law Rep. [1892] 2 Ch 124.

The broad question raised by this appeal is whether a limited company which has lost part of its capital can lawfully declare or pay a dividend without first making good the capital which has been lost. I have no doubt it can—that is to say, there is no law which prevents it in all cases and under all circumstances. Such a proceeding may sometimes be very imprudent, but a proceeding may be perfectly legal and may yet be opposed to sound commercial principles. We, however, have only to consider the legality or illegality of what is complained of. As was pointed out in *Lee* v. *The Neuchatel Asphalte Company* (5), there are certain provisions in the Companies Acts relating to the capital of limited companies, but no provisions whatever as to the payment of dividends or the division of profits. Each company is left to make out its own regulations as to such payment or division. The statutes do not even expressly and in plain language prohibit a payment of dividend out of capital. But the provisions as to capital, when carefully studied, are wholly inconsistent with the return of capital to the shareholders, whether in the shape of dividends or otherwise, except, of course, on a winding-up, and there can, in my opinion, be no doubt that even if a memorandum of association contained a provision for paying dividends out of capital such provision would be invalid. The fact is that the main condition of limited liability is that the capital of a limited company shall be applied for the purposes for which the company is formed, and that to return the capital to the shareholders either in the shape of dividend or otherwise is not such a purpose as the Legislature contemplated. But there is a vast difference between paying dividends out of capital and paying dividends out of other money belonging to the company, and which is not part of the capital mentioned in the company's memorandum of association. The capital of a company is intended for use in some trade or business, and is necessarily exposed to risk of loss. As explained in *Lee* v. *The Neuchatel Asphalte Company* (5), the capital even of a limited company is not a debt owing by it to its shareholders, and if the capital is lost the company is under no legal obligation either to make it good or, on that ground only, to wind up its affairs. If, therefore, the company has any assets which are not its capital within the meaning of the Companies Acts, there is no law which prohibits the division of such assets amongst the shareholders. Further, it was decided in that case, and, in my opinion, rightly decided, that a limited company formed to purchase and work a wasting property, such as a leasehold quarry, might lawfully declare and pay dividends out of the money produced by working such wasting property without setting aside part of that money to keep the capital up to its original amount. There is no law which prevents a company from sinking its capital in the purchase or production of a money-making property or undertaking and dividing the money annually yielded by it without preserving the capital sunk so as to be able to reproduce it intact either before or after the winding-up of the company. A company may be formed upon the principle that no dividends shall be declared unless the capital is kept undiminished, or a company may contract with its creditors to keep its capital or assets up to a given value. But in the absence of some special article or contract there is no law to this effect, and, in my opinion, for very good reasons. It would, in my judgment, be most inexpedient to lay down a hard and fast rule which would prevent a flourishing company either not in debt or well able to pay its debts from paying dividends so long as its capital sunk in creating the business was not represented by assets which would, if sold, reproduce in money the capital sunk. Even a sinking fund to replace lost capital by degrees is not required by law. It is obvious that dividends cannot be paid out of capital which is lost: they can only be paid out of money which exists and can be divided. Moreover, when it is said, and said truly, that dividends are not to be paid out of capital, the word "capital" means the money subscribed pursuant to the memorandum of association, or what is represented by that money. Accretions to that capital may be realised and turned into money which may be divided amongst the shareholders, as was decided in *Lubbock* v. *The British Bank of South America* (6). But, although there is nothing in the statutes requiring even a limited company to keep up its capital, and there is no prohibition against payment of dividends out of any other of the company's assets, it does not follow that dividends may be lawfully paid out of other assets regardless of the debts and liabilities of the company. A dividend presupposes a profit in some shape, and to divide as dividend the receipts, say, for a year, without deducting the expenses incurred in that year in producing the receipts would be as unjustifiable in point of law as it would be reckless and blameworthy in the eyes of business men. The same observation applies to payment of dividends out of borrowed money. Further, if the income of any year arises from a consumption in that year of what may be called circulating capital, the division of such income as dividend without replacing the capital consumed in producing it will be a payment of a dividend out of capital within the meaning of the prohibition which I have endeavoured to explain. It has been already said that dividends presuppose profits of some sort, and this is unquestionably true. But the word "profits" is by no means free from ambiguity. The law is much more accurately expressed by saying that dividends cannot be paid out of capital than by saying that they can only be paid out of profits. The last expression leads to the inference that the capital must always be kept up and be represented by assets which, if sold, would produce it; and this is more than is required by law. Perhaps the shortest way of expressing the distinction which I am endeavouring to explain is to say that fixed capital may be sunk and lost and yet that the excess of current receipts over current payments may be divided, but that floating or circulating capital must be kept up, as otherwise it will enter into and form part of such excess, in which case to divide such excess without deducting the capital which forms part of it will be contrary to law. The Companies Acts do not require even limited companies to keep accounts, still less to keep them in any particular form. The only enactment on the subject is section 26 of the Companies Act, 1862, and Form D in the third schedule, and these relate solely to the nominal capital and calls. But, although this is so, yet, as a matter of business, accounts of some sort must be kept; and in order to shew what has been subscribed by the shareholders and what has become of the money so subscribed, and to shew the results of the company's trading or business, it is practically necessary to keep a capital account and what is called a profit and loss account, and as a matter of business these accounts ought to be kept as business men usually keep them. Accordingly, we find provisions for keeping such accounts in Table A in the Appendix to the Companies Act, 1862 (see articles 78–82), and in the articles of association of most, if not all, companies. But there is no law which compels limited companies in all cases to recoup losses shewn by the capital account out of the receipts shewn in the profit and loss account, although care must be taken not to treat capital as if it were profit. This is in accordance with *Bolton* v. *The Natal Land and Colonisation Company* (8), which is the latest reported case on the subject. Further, it is obvious that capital lost must not appear in the accounts as still existing intact; the accounts must shew the truth, and not be misleading or fraudulent. The Acts of 1867 and of 1877 are in no way inconsistent with these observations. They provide for the reduction of the nominal capital mentioned in the memorandum of association. They do not render it obligatory on a company which has lost some of its capital to reduce the nominal amount mentioned in its memorandum. There are advantages in doing so, and the Acts were passed to enable limited companies to obtain these advantages; but there is nothing in these Acts, any more than in the Act of 1862, which prevents a company which has lost part of its capital from continuing to carry on business and declaring and paying dividends. A law forbidding this may well have been considered by the Legislature far too rigid, and in their desire to check dishonest and reckless trading Courts must be careful not to put tighter fetters on companies than the Legislature has authorised. It follows from what has been said above that the proposed payment of dividend in this particular case cannot be restrained. Mr. Justice Stirling has, in his judgment, examined the memorandum and articles of association so fully that I do not think it necessary to examine them again. It is plain there is nothing in them which requires lost capital to be made good before dividends can be declared. On the contrary, they are so framed as to authorise the sinking of capital in the purchase of speculative stocks, funds, and securities, and the payment of dividends out of whatever interest, dividends, or other income such stocks, funds, and securities yield, although some of them are hopelessly bad, and the capital sunk in obtaining them is lost beyond recovery. There is no suggestion of any improper juggling with the accounts, and there is no payment of dividend out of capital. There is no insolvency, and we have not to deal with a petition to wind up. Some capital is lost, but that is all that can be truly said, and that is not enough to justify such an injunction as is sought. The appeal must be dismissed.

KAY, L.J.—I should be sorry if it were held that a joint-stock trading company can properly estimate their profits in any way differing from that in which an individual or a partnership of individuals carrying on a similar business would do. An ordinary trader takes a yearly account of all the capital employed in his business, allows for any loss or depreciation in value, and carries the balance to the profit and loss account, from which he makes out the profit or loss of the year. In this mode a loss or depreciation of such capital affects directly the profit of the year which is thereby diminished. But if upon the whole capital account there is a gain, this goes to swell the year's profit. In my opinion a joint-stock trading company should do the same. The question in this case is whether the capital employed by this company in making investments is capital employed in the business for the purpose of this usual mode of taking the year's account. If the company were formed for the purpose of buying stocks, shares, and the like to sell again, and their business was to make profit on such resale, it is obvious that any profit or loss on such transactions must be estimated in the way I have stated. But this is not their business. They buy stocks, shares, and the like, and they have power to sell and change them. But they buy as investments, and do not look to the sale as the source of their profit. They buy, we are told, all sorts of investments which nominally pay a large rate of interest—those, in short, in which a prudent man would not invest his own money—and the source of their profit is that, having very large funds entrusted to them by the confiding public, they are able out of the income of these investments to pay in most years something more to their shareholders than the three or four per cent. which represents at present the utmost income that can be obtained from safe securities. The natural result of such a reckless dealing with the moneys entrusted to them has followed in this case. There has been an actual loss of invested capital to the amount of about 75,000*l.* If the depreciation below the cost price of other investments be added to this the loss is much greater. This company seem to have been courting the fate which has overtaken other similar companies which are now in liquidation. The company have power by their articles to form out of income a reserve fund before declaring any dividend, and if they were to do this in order to make good the loss they have sustained, the directors would be acting within their powers. So if the capital had been increased by a rise in value of the investments, I conceive that they might have realised some part of that increase and distributed it as dividend. The question is whether they were compellable to do either of these things. It is argued that in the events that have happened, if they do not replace the lost capital out of income they will, in effect, be paying dividends out of capital. That is only another mode of trying the same question. If they are not bound so to replace the lost capital, they may divide the whole income among the shareholders without devoting any of it to this purpose. I have not a very confident opinion in the matter, but on the whole I am not satisfied that there is any legal obligation on the directors to do this. The persons who have been so foolish as to take shares in this company seem to me with their eyes open to have entered upon a reckless and dangerous speculation, involving an almost certain loss and depreciation of capital. They seem to me to have authorised their trustees to make the investments which they have made. In the case of any ordinary trust it is not the right of any *cestui que trust* where an authorised investment has failed to require that it should be replaced out of the income of the remaining investments. That would be sacrificing the interest of a tenant for life to that of the remaindermen. In this company the effect would be to give the deferred shareholders a benefit out of the income of the preference shareholders. [His Lordship then referred to the provisions of the memorandum and articles of association above set out, and continued:] These provisions seem to me to mean that any income received may be divided whether part of the capital is lost or not. At present I do not know of any law to prevent this, and it might be difficult to frame such a law without unduly interfering with the liberty of commercial proceedings. I have no sympathy whatever with those who have become shareholders in such an undertaking. The object and the effect of the operation of such companies is to give a fictitious value to other speculations as unsound as their own by keeping up the market price of the stock and shares in which it is their business to invest; and the sooner that it is generally understood what the probable result of such transactions may be, the better it will be for the commercial and investing classes in general.

Solicitors—Flux, Leadbitter & Jackson, for plaintiff; Ashurst, Morris, Crisp & Co., for defendants.

THE DEPRECIATION OF MACHINERY AND PLANT

E. Hartley Turner

Leeds and District Chartered Accountants Students' Association.

THE DEPRECIATION OF MACHINERY AND PLANT.

By Mr. E. HARTLEY TURNER, A.C.A.

AT a meeting of the Society held on the 15th February 1894, Mr. TURNER delivered the following lecture :—

WHEN your late secretary, Mr. Butterfield, honoured me with the request that I would deliver a lecture before your society, I readily assented, as I felt that the students' societies connected with our Institute are doing exceeding good work, and are labouring to produce a race of accountants more and more worthy of the increasing confidence which is being reposed in us by the mercantile and investing public. And when I reviewed the ungrudging efforts that were made, in my student days, by our local seniors, I felt that I would be, in some slight degree, repaying an obligation, in rendering to others such humble return as is in my power.

Your secretary was kind enough to give me a wide choice of subject, and seeing that in 1891 I delivered a lecture on "*Calculations for Accountants*" before the Manchester and Newcastle-on-Tyne students societies, I felt that I could (somewhat selfishly, I admit), with advantage to myself, enlarge upon one section of that lecture. I therefore chose the subject of "*Depreciation of Machinery and Plant*" for my subject to-night. *Per contra* the selfish motive, I carefully read the lectures which have been previously delivered upon the subject, and found that, whilst excellent in themselves, they did not treat of depreciation in a mathematical sense, but rather dealt with the legal and individual aspects of the subject.

Profiting by the experiences there detailed, and my own observations, I have endeavoured to arrive at the principles underlying the question, and I now submit to your criticism my conclusions based upon those lectures.

In addition to the lectures delivered to societies connected with our Institute, I have carefully read, and derived considerable profit from, a book written by Mr. Ewing Matheson, C.E., entitled "The Depreciation of Factories, Mines, and Industrial Undertakings and their Valuation," 2nd edition. Published by Messrs. Spon, 1893, and a paper read before the Institute of Civil Engineers (1869-70) by Mr. E. Price Williams, C.E., on "The Maintenance and Renewal of Railway Rolling Stock," published by William Clowes & Sons, 1870, with which latter gentleman I was recently associated professionally, and both of which books I recommend to your careful perusal and study.

The following are the lectures which have been previously given upon the subject :—

I. "Depreciation and Sinking Funds." By Edwin Guthrie, F.C.A. 2nd April 1883.
II. "Treatment and Depreciation of Freehold and Leasehold Properties." By F. R. Goddard. Northern Institute of Chartered Accountants. 8th November 1882.
III. "Depreciation in relation to the audit of Accounts." By John Mather. Manchester Institute of Accountants. 3rd January 1876.
IV. "Wear and Tear and Depreciation." By A. Murray. Liverpool Chartered Accountants Students' Association. 6th October 1887.
V. "Writing off of Depreciation of the Wasting Assets of a Joint Stock Company." Prize Essay. By J. D. S. Bogle. London Students' Society. 20th November 1889.

By way of introduction, I will submit to you a few fundamental statements which will seem so obvious that they are not worthy of being mentioned, yet on the principle that Euclid found it necessary to lay down certain axioms, I will endeavour to formulate the principles underlying the question of depreciation, and we will see if we cannot, by a consideration of them, find a few suggestions which will be of value in dealing with some, if not all, of the very numerous variations of this difficult subject.

First let me draw your attention to the various classes of capital outlay.

These I will divide as follows :—

(1) Capital outlay incurred in preparing the earth as Nature left it for carrying on business operations where there is no tangible asset remaining should the business be discontinued, such as opening up a quarry or sinking a shaft.

In these cases no expenditure in the way of repairs can affect the residual breaking-up value, but only the value as a going concern, and, moreover, the cost is mainly for labour.

(2) Capital outlay where there will be *always* some residual value.

1. Land.
2. Buildings.
3. Engines and Machinery.
4. Tools.

The cost in these cases is for materials, and labour expended upon such materials, in order to produce a means of turning out the commodity dealt in.

We thus see that in all manufacturing businesses capital is expended in property at the commencement of the business, with the previous certain knowledge that when the business is given up and the assets realised, the sum so realised will be insufficient to replace the original capital expended.

This difference between the original capital expended and

the ultimate amount realised is due to one or more of four causes:—

1. That the original outlay was for labour only, as in the case of opening a quarry or sinking a shaft.
2. The fact that a second-hand article brought to auction is *ipso facto* reduced in value.
3. *In the case of a machine*: that since it was made the type has become obsolete or has been improved in such a manner that no addition to the old type can bring it up to the improved level.
4. In the case of a machine, further: that the productive power, both as regards quantity and quality, has been reduced by reason of so many years' wear and tear.

From whichever of these causes the fall in value springs, it has been incurred through the desire of the capitalist to employ his *capital* to produce *revenue*, and it has ever been an admitted principle that losses of capital must be made good before the return yielded by such capital can be treated as income.

Consequently, in preparing the Revenue Accounts of trading concerns, it is customary to charge against the gross revenue of each period such an estimated sum, *and it is always an estimate*, as will replace the loss of capital during that particular period.

And as it is obvious that all the four causes cannot be treated in the same way, I will mention the main principles which are adopted in dealing with each case.

First, outlay on quarries and mines:—Where the property is held on a short lease it is usual to write off the outlay in proportion to the number of years the lease has to run, but in the case of a long lease, say 999 years, or of freehold property, it is usual to write off the outlay *as the profits admit*, namely, by providing a reserve fund out of such profits. This may either be shown in the Balance Sheet as a Reserve Fund on the liabilities side, or it may be deducted from the outlay. There are differences of opinion about this (and I have a decided opinion myself), but it hardly comes within the province of my lecture to-night.

The second and third causes of the fall in value are usually provided for by a Reserve Fund, or, as is too often the case, they are not provided for at all.

The fourth cause is, undoubtedly, the most important to us as accountants, arising, as it necessarily does, from causes of which we can have no technical knowledge, and in which we must be guided by those who are best qualified to judge, but whose interests, in too many cases, are opposed to the proper provision being made.

The fourth case, therefore, is the one that we can most profitably discuss to-night. It has the advantage that it is the one about which there are the widest divergences of opinion, and the most variation in practice, but it has the disadvantage that it is a very wide subject indeed.

I do not, however, propose to go into individual cases, but shall endeavour to lay before you the principles which I think I can see underlying it, giving you the arguments *pro* and *con*, and, by leaving you to apply them to cases within your own practice, bring the light of experience to bear upon the question. In return I shall ask you to be kind enough to criticise my remarks freely and frankly.

Perhaps a definition will help us here, and I will confine it to the *Depreciation of Machinery and Plant*.

Ever since I promised to lecture to you I have been in quest of a definition and I have framed many. Here are a few:—

"The charge against the revenue of any particular "period, being that proportion of the cost of the finished "and partly finished production during that period "representing the value of the wear and tear of the "producing Machinery and Plant.

or

"The reduction in value of the producing Machinery "caused by the operations carried on during the "period."

or

"The repayment to Capital, out of the total gross "revenue earned during the period, of such proportion "of the original capital outlay as has been absorbed or "consumed in earning such gross revenue."

I prefer the latter, which I propose to adopt in my subsequent remarks, which will be directed to answering the question, *What part of the original outlay on Machinery and Plant should be written off to Revenue during each year it is used?* and I shall confine myself to the question of *wear and tear* only, leaving untouched the question of a fall in value from all other causes.

And right here I must draw a broad line, because it is evident that the life of a machine can be largely extended not only by repairs, but by judicious care of the machine in the matter of oiling and cleaning, and also in protecting it from the effect of injurious external agencies, such as damp, &c.

I do not propose to consider the fall in value caused by improper care of the machine, as this is not capable of being expressed in definite terms, but depends upon the particular circumstances of each individual case.

I have now narrowed down the enquiry to the question of finding the proper charge to revenue in respect of the wear and tear of a machine which is worked under good average conditions, and is kept in a proper state of repair at the expense of revenue.

It will be necessary here to divide machinery and plant into three broad classes, to avoid having to consider in detail the numerous kinds of machinery, and I propose to make the following classification.

I. Simple machines and plant which are incapable of repair or only so to a slight extent.
II. Compound machines where the running parts are only a small proportion of the whole, and may be renewed separately.
III. Machines in which the running parts predominate or where the power is applied in a violent or intermittent manner.

Before dealing with each class *seriatim*, I will briefly recapitulate the various forces at work which have to be taken into account in arriving at a proper estimate of the rate of depreciation. These are of two kinds:—

I. *Forces accelerating decay.*
   (*a*) The speed and regularity at which the machine is run.
   (*b*) The character of the work.
   (*c*) The environment of the machine.
II. *Forces retarding decay.*
   (*a*) Repairs.
   (*b*) Replacement of parts.

And we shall see that as these forces vary in intensity, the life of the machine may be compared to the resultant of these forces, and therefore the rate of depreciation to be charged to revenue will vary inversely as the life of the machine.

For diagram see next page.

Let us now consider the various classes of machines set out above.

I. *Simple machines* incapable of repair—a familiar instance of this class is found in the humble grindstone, which is certainly a machine, but yet cannot be much repaired. In such a case it is a very easy matter to estimate the rate of depreciation, but I will leave it over for the present, as I propose to deal later with the general principle which applies to all three classes.

Under this head I should like to refer to *Loose Tools*, which are very often treated on a perfectly erroneous principle. In many businesses these are treated as "plant," and are raised to the dignity of a Capital Account. All subsequent

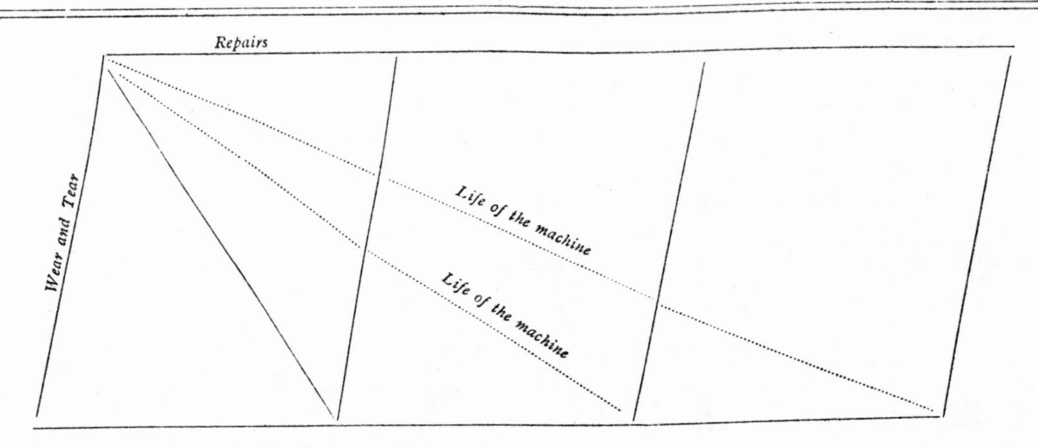

purchases are added to the account, and they are written down by a periodical charge for depreciation, which, in many cases, is quite inadequate to provide for the consumption during the period.

I consider that *Loose Tools* should be treated as an ordinary *trade expense*, and a separate account kept to which all purchases should be debited. At each stocktaking an inventory of them should be made and valued *as a going concern*, allowing for due wear and tear, and the balance of the outlay should be charged to revenue. In this way tools lost or stolen (by no means an uncommon experience) are charged to revenue, whereas if they are treated as a Capital Account and depreciated this leakage is not provided for. Further, the annual stocktaking would have a beneficial effect upon the foreman and workman which otherwise would not exist.

I think that in any well-arranged system of depreciation, the simple machines, to which I have before alluded, should be kept in a separate account, and that stock should be taken at each stocktaking, each item being valued periodically at such a reduction on the previous valuation as may be deemed necessary. In support of this contention I would remind you that these machines are a very heterogeneous assemblage, and depreciate in widely varying ratios, and although a very fair average rate might be fixed, yet it would vary from time to time. On the contrary, by taking an actual valuation periodically, a nearer approximation to the actual working value, and consequently the proper charge to revenue, would be arrived at.

II. *Compound machines where the running parts are only a small proportion of the whole, and may be renewed separately.*

A typical example is found in the lathe or similar engineering tools in which the running surfaces are hardened, the bearings are small in proportion to the machine and may be renewed separately, and the support or frame of the machine is bulky, and forms a large proportion of the initial cost by reason of sheer weight.

In these cases it is reasonable to conclude that the machine will last a considerable time, thus indicating a low rate of depreciation ; but during the life of the machine the individual parts will require frequent renewal, which should be charged direct to revenue as a trade expense.

Contrast this with simple machines of Class I., where we find that the proper method is to treat it as a Trade Expense Account purely, with a periodical actual valuation. In Class II. we have a mixture of the two, namely, a trade expense for renewal of parts and a periodical charge for that which cannot be renewed, and which has to be met by a charge for depreciation.

Class III. *Machines in which the running parts predominate, or where the power is applied in a violent or intermittent manner.*

Under this head I class all machines where the life of the machine is governed by the wearing parts. In these cases, under the most favourable conditions, it is not possible to do much more than replace parts which are accidentally broken, necessitating repair.

As the machine gets older it is found that its producing power, both as regards quantity and quality, is reduced, and it is not possible to say where the defect lies. In fact, it is getting "worn out."

As compared with Classes I. and II. we have a small charge to Revenue under the head of "repairs" and a steady "depreciation," consequently, this must be borne in mind in fixing the rate.

We see, therefore, from an analysis of the various kinds of machinery, that in fixing a rate of depreciation it is of the utmost importance to take into consideration the effect of repairs and renewal of parts, in prolonging the life of the machine.

Having done this, it ought to be a very simple matter for a practical business man to fix the *life* of a machine. He can also form a fair idea of the residual value of the machine when it ceases to be fit to be worked at a profit. Given the cost, and these two factors, it is a simple matter of calculation to the accountant to ascertain the annual charge for depreciation. How to do this I will point out later.

An important point in connection with depreciation, and a much debated one, is whether the depreciation should be calculated on the original cost, or on the reduced amount at the previous stocktaking. Let us see what it means. It is a generally accepted opinion that the repairs increase as the machine gets older, and it is also generally admitted that it is advisable to distribute the total charges to Revenue equally over the life of the machine, for, although the charge should not be so much during the earlier years, yet it is sound economics to make provision for old age.

Now, as between depreciating on the original cost or on the reduced amount, we find that the latter method has the effect of relieving the later years, when the repairs are generally heavier, whilst if we depreciate on the original amount the greater burden is thrown on the later years.

Perhaps, a theoretical case will make it clearer.

	1 yr.	2	3	4	5	6	7	8	9	10	11	
On original cost												
Depreciation	6	6	6	6	6	6	6	6	6	6	6	= 66
Repairs ..	1	2	3	4	5	6	7	8	9	10	11	= 66
Total annual charge ..	7	8	9	10	11	12	13	14	15	16	17	=132
On reduced amount												
Depreciation	11	10	9	8	7	6	5	4	3	2	1	= 66
Repairs ..	1	2	3	4	5	6	7	8	9	10	11	= 66
Total annual charge ..	12	12	12	12	12	12	12	12	12	12	12	=132

There are arguments on both sides, yet I think that with one reservation the most equitable way is to depreciate on the reduced amount for these reasons :—

1. There is no doubt that a new machine does not wear so rapidly as an old one.
2. The effect is to more nearly equalise the total charge to revenue for repairs and depreciation over the life of the machine.

The reservation I refer to is, that in fixing the rate of depreciation due regard should be had to the fact that, at the same rate per cent., it takes a very much longer time to write off the capital outlay by calculating the depreciation on the reduced amount than it does by calculating on the original amount. And, as a rule, the extent of this difference in time is hardly ever realised by business men.

I will give you an example showing the amounts remaining under each method at 5 per cent.

	Amount remaining, calculating on original amount	Amount remaining, calculating on reduced amount	Difference between the two methods expressed in percentage of original cost
Original cost ..	100	100	..
At end of year 1	95	95	..
2	90	90	..
3	85	86	..
4	80	81	..
5	75	77	= 2%
6	70	74	..
7	65	70	..
8	60	66	..
9	55	63	..
10	50	59	= 9%
11	45	57	..
12	40	54	..
13	35	51	..
14	30	48	..
15	25	46	=21%
16	20	44	..
17	15	42	..
18	10	40	..
19	5	38	..
20	0	36	=36%
25	..	28	..
30	..	21	..
40	..	13	..
50	..	7	..

From this you will see that (calculating on the original amount) by the time the whole is written off there is 36 per cent. of the original cost remaining if calculated on the reduced amount.

To put it another way. Assuming that a machine, when broken up, will be worth 10 per cent. of the original cost, this point will be reached, on the *original amount*, at the end of the eighteenth year, whereas on the *reduced amount* it will not be reached until the end of about the forty-fifth year, which is much beyond the "life" of the average machinery, which we find depreciated at 5 per cent.

The conclusion I wish to draw from these figures is this. My experience has been, and I do not doubt that yours has been the same, that when a mill or works has been sold the price realised has been far below the value at which it stood in the books. No doubt a large part of the difference has arisen from the fact that the sale has been a forced one, or that the machinery is old-fashioned; but, seeing that this difference occurs even on a friendly revaluation, we are forced to the conclusion that there are other causes at work.

In my opinion this fall in value is largely due to insufficient depreciation having been written off; and, as far as I can see, it has arisen in this way.

A manufacturer in the good old days, when prices were good and profits were large, looked upon bookkeeping, in anything approaching a scientific manner, as a waste of time. Many do so even now. We must also remember that in those days trained accountants were few and far between. Consequently, in providing for depreciation, the course of reasoning would be something like this: "This machine will last for 20 years if it is well looked after, therefore I must depreciate at 5 per cent." He did so at the end of the first year, and correctly so, but at the end of the second year he overlooked the fact that the depreciation should have been not only at the *same rate* but also should have been the *same in amount*, and took it on the *reduced* capital value remaining at the end of the first year, not realising that he was thereby extending the life from 20 to 45 years.

And so the error was perpetuated, and is still being perpetuated to-day in the majority of cases.

Our typical manufacturer had, and still has, one more chance of salvation, but he missed, and is still to-day missing it. At the end of the twentieth year the machine gave out as he had anticipated, and he sold it for £10 (it cost, we will assume, £100) which he credited sometimes to Capital Account; but as often as not, as I have often seen, the entry was made in the Day Book, and it was actually credited to *Revenue*.

Let us see what was the actual position at the time. The machine, as we have seen, stood in the books at the end of the twentieth year at £36. This was not *apparent*, as it was hidden in a large sum of, perhaps, many thousands of pounds, representing the whole of the machinery and plant. At the best he credited the Capital Account with the amount realised, viz., £10, bought a new machine, which he debited to Capital Account, and the result was that the Capital Account stood with a debit of £26, for which there was actually no asset, and which should at once have been written off to Revenue.

Imagine this going on every year, with an occasional renewal of a boiler or an engine, and we get a good explanation of the small amount realised as compared with the book value.

I have gone into this by no means uncommon case in some detail, because, on the face of it, it suggests one or two obvious safeguards.

First, in fixing the rate of depreciation to be calculated on the *reduced* amount, he ought to have seen that 5 per cent. would not write off the cost in twenty years. Having got so far, it is not a very difficult calculation to ascertain that the rate should have been nearer 11 per cent. than 5. *Secondly*, had his books been kept in such a manner as to show the original cost of each machine, and the amounts written off, he would have discovered the error when he sold the machine. But the books were not so kept. The whole of the machinery and plant was included in one item. I do not suggest that a Ledger Account should be opened for each machine, but if Ledger accounts were opened for groups, for instance, boilers, engines, mules, looms, lathes, and so on, and a subsidiary book kept for each group, agreeing with the total of the Ledger Account, he would have discovered the error. To show you that this is not impossible, I would mention the fact that some years ago I elaborated such a scheme, and shortly afterwards, on going to a new audit, found that they had been doing so since 1838. Truly, there is nothing new under the sun.

The system I refer to is certainly the most complete of

any that have ever come under my notice, and after an experience of it in practical working of nearly ten years, I do not think that I could improve it in the slightest degree were I given *carte blanche* in the matter.

Briefly, it may be described as follows: The manufacturing concern where it is used consists of spinning and weaving, the firm owning the land, buildings, cottages, and water rights. They make their own gas, the mills are lit by electric light, and they have their own mechanics' shop.

In the Private Ledger the various Capital Accounts are kept separately as follows :—

Land and Water Rights.
Cottages.
Other Buildings not used for Machinery, Boundary Walls, Fences, &c.
Buildings of Mills and Sheds.
Motive Power, including Engines, Shafting, Belting.
Machinery.

And for each of these accounts there is a subsidiary Ledger kept, where the gross amount is further analysed.

In carrying out this analysis various methods are adopted with the view of grouping the machinery, &c. For instance, each mill and shed is shown separately, and where similar property is used throughout the building it is all found under one head,—for instance, shafting and belting. The remainder is grouped in rooms.

Each group has one page allotted to it in the Subsidiary Ledger, and all property on the same page is depreciated at the same rate. The entries in each page at any stocktaking only occupy one line, the pages being provided with columns headed :—

1. Amount at previous stocktaking brought forward.
2. Additions since, being purchases or additions.
3. Transfers from other departments.
4. Total (1+2+3).
5. Depreciation at the rate specified at the head of each page.
6. Deductions, being value of articles worn out or replaced.
7. Transfers to other departments.
8. Value at the present stocktaking to be carried forward.

And in addition there is a broad blank column for "Remarks," where are entered particulars of the original machinery purchased, new additions and replacements, and also of amounts written off.

At the end of each period a summary is made showing the totals of each of the columns for the whole concern. Column 2 of the summary shows the total additions, and corresponds with the amounts in the Ledger charged to capital during the period. Column 3 agrees with Column 7, and is only a transfer from one account to another. Column 5 gives the depreciation to be charged to Profit and Loss Account, and Column 8 gives the present value as shown by the grand total in the Balance Sheet.

Column 6 deserves more than a passing mention. In it we get the items similar to the amount of £36 referred to above, that is, the amount remaining in the books as the value of a machine which has been broken up or sold. The procedure is very simple. Suppose a machine has been broken up, an entry is made to that effect at the proper page, the date when it was purchased, the original cost, and the rate at which it has been since depreciated are all given *on that page* without further reference to books, perhaps, long since destroyed, and from these data, a simple rule, deduced from the algebraical formula for a geometrical progression, gives the amount at which it stands included in the gross value of all the machinery in that room. So accurately can this be done that on one occasion when the last machine in one room was taken out, the amount so calculated was less than £1 out, and this in face of the fact that the account had been going for many years.

The total of all these amounts, as shown in the summary, is charged to revenue as being the excess of the *actual* depreciation over and above the *estimated* amount, and thus we get what very few concerns ever find out, namely, a practical test of a theoretical estimate.

One further advantage is afforded, that valuable data are obtained and used as a guide for the future, and as a consequence the property is kept at a fair working value, and which would be realised except on a forced sale by auction.

An incidental advantage is that all sales of old iron, old machines, etc., are credited to Revenue, so that there is not any fear of sales of capital assets being credited wrongly.

It may be asked: Does all this entail any extra labour? The answer is that if it does it is *necessary* and remunerative labour ; but taking into consideration the fact that proper appliances *always* reduce labour there must be an actual saving of time. Who has not experienced the almost hopeless task of trying to find out details of plant purchased many years ago and the fruitless search in dusty and dirty and damp invoice books. The saving, also, and the advantage to the management must be enormous in having a perfect life history of the concern at all times available.

As further bearing out my contention that the difference between the book value of a concern and the price realised on a re-valuation is largely due to the writing-off of insufficient depreciation, I would mention that although the firm in question write-off liberally yet in no single instance has the depreciation so written off been sufficient.

In striking contrast to this mathematical treatment of capital outlay I will mention to you an example of the old-fashioned method of lumping it all under one account, viz., Machinery and Plant, &c.

I have always considered that, speaking zoologically, a horse is an animal, but in this case it was treated as "plant," and included in this *omnium gatherum* account, which was depreciated at 5 per cent. on the reduced amount. When these accounts came under my notice I found a credit to the account of the following :—

Proceeds of sale of horse £20

And on referring back I found that it was in respect of a horse that had cost about £60 two years before, but had developed lameness. And allowing for the depreciation that had already been written off at 5 per cent., I suggested that at least a further £34 should be written off. Curiosity prompting me, I went further back in the evolution of this most interesting animal (only one was kept), and found, owing to its predecessors not having reached the good old age of 45 years predicted in fixing the rate of 5 per cent. on the reduced amount, that it was responsible for something like £200 of the total capital value. One has only to imagine the rate of equine mortality to be high for a few years, and the concern to be then sold at the book value, to realise what a handsome dividend may be declared out of keeping one horse.

With regard to the actual calculations required to be made in dealing with depreciation, time will not allow me to trouble you with the reasoning involved in deducing the rules from the algebraical formula for a geometrical progression, but I will merely refer you to a lecture which I delivered before the Students' Societies of Manchester and Newcastle-on-Tyne in November 1891, on *Calculations for Accountants with special reference to Inwood's Tables and Logarithms*, and which is fully reported in the Transactions of the Manchester Chartered Accountants Students' Society for 1891-2, in *The Accountant* for year 1892, pp. 337-356, and *The Accountants' Journal* of 1892-3, p. 77. I fear I am exceeding the time allotted to a lecturer, and can, therefore, only state the bare rules, which are as follows :—

A. Given the original cost of a machine, and the number of years during which it has been depreciated at a given rate per cent. upon the reduced amount. To find the residual amount *to which it has been written down.*

Let me illustrate this rule by the example I have previously mentioned, where £100 depreciated at 5% on the reduced amount for twenty years becomes reduced to £36.

Take the amount of £1 reduced by depreciation for one year	= £0·95
Find the logarithm of this amount	$\bar{1}$·9777236
Multiply it by the number of years	20
	$\bar{1}$·5544720
Add logarithm of the original cost, log. 100 =	2·
	1·5544720
and the remainder gives the log. of the amount remaining at the end of the term	£35·849 or £35 17 0

B. Given the original cost of a machine, the number of years that it may reasonably be expected to work efficiently under normal conditions, and the residual value at the end of that time. To find the rate of depreciation, to be calculated on the reduced amount.

I will use as an illustration one similar to the instance I have already mentioned, and will suppose that a machine, which originally cost £98, was at the end of 20 years sold for £9 10s. What has been the rate of depreciation?

Take the log. of the residual value £9 10. ..	0·9777236
Deduct the log. of the original amount £98	1·9912261
	$\bar{2}$·9864975
divide by the number of years, 20 [In order to divide a log. with a negative characteristic, add the divisor and reduce the characteristic of the dividend by 1]	20·
	20)$\overline{18}$·9864975
	$\bar{1}$·949324875

which is the log. of £1 reduced by depreciation for one year, or about ·89; consequently the depreciation has been at the rate of about 11 per cent.

C. Given the original cost of a machine, and the residual value when broken up, to find the number of years in which depreciation at a given rate per cent. (calculated on the reduced amount) will reduce the cost to such residual value.

Original cost, £100. Residual value, £20. Depreciation, 4 per cent. per annum.

From the log. of the residual value, £20	= 1·3010300
deduct the log. of the original amount, £100	= 2
	$\bar{1}$·3010300
and divide this log. by the log. of £1, reduced by 1 year's depreciation at 4 per cent. = ·96	= $\bar{1}$·9822712

reducing the negative logs. to positive numbers and then dividing as follows:

$$\frac{\bar{1}\cdot3010300}{\bar{1}\cdot9822712} = \frac{6989700}{0177288}$$

we find the result to be 39·423 years.

In the above rules for calculations I have expressed the time in *years*. In case the deductions are to be made at any other periods it is merely a question of so many periods at a certain proportionate rate per cent. For instance, if depreciation be deducted half-yearly, take double the number of years and half the rate per cent.

There is one question which ought not to be overlooked in dealing with the subject of depreciation. I refer to "*average*," which is an important factor, both with regard to depreciation and repairs.

Of course, where such a method is in vogue as that which I have described as perfect, it is not, perhaps, of so much importance in connection with the rate of depreciation, but I would direct your attention for a few moments to the question of average as applied to *Repairs*. Imagine a business where only *one* huge machine is used—which can only be repaired at stated intervals, and where the repairs, when undertaken, would cost a very large amount. It would, obviously, be unfair to the revenue of any one period to charge the whole of the repairs to the revenue of that period, especially in view of the fact that owing to the repairs taking place the production would cease, and the revenue thereby be diminished.

The remedy suggested is the equalisation of the incidence of the repairs over each period; and this opens up a very wide field of thought, depending, as it necessarily does, upon a proper estimate being made of the *average* repairs. In such a case it would seem proper that depreciation should be credited to a Repairs Reserve Account, out of which the cost of the repairs should be provided *as and when made*, and at the same time such an additional annual amount should be set aside out of revenue as would provide for the renewal of the plant when worn out.

Time will not allow me to enter more fully into this important side issue, but I commend it to you as being worthy of careful study.

I cannot pass over a method which is very common in private concerns, and which I always refer to as the *sudden death* principle.

I refer to the practice of writing off the outlay on machinery and plant, and even buildings and land, at a much quicker rate than is actually called for. I know of cases where new and *additional* boilers have been put in and charged to revenue, and even where the whole of the machinery and plant, still good, stands in the books as of no value.

The adoption of this method is inequitable in the case of a company as between successive generations of shareholders, and in a private partnership as between the partners, especially if the representatives of a deceased partner are, under the partnership deed, to be paid out on the basis of the last Balance Sheet.

The method is to be condemned even in the case of a private concern owned by one individual—as the Profit and Loss Account does not give a true idea of the cost of working, and we thus lose half the value of systematic accounts, in that the accounts of different periods are not comparable. If it is desired to write down the property below its actual value, which in itself is not to be commended, let us at least have the Profit and Loss Accounts correct for each period. To do this, it is only necessary to write off the ordinary depreciation to Profit and Loss Account, credit the profit so ascertained to Capital Account, and transfer from Capital Account any part of this profit that may be desired to a Reserve Account, keeping the Capital assets at their full value.

Another important question to accountants in connection with depreciation arises in connection with the accounts kept by municipal corporations of their revenue producing undertakings, such as gas and water works.

Here we have a statutory charge against revenue of an Annual Sinking Fund Instalment to provide for the redemption of the debt incurred in providing the works; but it is still the practice of a few corporations to charge in addition depreciation on the plant and works. I need not point out to you that the effect of this dual charge is to saddle the present generation of ratepayers with two burdens:—

1st.—That at the end of the term stipulated by Parliament, the municipality will own property free from debt, provided out of revenue, but

2nd.—This property will be handed over to the succeeding generation is as good a condition as the present generation provided it at the outset.

Our Manchester corporation, until recently, adopted this method, and we as accountants may be proud of the fact that it was entirely owing to the persistent and long-opposed efforts of my then principal Mr. Adam Murray, of the firm of Broome, Murray & Co., who was and now is a member of the Council, that a more equitable state of procedure was adopted, and at the present time, thanks to his perseverance, depreciation is not charged.

It should not be overlooked, however, that at the end of the term prescribed by Parliament, when the original debt has been repaid out of revenue, it will be necessary that the then generation of ratepayers shall provide adequate depreciation out of revenue so that they may hand over the property in as efficient a state as they succeeded to it.

I have not attempted to deal with the legal aspects of the question which have already been the subject of very learned discussions arising out of the decision in *Lee v. Neuchatel Asphalte Co.* These will be found in past numbers of *The Accountant* and *Accountants' Journal*.

It appears to me that the decision referred to has only the effect of *limiting* the extent to which the directors of a public company are bound to provide out of revenue for wasting assets.

In my opinion it is more important that, before certifying the accounts of any public company or private concern, we, as Chartered Accountants, should be satisfied in our own minds that the Balance Sheet (involving as it does the proper provision for depreciation) should present a full and true statement of the position of the company. Bearing this in mind, we should satisfy ourselves that the principle upon which depreciation has been deducted is sound economics, and we shall be on the safe side, leaving it to those shareholders who are anxious to have their pound of flesh to reduce what we consider should be the minimum provision, having regard to the fact that capital ought never to be distributed as revenue.

I am afraid I have unduly prolonged my lecture, and will therefore briefly sum up the points I have in my mind as being necessary to a proper understanding of the question.

1. That depreciation is, in too many cases, treated in a very loose and unsatisfactory manner.

   This arises from :—

   (*a*) The fact that the mathematical principles underlying the calculations are very rarely understood by business men.

   (*b*) That the books of many concerns are not kept in such a manner as will give reliable data for making the proper provision.

   (*c*) The fact that the charge to revenue does not affect the available cash assets, but is merely a book entry, and therefore open to considerable argument.

   (*d*) The fact that the interests of managers, directors, and others are often opposed to an adequate provision being made.

2. That the question of repairs is intimately bound up with depreciation, in that it is an important factor in assessing the rate of depreciation. So much is this so, that in some cases, as I have pointed out, it may be necessary to leave out depreciation altogether, its place being taken by a Reserve Account to provide for the periodical extensive repairs and the replacement of property, which, although depreciating rapidly, cannot be repaired to any great extent, except at intervals.

3. That in order to make proper provision for depreciation the books should be kept on such a system as will allow of sufficient information being readily obtained, in order to fix the rates.

   This system should have two main features.

   (*a*) The analysis and grouping of property which has the same rate of depreciation or thereabouts.

   (*b*) This grouping should be done in such a manner as will allow the management to test whether the rates, originally *estimated*, sufficiently meet the demands for renewal found necessary in practice.

If some such system as I have outlined were adopted generally, I think that the mode of treatment of depreciation would be raised from the rule-of-thumb level on which it stands at present, to a sound mathematical and economic basis. I consider that it is our duty as Public Accountants to endeavour to put it on this footing, notwithstanding the fact that we shall meet with opposition even from our clients, to say nothing of our friends, the Surveyors of Her Majesty's Inland Revenue Office who have charge of Schedule D.

CHARTERED ACCOUNTANTS AND THE PROFIT QUESTION

Ernest Cooper

Chartered Accountants Students' Society of London.

CHARTERED ACCOUNTANTS AND THE PROFIT QUESTION.

By Mr. Ernest Cooper, F.C.A.

At a meeting of the above Society held on 7th November, the following paper was read by Mr. Ernest Cooper :—

Six years ago yesterday, on the 6th November 1888, at the invitation of your Committee, I read a paper at a Meeting of your Society entitled "What is Profit of a Company?"

I accepted an invitation in June last to again read a paper, because I felt the importance to Chartered Accountants, and particularly to those entering the profession, of studying the question of ascertaining Profit. It seems as though the state of matters in regard to Profit, which in 1888 was doubt and uncertainty, is in 1894 something like confusion.

Unless I am misinformed, Counsel and Solicitors are in doubt how to advise upon questions connected with preparing Balance Sheets and ascertaining Profit.

It is not easy to suggest a subject of greater importance to Chartered Accountants. Profits are ascertained by accounts. It has been held that Directors paying a Dividend do so at their peril if they have not a Balance Sheet showing the true state of the Company (*Rance's* case, 6 Ch. 104). They expose themselves to the terrible penalties that Judges have attached to Sec. 165 of the Companies Act 1862, repealed and re-enacted as the 10th Section of the Act of 1890. Within the last few months a Judge has stated that Auditors are sufficiently Officers of a Company in his view to bring them within this section. If he be right, the already sufficient responsibilities and anxieties of an Auditor will be extended beyond those known to any trade or profession.

The principal object I have in view is to call attention to and endeavour to extract what is to be learned by us—for we are all students—from two important cases decided by the Court of Appeal since 1888, viz., *Lee v. The Neuchatel Asphalte Company* (41 Ch.D. 1) and *Verner v. The General and Commercial Investment Trust* (1894, 2 Ch. 239).

I shall point out difficulties which arise for accountants in giving effect to the judgments in these two cases as I understand them ; but references to law I shall take from Judges and Lawyers, and I shall be as careful as possible to apply the references in the same sense as I find them applied by Lawyers. Wanting legal training, I have found it impossible to reconcile the statements of Lord Justice Lindley in these cases with statements of Judges in other cases. To this fact neither you nor I would attach any importance. But we find one eminent Judge (Mr. Justice Stirling) expresses plainly his difficulty in agreeing whilst giving judgment in the *Commercial* case. Mr. F. B. Palmer argues against the soundness of the *Neuchatel* case (if I rightly understand the remarks in his book), supporting himself at every step by cases. No single case is cited in support of the main grounds of the decision in the *Neuchatel* case, and no case but the *Neuchatel* case in support of the decision in the *Commercial* case. The cases appear to stand alone, and do not profess to rest on any principle, but conflict with the two previously received principles that Capital must not be returned, and that dividend can be paid only out of Profit. I suggest, too, that they are impracticable in working, and encourage unsound accounting.

I will first refer briefly to some matters I dealt with in my paper of 1888, "What is Profit of a Company?"

I quoted from the 5th Edition of Mr. Buckley, Q.C.'s Book on the Companies Acts, published in 1887 (Preface, p. iv.), that "we are little nearer to knowing what Profit is than we were five years ago," and from Mr. F. B. Palmer's book on Company Precedents (4th Ed. 1888, p. 258), "There is a difference of opinion as to how Profit should be ascertained."

Of Mr. Buckley's views it is sufficient to quote the following (5th Ed. p. 487):—

"The writer has always understood the true principle to "be, that Capital Account and Revenue Account are dis- "tinct Accounts, and that for the purpose of determining "Profits you must disregard accretions to or diminutions of "Capital."

These words do not appear in the Sixth Edition of Mr. Buckley's book, but a similar statement appears now supported by the case of *Lee v. Neuchatel Asphalte Company* (41 Ch.D. 1).

To explain Mr. Palmer's views it is sufficient to quote the following (4th Ed. p. 258):—

"Profit is to be ascertained as in an ordinary Partnership, "namely, by a Balance Sheet showing the general results of "the Company's operations to date. That is to say, the "Capital Account and Revenue Account are to be treated as "one continuous Account."

By the term "Double Account System" I understand a form of Accounts by which the Assets and Liabilities representing or appertaining to the application of the Capital contributed (usually to a public work) are kept separate from other assets and liabilities of the concern, whether a Company, a Partnership, or an individual, be the owner.

By "Single Account System" I understand a form of Accounts by which the whole of the Assets and Liabilities of the Company are taken together in one Account, stated in practice in the form of a Balance Sheet, including a nominal account, created by double entry Bookkeeping, representing the Capital or the deficiency of Capital to make the balance.

You will see Mr. Buckley adopts the Double Account System, and Mr. Palmer the Single Account System.

I explained the constitution of what for shortness I called Companies Act Companies, that is to say, Corporations, distinct from their members, formed by registration under the Companies Acts, described by Sir George Jessel as "Commercial Partnerships," and as his Lordship said, "In the absence of express provisions, statutory or "otherwise, subject to the same considerations" as Partnerships (*Griffith v. Paget*, 6 Ch.D. 511), and described by Lord Justice Lindley (6th Ed. p. 8) as "Partnerships incorporated by Registration."

Then I considered the constitution of Parliamentary Companies for Public Works, such as Railways, Waterworks, Gas-works, Canals, and Docks.

In Parliamentary Companies the law concerns itself mainly with the work to be constructed, and very secondarily with the constitution of the Company. A Company is unnecessary. An individual may be owner of a Railway, and if so, is expressly included by the Act (The Regulation of Railways Act 1878, Sec. 2) in the term "Company," and made liable to the same regulations as to Accounts as a Company. The Companies Acts, on the other hand, concern themselves not at all with the work to be constructed nor with the objects of the Company, but almost solely with the constitution and winding-up of the Company.

In Parliamentary Companies, Parliament authorises a given amount of Capital to be raised for a public work. This power implies the limitation of the application of all money raised from Proprietors or by loans to the work and the equipment thereof, and the retention in the work of all money expended upon it. Thus the Capital forming the Capital Account of a Railway is not synonymous with the Capital of the Proprietors. The Debenture Capital forms part of it. A Railway Company not only cannot apply its Capital to Dividend, but it cannot as a Companies Act Company must do, if necessary, apply its Capital to payment of its Creditors. The cost of the work or its value is immaterial—all that is essential is, that all the Capital raised go to the work and stay there, and that the work be maintained. Thus Capital may be raised at 50 per cent. discount, or 50 per cent. premium, but the full 100 per cent., and no more, stands in the Accounts both as the Capital raised and as the cost of the work of a Parliamentary Company. Capital of a Companies Act Company cannot, as you know, be issued at a discount, and premium is of the nature of profit, and I know of no reason for doubting that it can be divided.

How natural, indeed necessary, it is that Parliament, when authorising a Company to construct a Public Work (usually a partial monopoly) should in the public interest require periodically a separate account of the work, showing that all money authorised to be raised has gone into the work and that the work has been maintained. This is "Double Account."

Some Companies Act Companies (but very few) keep their Accounts on the Double Account System, as, for instance, Indian Railway Companies incorporated under the Companies Acts, which, by contract with the Indian Government, keep their accounts in a form similar to that of English Railways, and a few Tramway Companies.

As an individual may be the Owner of a Railway or other public work, and so become liable to keep accounts of the work in the prescribed manner, so, of course, a Limited Company may become the owner of the public work and be required to keep such accounts; but these accounts do not become necessarily the accounts of the position of the Company, but only of the work. The Limited Company, like the individual, may have other property and other objects—may be a Banker or a Trader, or a Manufacturer—in which case the application of Double Account to the whole Company is impracticable, owing to the mixture of other funds with the Capital.

The mistake, if I may venture so to describe it, of Mr. Buckley's view that Capital Account and Revenue Account are distinct accounts, lies in his treating as a principle of general application what is a special restriction or regulation applied to but few Companies under the Companies Acts, and only possible of application in exceptional circumstances. It would seem that the Court of Appeal has, in the two cases referred to, adopted Mr. Buckley's view.

After pointing out that Mr. Buckley cited no authority, I referred to the cases cited by Mr. Palmer in support of the Single Account System.

Vice-Chancellor Kindersley in 1866 (*Helby's* case, 2 Eq. 167), Lord Justice Selwyn in 1879 (*Stringer's* case, 4 Ch. 475), and Mr. Justice Chitty in 1886 (*Midland Land and Investment Corporation, Palmer's Comp. Precedents, 5th Ed.* 358) and in 1892 (*Lubbock v. British Bank of South America* [1892], 2 Ch. 198) expressed opinions in favour of the Balance Sheet of Assets and Liabilities or the Single Account.

Mr. Buckley instances as a loss on Capital Account, which may be disregarded in determining profit, the loss of a ship by a shipowning company. This is a singularly unhappy illustration, as, apparently, even a Parliamentary Company could not divide until such loss had been replaced. This is shown by the New Tay Viaduct Act 1881. When years ago the Tay Bridge was blown down, Parliament allowed stock to be created to reconstruct the bridge, but required the Company to redeem the stock out of profits.

Lee v. Neuchatel Asphalte Company (41 Ch.D. 1) was decided by Mr. Justice Stirling in February 1888, and by the Court of Appeal in February 1889. The argument and Judgments in both Courts are reported together in the Law Reports in June 1889.

The Neuchatel Company was formed in 1873 by amalgamating six Asphalte Companies, the separate concerns being bought for £1,137,000 paid in Ordinary and Preference Shares of the new Company. The new Company acquired by the original purchase, and by renewals, concessions or leases, ultimately holding one of about thirty years. It was admitted that the whole of the asphalte could not be extracted within the term of the concession, so the value of material extracted did not affect the question, and the concession was in effect merely a lease. It was not contended that the amount of the shares was represented by assets of equal value. The Articles of Association provided that a reserve for renewal of any lease or concession need not be provided. In case of winding up the Ordinary and Preference Shares took the assets rateably. Evidence was given that the assets of the Company, including the concession, were of greater value than they were at the commencement of the Company. A Shareholder holding a few Preference and a large number of Ordinary Shares applied for an injunction to restrain the payment of a dividend to the Preference Shareholders on the ground that depreciation had not been provided for. Mr. Justice Stirling refused the injunction on the ground that the assets were of greater value than at the start, and so the Capital was intact, and he said it must not be assumed the Company would not cover depreciation in the future.

The head-note is not, I think, a quite accurate summary of the Report, but it will serve our purpose. With the first half of it, which is based upon a registered contract, we need not concern ourselves, as this may be taken to be already over-ruled by the House of Lords in the *Ooregum* ([1892] App. Ca., 125) case in 1892.

The other half is as follows:—

"There is nothing in the Companies Acts to prohibit a "Company formed to work a wasting property, as *e.g.*, a "mine or a patent, from distributing, as dividend, the excess "of the proceeds of working above the expenses of work- "ing, nor to impose on the Company any obligation to set "apart a sinking fund to meet the depreciation in the value "of the wasting property. If the expenses of working ex- "ceed the receipts, the accounts must not be made out so "as to show an apparent profit, and so enable the company "to pay a dividend out of Capital, but the division of the "profits without providing a sinking fund is not such a pay- "ment of dividends out of capital as is forbidden by law.

"Decision of Stirling, J., affirmed."

You will notice that no reference to a lease appears in the headnote, although the subject matter of the case was merely a lease, and neither a mine nor a patent. It is the fact that Mr. Justice Stirling's judgment is affirmed, but there is no other resemblance between the decisions of the two Courts. Both Courts refused the Plaintiff's request, and both expounded the law; but not one word of the head-note is applicable to the grounds of Mr. Justice Stirling's judgment.

Verner v. General and Commercial Investment Trust ([1894] 2 Ch. 239) was decided by Mr. Justice Stirling in March, and by the Court of Appeal in April of the present year, 1894.

The General and Commercial Investment Trust was formed with the main object of investing in Stocks and Shares its share capital and moneys borrowed on deposits and raised by the issue of Debentures. After taking off the income a sum to provide for expenses, the remaining income is applicable to dividend upon the 5 per cent. Preference Shares and the Ordinary Shares. The Company raised £300,000 by Debenture Stock and £600,000 by Share Capital, and invested the whole in securities. The investments had declined in value £250,000, equal to five-twelfths of the Share Capital, some being utterly worthless, so that if the decline in value be regarded as permanent, each so-called £10 share (if surplus income be not taken into account) had become a participation of seven-twelfths of £10, say £5 16s. 8d. There was a balance of income received on the Investments in excess of the expenses and interest on the Debenture Stock amounting to £23,000, so deducting this from the £250,000, on a sound Balance Sheet the company would appear to have lost £227,000 of its Capital. One of the Trustees—the Directors were given this name—brought a friendly action to have it declared that a dividend could lawfully be paid. The following extract from the headnote of the report in the Law Reports gives a sufficient summary of the judgments for our purpose.

" Held (by Stirling J. and by the Court of Appeal), that " it was within the power of the Company to declare a " dividend, for that there is no law to prevent a Company " from sinking its Capital in the purchase of a property " producing income and dividing that income without " making provision for keeping up the value of the Capital; " and that fixed capital may be sunk and lost, and yet the " excess of current receipts over current expenses may be " applied in payment of a dividend, though where the income " of a Company arises from the turning over of circulating " capital no dividend can be paid unless the circulating " capital is kept up to its original value, as otherwise there " would be a payment of dividend out of Capital."

You will notice from the extract from the headnote of the report of the *Neuchatel* case that the sanction to pay dividends without providing for waste is based upon the absence of provisions in the Companies Acts. I contend that there is no distinction material to the question as regards what is profit, and what is payment out of capital, and what is capital, between the case of an individual, of a partnership, or of a Company, and I find nowhere the contrary suggested. Why then should the Acts contain any provision on this subject? The Partnership Act 1890 does not.

When V.-C. Page Wood in 1864 told us (*Macdougall v. Jersey Imperial Hotel Co.*, 2 H. & M. 528) that Capital could not be withdrawn or returned, and that limited liability carried with it an implied contract to this effect, Limited Companies in regard to this question were shown to be in a position analogous to Partnerships with a fixed Capital, with the qualification that of course partners may at will alter their deed and agree to divide their Capital. Is it to be suggested that if I enter into Partnership and agree to contribute Capital and draw profits only, that I can against the will of my Partner draw out the surplus receipts without allowing for waste?

In the *Commercial* case, Mr. Justice Stirling said (p. 245):—

" So far as I know, the Court is now for the first time " asked to say whether a dividend can be paid out of excess " of receipts over expenditure when there has been a loss " upon capital."

His Lordship does not express surprise at nor suggest any explanation of this remarkable fact. Limited Liability has existed for 39 years, and many thousands of Companies are registered under the Companies Acts (over 18,000 Companies, the Registrar tells us, were carrying on business at the end of April last), and nearly all the Companies are issuing, year by year, Balance Sheets, and yet no one has ever raised in the Law Courts this question, an every-day question, and a momentous one for Directors, who are liable to refund dividends improperly paid. The reason I suggest why the question has been asked is that Mr. Buckley said in his book, that he had always understood that Capital account and Revenue account were distinct accounts, and that you can ignore a loss of Capital in ascertaining Profit.

An important point is that Creditors were not represented by Counsel in either case. It is fair to assume the Debenture-holders of the *Commercial* Company advanced their money against Capital double the amount of the Debentures and relying upon the law as it stood, that Capital may not be returned. In this case, too, the decision seems based upon the idea that only the Capital bought the Investments, and the fact that one-third were bought with Creditors' money is not noticed.

A peculiarity of the two cases is the manner in which the Judges use the words "profit," "revenue," and "income." Speaking generally, it may be said the words are treated as synonymous, and certainly the distinction between them is nowhere referred to. The Articles of Association of the *Commercial* Company give power to divide profit, and, apparently, nothing else, but this is nowhere noticed, and the surplus of receipts over expenses, without providing for depreciation, surely not profit, is tacitly treated as profit.

McCulloch's definition of profit, accepted by Lord Blackburn in the *Coltness Iron Co. v. Black* (6 App. Cas. 315, 329) was read to the Court in the *Neuchatel* case, and, apparently, not expressly dissented from. It is as follows:—

" Profits really consist of the produce or its value remain- " ing to those who employ their Capital in an industrial " undertaking after all their necessary payments have been " deducted, and after the Capital wasted and used in the " undertaking has been replaced."

No Judge, I think, has gone so far as to state expressly that a Company has made profit until waste has been provided for. It is evident that profit must, in some sense, be gain or increase, and not, as in the *Commercial* case, immense loss; yet the headnote of the report of the *Neuchatel* case says a

" Division of profits without providing a sinking fund," which seems a contradiction in terms, is not forbidden by law.

Even Mr. Palmer, in spite of the *Neuchatel* case (a mere question of a lease, bear in mind), says it is well settled that only profits can be divided. He cites these clear words of Chief Baron Kelly (*Knowles v. McAdam*, 3 Ex.D. 23):—

" Suppose a man pays £1,000 for a lease of a mine for one " year only; at the end of that year he has got all the coal " in the mine and sold it for £1,200, the expenses of labour " and materials being £100. Is his profit £1,100? It would " be an abuse of language to say so. His profit is what " remains in his pocket after deducting the expenses, viz., " £1,000 for the liberty to get the coal, and £100 for the cost " of getting it. That is, his profit is £100 only."

Then take the remarks of Mr. Justice Chitty in the case of *Lubbock v. British Bank of South America* ((1892) 2 Ch.D. 201) where a large increment on sale of part of the business was held to be profit. His Lordship says.—

" All that the Company is required to do, by force of the " Companies Act of 1862, is to keep its capital intact and not " to pay dividends out of its own Capital, in other words, to " keep that Capital for its Creditors and any others who may " be concerned therein."

"I put during the argument a humble illustration. A " man's business is to make boots and shoes. He has

"£10,000 which he takes into that business as his Capital. "He makes boots and shoes, and spends the whole of his "£10,000 in doing it, and he sells and gets back from his "customers a certain sum on the sale. He compares then—"assuming he has sold all—what he has got back with his "expenditure in producing the boots and shoes and putting "them on the market, and if he finds he has his £10,000 (I "am treating it apart from any question of debts out-"standing, supposing it is a good solid sale), then his "Capital is intact, and the rest, if there is a rest remaining "in his hands, is profit. On the other hand, if he has only "£9,000, his Capital is not intact, and he has lost."

It must be borne in mind that profit can be rarely more than an estimate, and not an absolute sum. In ascertaining profit some values are estimated and others are uncertain, and liabilities may exist which are not known. There must not be limitation of the latitude necessarily allowed in valuing or estimating assets. Hard and fast application of strict rules is impossible.

There is also difficulty in the two cases in gathering the meaning attached by the Judges to the word "Capital." It would appear that, in some instances, they use the word as applying to the Share Register total called Capital appearing on the left hand side of most Balance Sheets, and in other instances as applying to the assets, or some of the assets on the right hand side. It does not seem clear that they held the view for which I contend, that neither of these is the Capital, but that the difference between the Liabilities and Assets, or the surplus of assets, if there be a surplus, is the Capital.

Lord Justice Lindley, in the *Neuchatel* case, after enforcing (as I tried to do with explanatory reasons in 1888) that a Company does not owe its Capital, says (p. 23):—

"What it means is simply this: that if you want to find "out how you stand, whether you have lost your money or "not, you must bring your Capital into account somehow or "other."

Wanting to know how you stand is wanting to know what your Capital amounts to.

Probably if the question were put to you, "Which side of a Company's Balance Sheet is the real Capital on?" you might, some of you, answer without consideration "the left." This, of course, would be wrong, nor would it be accurate to say the right. The Capital is the difference between the Assets and Liabilities on both sides, and double entry Bookkeeping creates a fictitious or "nominal account" to show this difference and make a Balance, and enable a Balance Sheet to be prepared.

When there are liabilities the assets are not the Capital.

It may be as well to consider a little further what this Balance Sheet item called Capital Account really is. You will recollect the Companies Act 1862 requires a Company with Capital divided into Shares to distinguish each Share by its number, and to state in the Register the amount paid or agreed to be considered as paid on the shares. There is no power, without the sanction of the Court, and the formalities of the Acts of 1867 and 1877 to reduce the amount considered as paid on the shares. Of an individual or of a partnership, of course the Capital account and the amount of the shares of the partners rise or fall with the increase or decrease of Capital in the business. So in fact does the share of a shareholder in a Company. If a Company starts with £100,000, in 10,000 £10 shares, and loses £50,000, the £10 share is not a participation of that amount, but of £5. But the law requires you still to call the share £10.

If you want your share to really represent Capital you go to the Court and ask leave to perform the strange feat of cancelling capital which is lost. This is just as impossible as that power which the marvellous 3rd Section of the Companies Act 1880 tries to authorise, viz., to reduce the Capital by returning Profits. The lost Capital has already cancelled itself, effaced itself, and is gone. Even an Act of Parliament cannot cancel it. What the Acts mean is you may call your counterfeit £10 share an honest £5 share.

This leads one to express a hope that some day we may see Companies Balance Sheets drawn up in a more intelligible form. The capital of the proprietors might be stated under a separate head commencing with the Share Register total or so-called capital figure, and the Reserved Capital and the undivided profit added, or a loss deducted, and one figure, the balance representing the real capital in the concern, shown in the Balance Sheet.

Another small question I will refer to in passing. A gentleman addressing you last year told you it was not easy to see why the liabilities appeared on the left hand side of a Balance Sheet and the assets on the right, and he had given up putting the words "Dr." and "Cr." on Balance Sheets, and the Chairman of your meeting approved this. It would be precisely as reasonable to leave the words out of a Ledger. They are a necessary part of the account. In the Ledger the account is the account of the customer or others with the owner of the business. In the Balance Sheet the account is the opposite, that is to say, the account of the owner of the business with the customer and others. Those to whom I am Debtor are my Creditors. In my Ledger they appear as Creditors, for the Ledger shews their relation to me. In my Balance Sheet I state my relation to them, which is that of Debtor, so I put them on the left hand, or Dr. side. Therefore, when you have made out the trial balance from the Ledger, you must, of course, transpose the sides to make the Balance Sheet.

Then your lecturer of last year advised you to put Liabilities and Assets at the head of Balance Sheets. I advise you never to do so. Many years ago, Sir George Jessel severely censured this practice. Various items are found on both sides of Balance Sheets which are not strictly liabilities or assets.

The Judges cannot, I think, be taken to desire to alter the usual or dictionary meaning of words, and it is not, I hope, presumptuous in a Chartered Accountant to claim acquaintance with the technical terms of his business. If he does not know the meaning of such words as Capital, Revenue, Income, Loss, and Profit, he is surely not qualified to practise a profession which deals so much with these terms.

Then, without attempting exact definition, I say the word

Capital implies a measure of wealth, and the words Profit and Loss imply increase of wealth and diminution of wealth. Revenue implies product of working a property, when loss is not contemplated, and is not the proper designation of the result of trading which involves both Loss and Profit. You may have revenue from your property although it may have fallen in value, but you cannot have made profit until the fall in value is covered. Income is that which accrues or is received, whether profit of trading, produce of property, or earnings of labour, or from a gratuity, an annuity, or any other source.

I understand, of course, that the context may give to these words a special or qualified meaning.

Another peculiarity of the two cases is, what for lack of better terms, I will call an air of doubt and uncertainty in the judgments. Lord Justice Lindley, it is true, is not doubtful, but he begins his judgment in the *Neuchatel* case by the expression of an opinion that to assent to the plaintiffs' contention would paralyse the trade of the country, and ends with a hope that he is not "laying down any rule which would lead people to do anything dishonest": a warning reiterated by Mr. Justice Stirling with greater emphasis in the *Commercial* case.

Lord Justice Lindley, in the *Neuchatel* case, in regard to the sanctioning of dividend without providing for waste, says (p. 20):

"All I can say is, if that is a return of Capital it appears "to me not to be such a return of Capital as is prohibited "by law."

This seems to imply that it may be a return of Capital, and entitles us to retain our opinion that it is so, and it leaves us in doubt what kinds of return are sanctioned and what kinds prohibited.

His Lordship says (p. 21) a "Dividend, no doubt, presupposes a Profit in some shape," and after saying:

"There is nothing at all in the Acts about how dividends are to be paid," and "It is not a subject for an Act of Parliament to say how accounts are to be kept," his Lordship resorts to the Act to support his judgment thus:—

"It is, I think, a misapprehension to say that dividing "the surplus after payment of expenses of the produce of "your wasting property is a return of Capital *in any such* "*sense as is forbidden by the Act.*"

Lord Justice Cotton says (p. 17):

"There is nothing in the Act which says that dividends "are only to be paid out of profits."

What we want to know is, Can dividends be paid lawfully out of anything but profits?

Then Lord Justice Cotton in the *Neuchatel* case says: "The only thing here to be considered is, Is this really a division of Capital assets of the Company under the guise of making and declaring a Dividend?" Yet he puts the case upon the motives and intentions of the Directors.

"If it can be shown that this dividend has been declared "from improper motives, with the intention, not of dividing "Profit, but of returning Capital, I think the Court ought "to interfere."

It is not easy to see how intentions can alter the fact, or how the motives and intentions are to be ascertained. May not the motives and intentions of one Director have been bad and of another good? Yet if a Dividend is wrongly paid all may have to answer under the 10th Section of the 1890 Act, which does not discriminate.

Mr. Justice Stirling bases his decision in the *Commercial* case wholly upon the *Neuchatel* case, and, unlike the Court of Appeal, he says:—

"I base my decision on the peculiar nature of the consti- "tution of this particular Company,"

and adds that it is not to be assumed to apply to an ordinary trading company, and

"It follows . . . that the Shareholders would not be "entitled to divide . . . any increase in the value of "the Investments, however great."

It is difficult to understand this—surely the surplus would be profit, and the Shareholders are entitled to the profit.

Lord Justice Kay says:—"I have not a very confident opinion in the matter"; and he throws aside the Double Account. He says:—

"I should be sorry if it were held that a Joint Stock "Trading Company can properly estimate their profits in "any way differing from that in which an individual or a "partnership of individuals carrying on a similar business "would do. An ordinary trader takes a yearly account "of all the Capital employed in his business, allows for "any loss or depreciation in value, and carries the balance "to the Profit and Loss Account, from which he makes out "the Profit or Loss of the year. In this mode a loss or "depreciation of such Capital affects directly the Profit of "the year, which is thereby diminished. But, if upon the "whole Capital Account there is a gain, this goes to swell the "year's Profits. In my opinion a Joint Stock Trading "Company should do the same."

This corresponds with practice and with all cases I have seen excepting the *Neuchatel* and *Commercial* cases.

Lord Justice Kay finds a way of agreeing with Lord Justice Lindley in the analogy (an incomplete one, I would respectfully suggest) of an ordinary settlement Trust, and he accepted the Articles as authorising the distribution of income where capital is lost. In an ordinary settlement it is not Profit but income which goes to the tenant-for-life.

Assuming that the cases rest chiefly upon Lord Justice Lindley's great authority as a Company lawyer we are naturally led to look to his well known works on the Law of Partnership and Companies. We find there similar views expressed to those in his Lordship's judgments. He says (Lindley on Partnership, 6th Ed., p. 397):—

"Profit is the excess of receipts over expenses."

"The profits divisible in any year are ascertained by com- "paring the ordinary receipts with the ordinary expenses of "that year. . . . ."

These definitions must, I think, be difficult of comprehension by Accountants.

Further—

"But, if the current receipts exceed the current expenses, "the writer apprehends that the difference can be divided "as profit, although the capital may be spent and not be "represented by saleable assets. . . . ."

And his Lordship says (*Lindley on Companies*, 5th Ed., p. 430):—

" And if a Company, after defraying all current expenses " and the interest of its debts, has a surplus arising from its " current receipts, there is no principle either of law or " morality which requires that such surplus shall be " accumulated, or forbids its division as profit amongst the " Shareholders. . . . ."

" And it has been decided that if the articles allow it, " dividends may be paid even by a Limited Company, if its " income exceeds its expenditure, although its whole capital " may have been sunk in obtaining wasting property. . ."

The following is easily assented to, but hard to reconcile with what goes before:—

" To pay what are called profits or dividends out of " Capital is, under whatever disguise, tantamount to " returning so much Capital to the Shareholders. . . ."

Another point, to which I refer with diffidence, is the absence of expert evidence in both cases.

The question seems to have been really, Was there profit? The only way of ascertaining this is by an account. If a properly drawn up account showed profit there would have been no question. Then why should not Accountants have been called, to tell the Court how, in practice, accounts are prepared? An Accountant would have explained to the Court the impossibility of preparing a Balance Sheet to show profit without allowing for waste, or I should contend, to conceal the fact that the Capital was being returned.

The law says Capital may not be returned. I submit that the fact whether in a given case Capital is returned by the Dividend which is paid is an Accountant's question, a question to be ascertained by accounts and by no other means. Then I see little more reason in deciding the question without expert evidence than deciding without expert evidence on the best kind of steam boiler, or the best way of building a ship.

The following extracts from the *Neuchatel* case are interesting.

Lord Justice Lindley says (p. 22):—

" If they think their prospects of success are considerable, " so long as they pay their creditors, there is no reason why " they should not go on and divide profits, so far as I can " see, although every shilling of the Capital may be " lost."

This is startling, but it is apparently a necessary result of the decisions. If a partial loss of Capital need not be made up, it is difficult to understand on what principle it can be necessary to replace the whole.

His Lordship continues (p. 25):—

" There is nothing in the Acts to show what is to go to " Capital Account or what is to go to Revenue Account. " We know perfectly well that business men very often " differ in opinion about such things."

There seems to be a misapprehension here.

It is true business men differ as to what is to go to so-called Capital and Revenue Accounts, but it is not, I think, the fact that they ever differ as to depreciation or waste being a charge to Revenue or Profit and Loss.

P. 25—" The Act does not say what expenses are to be " charged to Capital and what to Revenue. Such matters " are left to the Shareholders. They may or may not have " a sinking fund or a deterioration fund, and the Articles of " Association may or may not contain regulations on those " matters. If they do, the regulations must be observed; if " they do not, the shareholders can do as they like, so long " as they do not misapply their Capital and cheat their " creditors."

Is it not manifest that if you have not a depreciation fund by which it must be assumed his Lordship means that depreciation is provided for), you cannot ascertain profits? I shall try to show that it is also manifest that by dividing anything but profit, Capital is returned or misapplied. To do this is held to be *ultra vires*, and Lord Macnaghten, in *Trevor v. Whitworth* (12 App. Ca., 436), said the Memorandum of Association could not give the power in that case to misapply Capital; and Lord Justice Lindley himself says (*Commercial* case, p. 264):—

" There can, in my opinion, be no doubt that even if a " Memorandum of Association contained a provision for " paying dividends out of Capital such a provision would be " invalid."

In the *Commercial* case Lord Justice Lindley says (p. 266), " The law is much more accurately expressed by saying " that dividends cannot be paid out of Capital, than by " saying that they can only be paid out of profits."

My contention being that a Company has only Capital and Profits, I consider, of course, that both these expressions are of the same effect. His Lordship continues (p. 267):—

" It is practically necessary to keep a Capital Account and " what is called a Profit and Loss Account, and as a matter " of business these accounts ought to be kept as business " men usually keep them."

Here it must be said that the fact is that Companies under the Companies Acts very rarely keep a Capital Account at all—*i.e.*, a real Capital Account showing the application of the Capital. The Balance Sheet is the only Capital Account. There is a Profit and Loss Account, but that is part of the Balance Sheet and so part of the Capital Account of a Companies Act Company.

Lord Justice Cotton and Lord Justice Lindley both assent to the proposition that Capital must not be returned. The former says—

" It is established, and well established, that you must not " apply the assets of the Company in returning to the share- " holders what they have paid up on their shares."

And again it is

" Firmly fixed that Capital assets "

are not to be applied to dividend, and Lord Justice Lindley says the provisions of the Act

" Are wholly inconsistent with the return of Capital to the " shareholders."

There are many cases culminating in the decision of the House of Lords in *Trevor v. Whitworth* (12 App. Ca. 409), which establish that Capital cannot be returned.

Therefore I shall assume this to be so, and shall try to see whether the judgments in the two cases do or do not sanction a return of Capital.

The only other question I shall seek for an answer to is, Are there such assets of a Company as can be properly comprised in Lord Justice Cotton's words (*Neuchatel* case, p. 19), which were expressly adopted by Mr. Justice Stirling as the basis of his judgment in the *Commercial* case, viz. :—

"Using 'Capital' in the proper sense of the word—by "which I mean permanent assets, and assets not to be ex- "pended in providing for the profit earned by the Com- "pany."

In considering this it may be as well to bear in mind Lord Justice Lindley's expression,

"Fixed Capital, which may be sunk and lost, and yet the "excess of current receipts over current payments may be "divided,"

as distinguished from

"Floating and circulating Capital must be kept up ;"

and Lord Justice Lopes' expression,

"Nominal or Share Capital diminished in value . . . "by reason of causes over which the Company has no "control,"

and the words of the headnote of the report of the *Commercial* case (p. 240),

"Fixed Capital may be sunk and lost, and yet the excess of "current receipts over current expenses may be applied in "payment of a dividend, though where the income of a "Company arises from the turning over of circulating "Capital no dividend can be paid unless the circulating "Capital is kept up to its original value, as otherwise there "would be a payment of Dividend out of Capital."

The question is, Are there Capital Assets as distinguished from other Assets? Are some of the Assets Capital and others not ?

I hope I have carried you with me when I say that Capital is the surplus of Assets. We may accept the definition of Capital in Mill's Principles of Political Economy,

"Capital is wealth appropriated to reproductive employ- "ment,"

or that in Mozley and Whiteley's Law Dictionary—

"The net amount of property belonging to a merchant "after deducting the debts he is owing."

I, of course, contend that it makes no difference whatever whether the merchant be an individual, a partnership, or a Companies Act Company.

You will not contend that the Assets are the Capital, for you see at a glance at, say, the Balance Sheet of the London and County Bank, there are forty millions of Assets and only two millions under the word "Capital" on the other side, and you will find it impossible to say which of the assets is or is not Capital. On the other hand if you look at the Capital Account of a Railway, you will see the assets and the contributed Capital are equal if you include any unexpended or over-expended balance.

Then you will agree that if a merchant chooses to allow this surplus of Assets over Liabilities to stand in his Balance Sheet in three parts, say, "Capital," "Reserve," and "Profit undivided," he does not thereby change its character, and it all remains Capital, for by putting his pen through the two other names Capital absorbs them.

I will not occupy much time in trying to prove that to pay a Dividend when there are no profits is to return the Capital. If you agree with me that the Capital is the surplus of assets, then when there is profit it is included in and forms part of the Capital, and when there is loss it reduces the Capital, and it follows that when you pay a dividend you always reduce the Capital. If you pay away in Dividend more of the Capital than represents profits, *i.e.*, if you pay away so much that you do not leave a surplus of assets equal in amount to what was contributed as Capital by the members, then to that extent you return Capital. But you may say Supposing all the Capital is lost, how then can you return it? If you have no Capital, *i.e.*, no property of your own, then you pay to your shareholders what in effect is the property of the creditors, but if you have any earnings above your debts they constitute the replacement of Capital, so to that extent your capital is regained. But until you have regained all the capital originally contributed you have no profit, and there are only two things you can have—

(1) Capital contributed ; and

(2) Capital added to it, *i.e.*, profit. A Company, or an individual, or a partnership, has nothing else. Accretions to Capital, Increment, and such terms all are comprised in Capital and Profit. Therefore, a dividend to shareholders is either a return of part of the Capital contributed, or it is profit, *i.e.*, accretion or increment to the Capital; and it matters not how an accretion comes, so it matters not how the diminution arises. All the cases before the *Neuchatel* and *Commercial* cases which I have seen make this plain by insisting on a Balance Sheet of the actual position.

How does a Company ordinarily ascertain profit? If, as is usual, the Books are kept by double entry, the necessary adjustments are made in the Books and a Balance Sheet is drawn up. The Assets are looked over, waste of leases and the depreciation of assets are written to Profit and Loss Account, and any ascertained or expected loss from bad debts is written to the debit of that account. Interest and Commission are calculated on money borrowed and lent, and these and other earnings and outgoings are credited and debited to Profit and Loss Account. If the result shows that the Assets, after being examined and adjusted, exceed in amount the Capital brought in and the Liabilities, there will appear a profit. If the reverse, a loss.

Mr. Palmer says (5th Ed. p. 353) according to the system of the *Neuchatel* case no Balance Sheet is necessary in order to ascertain Profits. He might have said, it is not even possible in a proper sense, if you are, as you seem to be required to do, to keep the full amount of contributed Capital on the left hand side. How can you fill up the right hand side? Clearly only by such words as "waste" or "loss" or "Capital deficient," for Lord Justice Lindley is particular to say your accounts must not show Assets that are gone. In a partnership as, of course, you know, you would reduce the Capital figure on the left hand side. Does not this make it clear when Capital is returned?

Bearing in mind that partners are by the transfer of shares continually entering and retiring from Companies, and that the shareholders have personally seldom acquaintance with the details of the business, the obligation to make the

Balance Sheet a true statement of the position seems greater, or, at all events, not less, than in an ordinary partnership.

I contend that no one asset of a Companies Act Company, a partnership, or an individual more than any other is Capital. Fixed or permanent assets, such as a factory, a mine, or (if they be fixed, and I hold they are not) the investments of a Trust Company, or a Lease or Goodwill, are none of them clothed with any special character of Capital, not even a Railway which belongs to a Companies Act Company. The Balance at the Bankers or the Book Debts or an amount received as dividend on an Investment are neither less nor more Capital than the Factory, the Mine or the Lease. It makes no difference as regards this question whether the asset be paid for out of Capital or out of money obtained by borrowing or by credit in any form.

There is a distinction as to the method of valuation of less liquid or convertible assets, such as stock-in-trade, and more fixed assets, such as a factory, but otherwise they differ, I contend, in no respect as regards any question before the Court in the *Neuchatel* and *Commercial* cases from the other assets of the Company. The Capital of an individual (as of a Company) is that which he is worth. His assets are all subject to his debts. If he have a factory worth £40,000 and other assets worth £20,000, together £60,000, and he owes £50,000, he cannot say his factory is his Capital, for he is only altogether worth £10,000, and if he only owes £5,000, his Capital is £55,000, still the factory is not any more his Capital than the other assets, for if he sell the factory for an equal amount of cash, he does not thereby reduce his Capital. It is precisely the same of a Companies Act Company. But in the case of a Parliamentary Company the law only gives the Company control, of a certain fixed amount of Capital to place it in a certain work. Neither it nor the Railway or other work was ever, speaking strictly, the Capital of the Company, but it was the Capital of or invested in the Railway. All the assets of a Companies Act Company are interchangeable at will of the Company from time to time. But a Parliamentary Company can never dispose of its public work.

If, as I have said, I sell my factory, is the amount of my Capital altered by exchanging the factory for cash? Manifestly not. But, it is said, I have changed my permanent Asset into a floating Asset, and I might have paid a Dividend, notwithstanding the factory was blown down, whereas, if I invest the proceeds of my factory in Stock-in-trade and that is destroyed, I cannot pay a Dividend, as this would be paying away Capital.

Sir George Jessel says (*Robinson v. Ashton*, 20 Eq. 28.)

"The rise or fall in value of fixed plant or real estate "belonging to a partnership was as much profit or loss of "the partnership as anything else."

Then what is a permanent Asset, the waste of which need not be provided for? I presume land and houses are permanent. A factory, too; but the factory contains boilers which have only a limited life. Are ships permanent? Their rigging lasts a limited time; and steamers, too, have boilers. Are the cars of a Tramway Company permanent? Then, are their horses? They live about as long as boilers, and all these may be destroyed. I contend these cases are based on no principle. If they are we should be able to find means of applying the principle to answer these questions. To establish a principle there must be some dividing line, on either side of which you can place Lord Justice Lindley's two classes of Capital—Fixed Capital and Floating or Circulating Capital. I hope you will agree with me it is impossible to draw such a line.

The investments of a Trust Company are treated as permanent Assets by Mr. Justice Stirling, following Lord Justice Cotton, who had held the Lease of the Neuchatel Company to be such a permanent asset. But the investments were convertible at any moment at the will of the Company from Investments in Stocks and Shares into Cash. Cash, if anything, is apparently what is described as Floating or Circulating Capital. Therefore I cannot, according to Lord Justice Lindley, pay away this in dividend. But supposing I buy with the cash a three years' lease of a coal mine, or a one year's lease, to adopt Chief Baron Kelly's example I have quoted, I can, according to the *Neuchatel* case, divide the proceeds of the coal without replacing to Capital the cash used in buying the lease. Manifestly this is not dividing profit only. Then, what is it I divide? Surely the answer is simple, I divide or return capital. To square this with the *Neuchatel* case it is only necessary to reduce that Company's lease for 30 years to a lease for one year.

Then if the income of the Stocks and Shares of the Commercial Company may be divided, how long may this process continue? Nearly half or five-twelfths of the Capital had gone. If all went, and the remaining assets equal to £300,000 bought with borrowed money produced sufficient to pay the Debenture interest and left a surplus, could the shareholders take it? Not, perhaps, unless sufficient value remained to pay the Creditors, according to Lord Justice Lindley's view (*Neuchatel* case, p. 22); but where does the necessity to keep only enough for the Creditors come from? Not from the Acts. And what is the effect of a mistake by the Directors? An unseen liability or a claim for damages may come upon the Company, and the Creditors in a winding-up will then go unpaid. Will they not say that the Capital has been returned by the Directors to the Shareholders, and ask the Court to compel the Directors to replace it? The answer of the Directors must be "But our motives and intentions" (to use Lord Justice Cotton's words) "were good." Will this satisfy the House of Lords? Or, in other words, can it be reconciled with Lord Herschell's words in *Trevor v. Whitworth* (12 App. Cas. 415):

"They [the Creditors] have a right to rely, and were in- "tended by the Legislature to have a right to rely, on the "Capital remaining undiminished by any expenditure out- "side these limits, or by return of any part of it to the share- "holders."

It seems simply inaccurate to say, under the two decisions we have been considering, that Capital may not be returned. Capital may not be openly returned, perhaps, but if you introduce a simple subterfuge, say you acquire wasting assets and fail to maintain them out of profit, then the effect of these cases is that you may divide Capital. Strangely, Mr. Buckley says that these cases which seem to make an end of protection to the Capital Account show that Capital Account and Revenue Account are distinct accounts or that the Double Account is applicable, whereas the chief object of Double Account is the protection of the Capital Account. Sir George Jessel says (*Davison v. Gillies*, 16 Ch.D. 347) there is not profit, and, of course, Accountants know there is not profit until depreciation is provided for.

Parliament, having granted the privilege of limited liability, provided a scheme for the protection of those giving credit to limited Companies: Registration of information at a public registration office, a register of members open to the public, a register of mortgages open to creditors, the registration of contracts for payment of Share Capital by anything but cash, are all enforced by law. Judicial interpretation of the law has held that Capital once contributed cannot be withdrawn. There is, it is true, a hiatus in the scheme, owing to the absence of requirement that loss of Capital in carrying on the operations of the Company be publicly disclosed, but otherwise we have a fairly complete system by which a careful trader, before these two cases, might consider he had means of testing the credit of a limited Company he intends to trust, and if he found the Company was paying dividends he might reasonably think the Capital was intact. The *Neuchatel* and *Commercial* cases have gone far to destroy this scheme.

Surely, Mr. Palmer is right when he says the protection to Creditors supposed to be afforded by the Acts is now found to be a delusion and a trap, and that the system propounded by the Court of Appeal is not unlikely to mislead the public. He says, too (5th ed. p. 356), that before placing reliance upon Articles of Association to the effect that waste need not be provided for, "it may be wise to wait for further elucidation of the law." It may be wise for Accountants, when certifying Balance Sheets, to bear this advice in mind.

At the conclusion of the paper Mr. Welton said that he wished to put one or two points to the author of it. Firstly, as he understood it, it appeared that if the surplus of total assets over total liabilities represented Capital, all dividends would, under any circumstances, have to be paid out of Capital. This seemed a peculiar principle to announce, for surely it was wrong to pay dividends out of Capital. Secondly, it certainly seemed to him that goodwill should be put in the Balance Sheet as an asset; and, further, if the real value of all assets had to be brought in on the asset side of the Balance Sheet (so that the difference between the real value of the assets and the real amount of liabilities might show what the capital was, and so much of that capital as was not represented by shareholders' contributions would be divisible, as he understood Mr. Cooper had contended), what law was there, in a case like that of *Eley Brothers*, where the shares were worth four times their nominal value, to prevent them from valuing up their works and declaring an enormous dividend at once amongst the shareholders?

Mr. Cooper, in reply, said that as regards the first point, he had already stated in his paper that in his opinion the surplus of assets over liabilities was capital, and that every payment of dividend, therefore, was payment of Capital, and that in consequence all money paid away in dividends left the Capital contributed reduced. With regard to the second point, his reply would be that goodwill should never, under any circumstances, unless it was being sold, be put into the Balance Sheet.

Mr. Welton instanced the controversy between the London County Council and the Tramways Company, in support of his contention, pointing out that the Tramways Company was maintaining that it was a going concern, and that its value had to be measured in regard to its earning power.

Mr. Cooper replied that the case of the Tramways Company was a case where the goodwill was being sold, and that under no other circumstances could the goodwill of a Company or a concern find its way into the Balance Sheet.

Mr. Welton remarked that in his opinion a well kept Profit and Loss Account was of far more value in regard to the condition of a Company than any Balance Sheet ever constructed, more especially as it appeared that in the case of the Balance Sheet some of the legitimate assets could not be shown.

Mr. G. van de Linde wished to ask Mr. Welton one question. Mr. Cooper had laid it down that goodwill ought never to be put down in the Balance Sheet unless it was being purchased. Then he would ask how that goodwill was to be dealt with?

Mr. Welton said that, for instance, in the case of a Company going from good to bad, the way to extinguish goodwill was not by taking it out of profits, but by writing it down in the assets, in the way which Mr. Cooper regarded as so illogical, but which was at all events practical.

Mr. Dexter said that it seemed to him that Mr. Cooper's method was impracticable, taking, for example, the case of a mine.

Mr. J. D. S. Bogle, putting a further question regarding the writing off of goodwill, Mr. Cooper pointed out that he had not dealt with the question of goodwill in his paper in any way whatever.

Mr. C. R. Trevor said that, in dealing with the profits of a Company, the question ranged itself under two heads. In the first place, there were Companies in which it was impossible to do anything else than divide the earnings. Take the case, for example, of ships. It was the practice amongst shippers to divide the earnings amongst the owners, and the owners constituted practically a Company, although not registered as a Company. In all cases the earning power was reckoned without writing off the cost of the maintenance of the ships. Therefore, he did not think any objection could be made to the practice of dividing earnings as they were obtained. The same practice applied to collieries. The capital cost of collieries was not reduced. In the case of manufactories also, it was generally a very difficult matter indeed to ascertain, for Balance Sheet purposes, the exact value at any identical moment of the mills and works. Then there was the further difficulty of dividing Capital Loss from Revenue Loss. This question seemed to require very great consideration, and he would not like to assent to the proposition that goodwill should always be maintained; for when a Company had got into difficulties, or into a low position, and the goodwill stood as an asset, it would often be found to create a difficulty in settling matters, or in making a transfer, or in disposing of the assets to the best advantage. In fact, if goodwill was allowed to stand at full value, the shareholders would always run the risk of an irreclaimable loss.

Mr. A. F. Whinney said that it seemed to him that they had got a little beyond the point to which Mr. Cooper intended his paper should carry them. He did not think that any mention of the question of goodwill had been made by Mr. Cooper in his paper. He was sure they were very much obliged to Mr. Cooper for the points he had raised, but he was not disposed to think personally, that the Judges in the *Lee v. Neuchatel* case had laid down a principle which was to be considered as a principle in all cases. It seem to him that in this case there was a special article to be considered and a judgment was arrived at with regard to that special article. This case did not lay down a principle which they could safely adopt on every occasion. In proposing a vote of thanks to the Chairman of the meeting he would like to hear his opinion upon these two cases.

Mr. Clare Smith in seconding the vote of thanks said he should like an explanation of how it was that in the case of one of the Eastern banks the directors had been advised that, although their capital had been invested in silver, and silver had depreciated, it must be replaced before they could divide the profits which had been fairly earned on the year's work.

The Chairman (Mr. Hawkesley), said that he had listened to the paper that night with the very greatest interest. Mr. Cooper had said that what they wanted to know was, could dividends be paid lawfully out of anything but profits? He, Mr. Hawkesley, had noted the two findings which Mr. Cooper had quoted, but for his own part he should be content to take his stand upon the case of *Trevor v. Whitworth* in the House of Lords. They were really dealing with Limited Liability Acts. As he understood the policy of the Legislature it was this, that when a corporation was allowed to complete a limited liability, that is to say, that members were not liable beyond the amount of their subscriptions, then Parliament intended that—to the extent of the amount of this subscription—the capital of the company was to remain for the benefit of the creditors. There was a contract, it seemed to him, between the creditors of a limited liability company and the members of that company; and, consequently, if the capital of the company were reduced by the payment of dividends, that was doing precisely what the Legislature desired to prevent, namely, that a return had been made, not contemplated by the Act of 1862, and not authorised in any way. This seemed to him to be the point involved in the question of the payment of dividends out of capital.

Mr. Welton, referring to the question of goodwill, said that he did not think a banker would expect a customer who brought in a Balance Sheet with a view to an overdraft to include in it the value of the goodwill.

With regard to an observation made by Mr. Trevor, he would like to say that, in his judgment, lawyers and accountants went a good deal beyond their scope when they talked about making valuations. It certainly seemed to be the case that Chartered Accountants and auditors generally had got into the habit of allowing the public to believe that they were valuers when they were nothing of the sort. He thought they would find that as accountants they would get into very troubled waters unless they plainly stated, where they were asked to make an audit or to certify a Balance Sheet, that such Balance Sheet had been made without any responsibility being taken as regards the real value of the assets. He could not see that in a Balance Sheet, certified by an auditor, it could be expected that it should carry with it any responsibility on the part of the auditor as to the value of the assets. Mr. Trevor had referred to the practice of putting into the Balance Sheet, goodwill at cost price. This would be generally very much less than the actual value—realisable value.

If a Balance Sheet were taken, and the goodwill were put at a lower price than its realisable value, as much injustice would be done as if it were put above its real value, for, by doing so, men would be induced to part with their shares at less than their real value.

In the case of *McDougall v. The Jersey Hotel Company* the view was taken that there was an absolute contract that capital should not be returned to the shareholders in the shape of dividends. That was the particular point which he thought Mr. Cooper had really started for them, and he agreed with Mr. Whinney, who had hit the nail on the head in saying that the judgment in regard to the case of *Lee v. Neuchatel Asphalte Co.* applied only to this particular case, and therefore they were entitled to say that even in the Court of Appeal there was no principle laid down which could be used against the higher authority of the House of Lords in the case of *Trevor v. Whitworth.* There seemed to him to be a dense fog in regard to the two cases which Mr. Cooper had quoted, and he believed that accountants might employ themselves much worse than in taking cases of this kind to the House of Lords.

A vote of thanks having been carried *nem. con.*, and briefly acknowledged by Mr. Cooper and Mr. Hawkesley, the meeting terminated.

The History of Accounting

An Arno Press Collection

Bennet[t], James [Arlington]. **The American System of Practical Book-Keeping** and Foster, B[enjamin] F[ranklin], **The Origin and Progress of Book-Keeping.** 1842/1852. Two vols. in one

Brief, Richard P., editor. **The Late Nineteenth Century Debate Over Depreciation, Capital and Income.** 1976

Brief, Richard P. **Nineteenth Century Capital Accounting and Business Investment.** 1976

Bruchey, Stuart W[eems]. **Robert Oliver and Mercantile Bookkeeping in the Early Nineteenth Century.** 1976

Church, A[lexander] Hamilton. **Production Factors in Cost Accounting and Works Management.** 1910

Cole, William Morse. **Accounts:** Their Construction and Interpretation for Business Men and Students of Affairs. 1908

Dicksee, Lawrence R[obert]. **Advanced Accounting.** 1903

Dicksee, Lawrence R[obert]. **Auditing:** A Practical Manual for Auditors. 1892

Dicksee, Lawrence R[obert]. **Auditing:** A Practical Manual for Auditors. Authorized American Edition, Edited by Robert H. Montgomery. 1905

Dicksee, Lawrence R[obert]. **Depreciation, Reserves, and Reserve Funds.** 1903

Dicksee, Lawrence R[obert] and Frank Tillyard. **Goodwill and Its Treatment in Accounts.** 1906

Folsom, E[zekiel] G[ilman]. **Folsom's Logical Bookkeeping:** The Logic of Accounts. 1873

Garcke, Emile and J[ohn] M[anger] Fells. **Factory Accounts, Their Principles and Practice.** 1893

Hatfield, Henry Rand. **Modern Accounting:** Its Principles and Some of its Problems. 1916

Kehl, Donald. **Corporate Dividends:** Legal and Accounting Problems Pertaining to Corporate Distributions. 1941

Leake, P[ercy] D[ewe]. **Depreciation and Wasting Assets and Their Treatment in Assessing Annual Profit and Loss.** 1912

Lisle, George. **Accounting in Theory and Practice.** 1900

Matheson, Ewing. **The Depreciation of Factories, Mines and Industrial Undertakings and Their Valuation.** 1893

Montgomery, Robert H. **Auditing Theory and Practice.** 1912

Norton, George Pepler. **Textile Manufacturers' Book-Keeping for the Counting House, Mill and Warehouse.** 1894

Paton, William A[ndrew] and Russell A[lger] Stevenson. **Principles of Accounting.** 1916

Pixley, Francis W[illiam]. **Auditors:** Their Duties and Responsibilities Under the Joint-Stock Companies Acts and the Friendly Societies and Industrial and Provident Societies Acts. 1881

Reiter, Prosper, Jr. **Profits, Dividends and the Law.** 1926

Scott, DR. **Theory of Accounts.** 1925

Scovell, Clinton H. **Interest as a Cost.** 1924

Sells, Elijah Watt. **The Natural Business Year and Thirteen Other Themes.** 1924

Soulé, Geo[rge]. **Soulé's New Science and Practice of Accounts.** 1903

Sprouse, Robert T[homas]. **The Effect of the Concept of the Corporation on Accounting.** 1976

Zeff, Stephen A., editor. **Asset Appreciation, Business Income and Price-Level Accounting: 1918-1935.** 1976